Noir and Blanchot

Noir and Blanchot

Deteriorations of the Event

William S. Allen

BLOOMSBURY ACADEMIC
NEW YORK • LONDON • OXFORD • NEW DELHI • SYDNEY

BLOOMSBURY ACADEMIC
Bloomsbury Publishing Inc
1385 Broadway, New York, NY 10018, USA
50 Bedford Square, London, WC1B 3DP, UK
29 Earlsfort Terrace, Dublin 2, Ireland

BLOOMSBURY, BLOOMSBURY ACADEMIC and the Diana logo are trademarks
of Bloomsbury Publishing Plc

First published in the United States of America 2020
This paperback edition published in 2021

Copyright © William S. Allen, 2020

For legal purposes the Acknowledgements on p. ix constitute an extension
of this copyright page.

Cover design by Eleanor Rose | Untitled from Vertigo, 2014 © Daisuke Yokota

All rights reserved. No part of this publication may be reproduced
or transmitted in any form or by any means, electronic or mechanical,
including photocopying, recording, or any information storage or retrieval
system, without prior permission in writing from the publishers.

Bloomsbury Publishing Inc does not have any control over, or responsibility for, any
third-party websites referred to or in this book. All internet addresses given in this
book were correct at the time of going to press. The author and publisher regret any
inconvenience caused if addresses have changed or sites have ceased to exist, but can
accept no responsibility for any such changes.

Library of Congress Cataloging-in-Publication Data
Names: Allen, William S., 1971– author.
Title: Noir and Blanchot : deteriorations of the event / William S. Allen.
Description: New York : Bloomsbury Academic, 2020. |
Includes bibliographical references and index. |
Summary: "An examination of how art responds to dark times by way of the
writings of Maurice Blanchot and film noir"– Provided by publisher.
Identifiers: LCCN 2019039859 | ISBN 9781501358913 (hardback) |
ISBN 9781501358920 (epub) | ISBN 9781501358937 (pdf)
Subjects: LCSH: Blanchot, Maurice–Criticism and interpretation. |
Film noir–History and criticism. | Arts and society.
Classification: LCC PQ2603.L3343 Z5285 2020 | DDC 843/.912–dc23
LC record available at https://lccn.loc.gov/2019039859

ISBN: HB: 978-1-5013-5891-3
PB: 978-1-5013-8463-9
ePDF: 978-1-5013-5893-7
eBook: 978-1-5013-5892-0

Typeset by Newgen KnowledgeWorks Pvt. Ltd., Chennai, India

To find out more about our authors and books visit www.bloomsbury.com
and sign up for our newsletters.

Second Gentleman: Have you seen the new play? A tower of Babylon! A maze of arches, staircases, walkways, and all thrown so lightly and boldly into the air. One gets dizzy with every step. A strange conception. [He stands still, embarrassed]

First Gentleman: What's the trouble?

Second Gentleman: Ah, nothing! Your hand, monsieur! It's that puddle. Thank you. I could scarcely get past it, it could be dangerous!

First Gentleman: You weren't afraid?

Second Gentleman: Oh yes, the earth is a thin crust, I always think I could fall through where there's a hole like that ... You've got to step carefully, you could break through. But go to the theatre, I urge you.

GEORG BÜCHNER, *DANTONS TOD*, 1835

CONTENTS

Acknowledgements ix
Abbreviations xi

1 Dark time 1

2 Ruptures and deviations 21

3 Chiaroscuro 47

4 Between deaths 77

5 Damnation 107

6 Rewriting history 127

Notes 147
Index 177

ACKNOWLEDGEMENTS

Two of these chapters have appeared elsewhere in earlier forms: 'Melancholy and Parapraxis: Rewriting History in Benjamin and Kafka', *MLN* 123.5 (2008); and 'The Cracks in the Surface of Things: On Béla Tarr, Rancière, and Adorno', *Screening the Past* 39 (2015). My thanks to the Johns Hopkins University Press and the Screening the Past Group for permission to reprint them here. I must also express my warmest appreciation to Haaris Naqvi and Amy Martin at Bloomsbury for all their work and support in turning these pages into a book. And my profoundest thanks to Daisuke Yokota, and Naoko Hatta at the G/P Gallery, Tokyo, for permission to use an image from his *Vertigo* series (2014) on the cover of this book.

ABBREVIATIONS

Where double page references have been used they refer to the French or German text, and then the English versions, as translations have been modified throughout.

A   Theodor W. Adorno, *Ästhetik (1958/59)*, ed. Eberhard Ortland (Frankfurt am Main: Suhrkamp, 2009); *Aesthetics 1958/59*, trans. Wieland Hoban (Cambridge: Polity, 2018).

AM   Maurice Blanchot, *L'Arrêt de mort* (Paris: Gallimard, 1993); trans. Lydia Davis as *Death Sentence* in *The Station Hill Blanchot Reader: Fiction and Literary Essays*, ed. George Quasha (Barrytown, NY: Station Hill, 1999).

BD   Pierre Klossowski, *Le Bain de Diane* (Paris: Gallimard, 1980); trans. Stephen Sartarelli as 'Diana at Her Bath' in *Diana at Her Bath and The Women of Rome* (New York: Marsilio, 1998).

BT   Jacques Rancière, *Béla Tarr, le temps d'après* (Paris: Capricci, 2011); trans. Erik Beranek as *Béla Tarr, the Time After* (Minneapolis: Univocal, 2013).

CBT   András Bálint Kovács, *The Cinema of Béla Tarr: The Circle Closes* (New York: Wallflower Press, 2013).

DI   Billy Wilder and Raymond Chandler, *Double Indemnity* (Berkeley: University of California Press, 2012).

ED   Blanchot, *L'Écriture du désastre* (Paris: Gallimard, 1980); trans. Ann Smock as *The Writing of the Disaster* (Lincoln: University of Nebraska Press, 1986).

EI   Blanchot, *L'Entretien infini* (Paris: Gallimard, 1969); trans. Susan Hanson as *The Infinite Conversation* (Minneapolis: University of Minnesota Press, 1993).

EL   Blanchot, *L'Espace littéraire* (Paris: Gallimard, 1955); trans. Ann Smock as *The Space of Literature* (Lincoln: University of Nebraska Press, 1982).

GS2	Walter Benjamin, *Gesammelte Schriften II*, ed. Rolf Tiedemann and Hermann Schweppenhäuser (Frankfurt am Main: Suhrkamp, 1977); *Selected Writings: Volume 2, 1927–1934*, ed. Michael W. Jennings et al. (Cambridge: Harvard University Press, 1999).
KF	Adorno and Hanns Eisler, *Komposition für den Film*, ed. Rolf Tiedemann (Frankfurt am Main: Suhrkamp, 1976); trans. Norbert Guterman as *Composing for the Films* (London: Athlone, 1994).
MM	Adorno, *Minima Moralia. Reflexionen aus dem beschädigten Leben*, ed. Rolf Tiedemann (Frankfurt am Main: Suhrkamp, 1979); trans. E. F. N. Jephcott as *Minima Moralia: Reflections from Damaged Life* (London: New Left Books, 1974).
OC	René Char, *Œuvres complètes* (Paris: Gallimard, 1983); *Furor and Mystery & Other Writings*, ed. and trans. Mary Ann Caws and Nancy Kline (Boston: Black Widow Press, 2010).
P	Adorno, *Prismen* (Frankfurt am Main: Suhrkamp, 1955); trans. Samuel and Shierry Weber as *Prisms* (Cambridge: MIT Press, 1967).
PAD	Blanchot, *Le Pas au-delà* (Paris: Gallimard, 1973); trans. Lycette Nelson as *The Step Not Beyond* (Albany: SUNY Press, 1992).
PF	Blanchot, *La Part du feu* (Paris: Gallimard, 1949); trans. Charlotte Mandell as *The Work of Fire* (Stanford: Stanford University Press, 1995).
PFN	Raymond Borde and Étienne Chaumeton, *Panorama du film noir américain (1941–1953)* (Paris: Minuit, 1955); trans. Paul Hammond as *A Panorama of American Film Noir 1941–1953* (San Francisco: City Lights, 2002).
PG	G. W. F. Hegel, *Phänomenologie des Geistes*, ed. Wolfgang Bonsiepen and Reinhard Heede (Hamburg: Felix Meiner, 1980); trans. A. V. Miller as *Phenomenology of Spirit* (Oxford: Oxford University Press, 1977).
QC	André Bazin, *Qu'est-ce que le cinéma?* (Paris: Éditions du Cerf, 1985); trans. Hugh Gray as *What Is Cinema?* (Berkeley: University of California Press, 1967).
UDT	Benjamin, *Ursprung des deutschen Trauerspiels*, in *Gesammelte Schriften I*, ed. Rolf Tiedemann and Hermann Schweppenhäuser (Frankfurt am Main: Suhrkamp, 1974); trans. Howard Eiland as *Origin of the German Trauerspiel* (Cambridge: Harvard University Press, 2019).

WL1/2 Hegel, 1: *Wissenschaft der Logik. Die Objektive Logik (1812/1813)*, ed. Friedrich Hogemann and Walter Jaeschke (Hamburg: Felix Meiner, 1978); 2: *Wissenschaft der Logik. Die Lehre vom Sein (1832)*, ed. Friedrich Hogemann and Walter Jaeschke (Hamburg: Felix Meiner, 1985); *Science of Logic*, trans. A. V. Miller (London: Allen & Unwin, 1969).

1

Dark time

What is the status of the work of art in desperate times? The fictional and critical writings of Blanchot, much like the films noir coming out at the same time, are, however obliquely, both an expression of and a commentary upon the situations in which they arose. Thus, what is significant about these works is not just their darkness and strangeness but the fact that these qualities partly come from the obscure material aspects of their situation, which leads to a different mode of experience in their audiences. And so, as this mode derives from the pressure of the times, it is as political as it is aesthetic, thereby indicating how the times can give rise to works that reflect the times, a demand raised most pointedly in Hölderlin's question, 'what are poets for in meagre times?' in which its interrogative seems to become its own answer. While these political and aesthetic aspects are not merged into each other, it can be shown that the unique aesthetic form of film noir, for example, is its own political interrogation, just as is the case for Blanchot's narratives. But this interlinking also shows that a more extrinsic association of politics and aesthetics in the work fails to the extent that it does not recognize this prior intimacy, which then affects how we think about that pre-eminent political and aesthetic problem in such desperate times: the event. It is thus of considerable interest that the relation of politics and aesthetics in Blanchot's writings (much like film noir, as will be found) does not take place through the revelatory institution of an origin but via the rather more ambivalent form of a chiaroscuro, in which each aspect negates the other without eliminating or assimilating it, since the negation of politics by aesthetics, and vice versa, leads not to a mere emptiness or indistinction but to a shattering, stuttering reversal from one side to the other, in which is found the contingency of the times.

Hölderlin's elegy 'Brot und Wein' was written in the winter of 1800–1, after his separation from Susette Gontard. It is written along the lines of a classical elegy with nine verses that fall into three sections, and at the beginning of the final section is the verse that ends with the question cited earlier:

Indessen dünket mir öfters	Meanwhile often it seems to me
Besser zu schlafen, wie so ohne	better to sleep than to be without
Genossen zu seyn,	comrades as we are,
So zu harren und was zu thun	so to wait, and what to do and say
indeß und zu sagen,	in the meanwhile
Weiß ich nicht und wozu Dichter	I don't know and what are poets for
in dürftiger Zeit?	in meagre times?
Aber sie sind, sagst du, wie des	But they are, you say, like the wine
Weingotts heilige Priester,	god's holy priests
Welche von Lande zu Land	Who drifted from land to land
zogen in heiliger Nacht.	in holy night.

The poem was dedicated to Hölderlin's friend, the novelist Wilhelm Heinse, and it is his words that form the answer in the final lines. That Hölderlin was unconvinced by this response is confirmed by the fact that this verse was entirely rewritten in the following years as he continued to revise the poem, leaving in its place a more severe and enigmatic turning to the earth and to the night.[1]

Although this revision is highly significant for understanding Hölderlin's changing thoughts, and his concomitant move away from the strictures of classical poetry, these lines were nevertheless written, here, at the beginning of the nineteenth century, although they were not fully published until its very end. It is from this situation that Heidegger will configure his epochal reading of Hölderlin, for which this question will prove instrumental, but it is more important for present purposes to consider the broader stakes to which Hölderlin's question refers, which remain outstanding. The word that Hölderlin uses, *dürftig*, has a range of meanings (poor, meagre, thin, wretched, humble, scanty, weak, needy) that all point to a lack, and the lack he is referring to is onto-theological, which is to be understood as a fundamental lack of authority or law; there is no centre or ground that can orientate people and in which art could find its raison d'être. That this situation still pertains is the mark of modernity, but it is part of the double-edged ambivalence of this situation that it is not only the case that we are in a time of need but that time itself is poor or weak. For the lack of authority that Hölderlin has detected also unravels the flow of history and, as his later works will begin to explore, this leads to what he will call the categorical turning, the turning back of time upon itself. This time of darkness is thus also a dark time, one obscured in or by itself, which has as much impact on the historical path of the political, on the revolutionary event, as it has on the work of art and its artists.

It is worth looking more closely at what Hölderlin says here, for twice he remarks that this time of need exists in the meanwhile. For something to be in the meanwhile is for it to exist between events, and removed from them, and it is perhaps as such that time is poor or weak, since it would lack substance insofar as it is uneventful. It is thus that it is a mean time in all senses of the word. If time itself is impoverished, then this is because it is unable to accomplish itself and instead has become empty or idle; it falls into neglect and becomes prey to other forces. The practice of revolution is in this way metaphysical as it seeks to rescue the time of the event, to put time to work again and prevent it from collapsing under the pressure of its own deterioration. But doing so requires recognition of this decay before there can be any kind of intervention that would seek to rectify it. Hence, the revolution is intrinsically related to this mean time as it is derived from it, and the same is true of the work of art, such that it is also subject to this deterioration of time, the effects of which are distinct from any interiorization or exteriorization and instead concern the dissolution of terms and events. This is not to privilege the decay of time but to realize that through it the work of art is exposed to its own disruption in which another mode of experience is found, from which any thought of change must come.

In Marxist thought the idea of permanent revolution denotes a specific problem in the development of socialism. First with Marx himself, and then later and more substantially with Trotsky, permanent revolution is concerned with the problem of how the revolution should proceed given the differing situations to be found in different countries and at different times, as well as the problem of how revolutionaries should engage with existing class structures, parties and ideologies. To a large degree permanent revolution describes the absolute lack of compromise that revolutionaries should take towards these existing structures, as well as to the idea of allowing capitalism to fall into decline before socialism can emerge. Trotsky's thought on the latter point is most distinctive, as he insisted on the possibility of a socialist revolution even in situations where capitalism had not fully emerged, on the basis that it embeds itself, with this uncompromising attitude, in the pre-existing structures, and takes advantage of what can be gained by internationalizing the revolution so that it is not limited to its local conditions.

It is thus that the revolution can be understood as permanent, for in its lack of restraint it occurs continuously and throughout society, regardless of any structures or borders. Aside from this pervasive lack of compromise, I will not be discussing permanent revolution but will be seeking to understand what occurs in thought and language when history is subjected to such an imperative. This is not to abdicate from the sociopolitical but to find that which is captured by the idea of permanent revolution that is not part of Marxist doctrine. What is fundamental to Trotsky's innovation is the notion of a mode of historical change that does not occur through a series of structured stages, and so can apply to art just as much as it does to politics.[2] But in departing from this conventional model to essay a notion of radical, thorough and continuous change permanent revolution almost becomes an impossible thought, if it is not rendered banal, insofar as it holds a paradoxical combination of permanence and revolution. And when it is understood that whatever passes by the name of revolution involves both negation and desire, destruction and creation, then the implications of this change, once it is made permanent, are profoundly challenging. A notion of history as constant negation and desire presents considerable difficulties for thought and language, but it also opens up a relation to such convulsions that history, politics and aesthetics attempt to conceal through their formations. Understanding what happens when this relation of form and rupture is inverted makes it possible to understand the desire that revolution bears, whether it is political or artistic, and what is at stake in its demands.

The sense that there is a mode of time that is neither linear nor circular is found in situations of rupture, which is also the form by which thought or language responds to these moments. What is then problematic is the relation between this anomalous mode of time and these condensed and fragmentary forms, which in responding to this breach also expose it further. To begin I will look at how Blanchot discusses this problem in relation to the works of René Char, where the experience of this anomaly is marked by a form of writing that conveys the rupturing of worldly order, before moving on to his 1948 narrative *L'Arrêt de mort*, in which this breakdown undermines the very possibility of the event as that which happens, with all that this implies for the 'moment' of death. Blanchot's rethinking of the event thus leads to a revision of the nature of historical change as well as of the work of art. In their place a materialist thought emerges that is based in contingency, in a time of error, of accidents and mistakes, where occurrences are strange and opaque and in which time comes to feel like it is following a path that is inevitable or repetitive but that is simply a result of its contingency. These ruptures and deviations may become blind spots for thinking, but they also lead into a time that is unpredictable, where chance emerges in a thought of alienation. It is for this reason that I will examine two key noir films, *Double Indemnity* and *Vertigo*, for what they indicate about the nature of a world constituted by such breakdowns and accidents and its social and personal consequences. Finally, I will turn to two studies of historico-material disruption, Béla Tarr's film *Damnation* and Benjamin's reading of Kafka, which delineate the almost impossible demands on thought in encountering this negativity.

An example will help to show how the different aspects of this reading come together: when Marcel Carné's *Le Quai des brumes* was released in May 1938 it was strongly criticized by Jean Renoir, who accused it of being propaganda for fascism. This outburst seemed out of character for Renoir and he later tried to retract it, and even though the film was very well received it attracted many similar comments. While other considerations may have played a role in Renoir's reaction, the explanation he gave for condemning the film so robustly, which was reflected by other critics, was that it portrayed a society that was weak, corrupt and fragmented and thus open to the influence of fascist demagoguery; indeed, in his words, it seemed to need a dictator. France was enduring a very confused and unstable time in 1938, and already it seemed as though the spectre of defeat was hanging over it, as if the disaster were prefiguring itself, to such a degree that, as Georges Sadoul reported, representatives of the Vichy regime later claimed that if France was defeated it was because of *Le Quai des brumes*.[3] It is evidence of the disturbing quality of the film that it provoked such comments, and many factors contributed to this sense of unease – from Jacques Prévert's poetic rendition of Pierre Mac Orlan's morbid novel, to the gloomy camerawork and set designs of Eugen Schüfftan and Alexandre Trauner, alongside Maurice Jaubert's funereal score and a cast of characters who are either wretched, despicable or doomed. The scenario proceeds as if in a dream and yet is just as firmly anchored in a world of crime and decay so that it is not possible to know if the former arises from the latter or vice versa (which is exactly what is at issue in Mac Orlan's notion of the 'fantastique social'). It is this uncertainty that appears to have provoked Renoir's condemnation, but it is important to see that it is the focus of the film. In dark times it is not possible simply to assert the social possibilities of hope, since these are unconvincing, but nor is it acceptable simply to portray their apparent impossibility. In place of this antinomy, it is necessary to look closely at the fabric of what is historically and materially current and explore both its complexities and its implications, and to do so without any assumptions as to their possibilities. This leaves the situation open to the worst, but such a possibility can never be ignored, but nor should it displace the sense in which the interval in which it may arise is also one in which the materiality of time is exposed, which is not an experience of its possibilities as much as of that which remains outside history, and is elusive or resistant to its movements. Only in becoming aware of this exteriority can any sense of historical change be thought, even if it becomes that in which thought is exposed to its own disaster.

The extent of this ambivalence can be gauged by the way *Le Quai des brumes* was also condemned by Lucien Rebatet, who was one of the most sophisticated and widely read critics of the 1930s but who was also violently fascist and anti-Semitic. Although Rebatet was largely dismissive of the films that went by the name of 'poetic realism', because of their supposed decadence, he was equally aware of what made these films distinctive, and he was one of the first (and one of the most enthusiastic) critics to use the term 'noir' in a consistent way to describe (and condemn) these films. But what is of considerable interest is that the language he uses to criticize *Le Quai des brumes* is also used in his response to Blanchot's first novel, and although this could be adduced to the fact that his political views necessitated a similar vocabulary in relation to all cultural products of which he disapproved, it is highly significant that the same parallel would be marked by Sartre a few years later, when he would dismiss Blanchot's writings with the same criticisms that he would use to condemn *Citizen Kane* (Orson Welles, 1941). That writers from such opposing political positions could find themselves in agreement in relation to these works is very suggestive and points to the profound political-aesthetic uneasiness that they aroused. It is the aim of this book to examine how and why this disturbance arises and what it may be exposing that appears to disrupt the possibility of historico-political positivism.

Examining what Rebatet writes about these works is thus very revealing as his language clearly delineates their anomalous nature. The 'sins' of *Le Quai des brumes*, in his words, lie in its vagueness: we do not learn much about who the characters are or what they feel, everything is wrapped in the mists of its title and, although he appreciates the visual deployment of this motif, the vagueness of the characters only confirms their inconsequentiality, which is compounded by a poetic script that he does not hesitate to condemn on the basis of Prévert's Surrealist background. However, as has often been noted, there is a sleight of hand here, as Rebatet emphasizes this vagueness in order to dismiss the film as inconsequential; for instance, he describes the film's prologue in which the characters gather at a remote hut on the coast and then complains that the 'narrator' refrains from illuminating their lives. But in saying this he has ignored those elements that do not interest him, which then enables him to dismiss the lives of these characters and, indeed, their whole 'milieu'. For each of them, in their own ways, expresses the poverty, abuse or bitterness that has subsumed them and has led them to this strangely idyllic place cut off from the rest of the world, the bar known as Panama's (as its owner explains, Panama is a marvellous place, 'America, cut in two'). Prévert's script differs from Mac Orlan's novel, which is bleaker and more violent, but the poetry that, for Rebatet, simply casts a cheap halo of mystery around the characters, particularly in relation to the character of the army deserter, Jean (Jean Gabin), is not there to create an image of 'chivalry', as he claims. Instead, as Rebatet himself notes, Jean is merely 'a larva swept by the wind of fate', and it is this contingency that the poetry of his language reflects as, for example, when he shows his disgust for Zabel (Michel Simon) by comparing him to a giant centipede, a detail drawn from his experience of fighting in Indochina.[4] This point is expanded upon in Mac Orlan's book where the character of the soldier discusses the particular kind of delirium that can occur in the Foreign Legion, which is characterized by a form of mental irritation known as the 'cockroach' (*cafard*). The *cafard* describes the effects of the boredom, exhaustion and pointlessness of colonial military life that draws soldiers into a lethargy in which they become exposed to an excessive imagination, which can then explode into violence towards others or themselves.[5] In this case, the violent response that Jean has to Zabel (or Lucien (Pierre Brasseur)) is a result of the fact that the latter exemplifies the degradation and corruption he endured in his military service. Thus the poetry in Prévert's script is not a hollow

Surrealist embellishment of insignificant lives but evidence of a concrete imaginary that arises in specific circumstances of desolation. But all of this is dismissed by Rebatet as 'the most vulgar clichés', and it is notable that the only character for whom he expresses an 'indulgence' is the petty gangster Lucien, the one who is closest to a nascent form of fascism.

Turning to Rebatet's review of Blanchot's *Thomas l'Obscur*, it is apparent that the same arguments and vocabulary are being used. As with *Le Quai des brumes*, Rebatet begins by disputing the very status of Blanchot's work, which is deformed beyond hope by his misguided artistic ambitions, since he has ignored reality in order to develop his own faded recapitulation of Surrealist influences. What emerges from this disorder is bland and shapeless and extremely tiresome, nothing but 'insubstantial larvae passing through a kind of humid fog'.[6] This artistic condemnation is repeated in Sartre's review of Blanchot's second novel, which claims that Blanchot has failed as a novelist because he has simply recycled motifs from Kafka but with less insight and sophistication. In both cases it is not enough for these writers to criticize the works, but rather to attack their author on the basis that his attempts are flawed in principle because of a faulty grasp of the necessary relation of art to the world (for Rebatet, *Thomas l'Obscur* is flawed because of the author's 'Jewish art'; for Sartre, it is Blanchot's 'transdescendence tinged with Maurrasism' that is the underlying problem).[7] Hence, it is not sufficient to condemn the work technically but to reject its very existence because it sets out from the wrong kind of historico-political relation between art and the world. Both Rebatet and Sartre subordinate literature to a prior political assumption about the nature of art, and thus find themselves disoriented by works that first seek to examine literature on its own terms before considering its relation to the world. By starting from an examination of the work as such, its political implications are put in suspension, and it is this uncertainty that leaves Sartre and Rebatet uneasy, whereas for Blanchot no examination of politics can develop without passing by way of an examination of what literature exposes about language. In place of the urge towards decisive action, which determines the relation to history, Blanchot's narratives are drawn to what subtends the possibility of decision or action, the formlessness of thought and relation that has so tellingly been called 'larval'. It is thus essential to recall that the right-wing rhetoric of Blanchot's own journalistic writings of the period occurred alongside, before giving way to, the composition of works that sought to investigate the nature of this language of corruption.

For in Blanchot's fictional writings, just as in these dark or 'noir' films, there is an investigation of the opening that occurs in time when it seems to lose itself in materiality and becomes obscure, which is precisely what happens when the apparently steady movement of progress and development fails, when history is disconnected from the anthropocentric illusion of hope, leaving, in Sartre's words, a complete world where things manifest a captive and tormented thinking, at once changeable and enchained, that gnaws away from below at the linkages of the mechanism, without ever managing to express itself. Matter is never entirely matter, since it offers only a perpetually thwarted outline of determinism, and mind is never entirely mind, since it has fallen into slavery that matter impregnates and coarsens. All is woe: things suffer and tend towards inertia without ever achieving it; the humiliated, enslaved mind strives towards consciousness and freedom without reaching it. The fantastic offers the inverse image of the union of soul and body: the soul takes the place of the body, and the body that of the soul, and we cannot use clear and distinct ideas to think this image; it is necessary to resort to confused thoughts, themselves fantastic, in a word although wholly awake, wholly mature, and wholly civilized, we let ourselves give in to the magical 'mentality' of the dreamer, the primitive, and the child.[8]

Thus, the reactionary politics of this position merges with a philosophical obscurity to create a work that is at best irrelevant, and at worst, dangerously atavistic. Sartre is not describing Carné's film but Blanchot's second novel, *Aminadab*, and in doing so his personal fears and convictions have taken the place of careful reading. Instead of the blind confidence in civilization that Sartre espouses, Blanchot's later analysis of this historico-material interval and its consequences is more perceptive:

In the trembling interval [*entre-deux*] between a consciousness that is not formed and an unconscious that lets itself be seen and thereby turns the visible into the fascinating, we are able to learn one of the versions of the imaginary according to which man – is it man? – can make himself according to the image, and is more certainly exposed to the risk of unmaking himself according to his image, thus opening himself to the illusion of a similitude, perhaps beautiful, perhaps fatal, but of an elusive death that is wholly in the repetition of a mute ignorance.

ED: 194/126

It is precisely this interval that is to be explored, since it is not an interval that can ever be closed as it is an exposure to the evasiveness of death, to which we are exposed in the work of art. But first it is necessary to examine how such negativity takes place in thought and language.

I. The vertigo of negation

In a very useful article Badiou discusses the different forms of negativity as they appear in logic. These forms derive from Aristotle's distinction of statements that are classical from those that violate the principle of non-contradiction or the principle of the excluded middle, or both. As Badiou points out, this gives four forms of negation:

1. The negation obeys the two principles. It's the classical logic.
2. The negation obeys the principle of non-contradiction,
    but not the principle of the excluded middle.
3. The negation obeys the principle of the excluded middle,
    but not the principle of non-contradiction.
4. The negation obeys neither the principle of the excluded middle,
    nor the principle of non-contradiction.

As he goes on to spell out, the force of negation progressively weakens through these forms until in the last case there is a complete dissolution of all potency of negativity.[9] That is, the force of negation disappears as every negation is itself negated. To understand how this sequence develops it is necessary to go through the four stages carefully, and to explicate their role in Badiou's thought since they constitute his logic of worlds. From this position it is then possible to understand why Blanchot would persistently refer to the weakness of the negative, and how this will come to affect his understanding of existence, which will then mark out his difference from Badiou.

If we take a statement closer to Blanchot's thought, then it will be easier to see how negation works for him. For example, if we say of a text that 'this is a work', then for this statement to be logically consistent it must be the case that it does not violate the principles of non-contradiction and the excluded middle. That is, it is not possible for the statement to be both true and not true (non-contradiction) and, conversely, it is either true or false; there is no third state (excluded middle). But classical logic does admit of deviations from these rules that have been termed intuitionist and paraconsistent. In the first case (form two earlier), a statement obeys the rule of non-contradiction but not that of the excluded middle. An example of this can be found in the idea that a work exists but admits of variations of appearance, so that it appears in such a way that it seems to be neither a work nor not a work but something else. This form of negation is at the heart of the logic of appearance for Badiou, as appearances emerge precisely in this space between truth and falsity. The equivocation of this form of negation is important for his understanding of politics as it indicates how such intuitionist logic undermines activism by blurring the states of appearance. In the second case (form three earlier), a statement obeys the rule of the excluded middle but not that of non-contradiction. For Badiou, this is the logic of the event, insofar as its appearance is such that it both appears and does not appear, thereby violating the rule of non-contradiction, but in doing so presents itself in an irrevocable form as there is no equivocity about its appearance. This paraconsistent logic would then suggest of a text that it is both a work and not a work, that is, its existence rather than its appearance is at issue. In this case the political dimension is clearer, as the appearance of the work is not equivocal but its existence requires a decision in relation to it. The last form of negation (form four earlier) is thus one in which both its existence and its appearance are in question, and so the force of negation has encompassed the statement itself (by violating its non-contradiction), and also the space of its appearance between truth and falsity (the excluded middle). Hence, there is nothing left of the force of negation, as it has devoured itself by leaving a statement that is both true and not true, and that occurs in such a way that it is neither true nor false. This would lead to an abyss of ambiguity insofar as the sense of the statement has become ungrounded, or bottomless.

The political consequences of this last position seem clear, which is why Badiou dismisses it in order to focus on the tension between intuitionist and paraconsistent logic as they play out in the relation between the event and the everyday. But what is intriguing about Blanchot's position is that although he clearly states that the disaster affects everything while leaving everything in its place, thereby fulfilling the paraconsistent form of the event, he just as emphatically remarks on the space of the work as that between truth and falsity. For him the work puts in question the possibility of stating whether it exists at all, as well as how it appears. Thus he occupies the fourth position in Badiou's schema, but it is important to remember that this does not lead to formlessness and equivocation, as he remarked:

> To write in ignorance and rejection of the philosophical horizon, a horizon punctuated, gathered together or dispersed by the words that delimit it, is necessarily to write with facile complacency (the literature of elegance and good taste). Hölderlin, Mallarmé, so many others, do not allow us this.
>
> ED: 159–60/102–3

There is here an absolute rupture and a concomitant responsibility; we cannot turn away from that which turns away, even as we are drawn into its turmoil. This was also Blanchot's verdict twenty years earlier, when he stated with a resolve that was no less severe for its uncertainty:

> Will you allow this certainty: that we are at a turning point?
>
> – If it is a certainty that it is not a turning. The fact of belonging to this moment at which a change of epoch (if there is one) is being accomplished also takes hold of the certain knowledge that would want to determine it, making certainty as inappropriate as uncertainty.
>
> EI: 394/264

The weakness of the negative does not permit of a weakness of responsibility but makes its task more demanding. For we can only say that we are at a turning if it is not possible to say so definitely, as it is of the nature of the turning that it disables the possibility of determining it as such. In relation to the turning we can neither be certain nor uncertain (intuitionism), since it is only insofar as it also is not (paraconsistency). Badiou's emphasis on the qualities of the militant – on fidelity, affirmation and decisiveness – may be drawn from the thought of Lenin, via Althusser, and may preclude a negotiation with this weakness as risking equivocation, but it also refers to his understanding of being as mathematical, which places his thought at a distance from the literary thinking of Blanchot.

Being is understood by Badiou as a pure multiple, that is, not as substance or essence but as a multiple without qualities or determinations, the empty set or void, which is thus infinite. Being is the infinite site and point of finite existence, as well as its horizon. Badiou thereby affirms the position that passes from Parmenides to Descartes that being and thought are one in their infinity, which is, moreover, an infinity of infinities as in each case it is possible for there to be a further extension, since each infinity gives onto the possibility of an infinity plus one. This last point provides evidence of the mathematical positioning of Badiou's ontology, since it would not be possible to render the indeterminacy of being in such a way from a purely philosophical point of view, as in Hegel's thought, for example, let alone in Blanchot's understanding of literature. Badiou's decision to opt for a mathematical ontology comes from two factors: the first being the materialist injunction that philosophy cannot be a science as it is not objectively grounded; and the second that mathematics, and particularly set theory, allows for a rational but meaningless understanding of that which exceeds the capacities of thought, and thus permits a non-subjective, non-anthropocentric ontology. As such, set theory replaces ontology, as there cannot be a logic of being for Badiou since the pure multiple admits of no relations; hence there can only be a mathematics of being and a logic of appearances, or worlds. The possibility that mathematics may itself not be abstract enough to admit of this kind of sheer indeterminacy, insofar as it remains a form of mental construction (as Brouwer, the founder of intuitionism, believed), and furthermore, remains bound to digital quanta (even in its post-Cantorian developments), does not divert Badiou, but leaves open the possibility of how this indeterminacy might otherwise be construed.

Number as an abstract ordering system would seem to derive in part from the Kantian forms of intuition, as a synthetic a priori that enables counting and measuring in relation to the experiences of space, time and objects (particularly property), but it also develops through social-historical variation to an immense degree of differentiation. As such it achieves a formidable internal sophistication, much like the related disciplines of economics and theology, as it develops through arithmetic, algebra, calculus and geometry. But the uncertain ontological status of number is revealed in the way that the abstraction it depends upon removes it from the realm of concepts and objects while it nevertheless remains a material product of this abstraction, which means that it cannot achieve the status of a pure symbol or form (if such can ever exist).[10] Comparing this approach to Blanchot's, where the focus is on literature as the form of written language that is concerned with its own exploration, reveals a very different understanding of what may constitute existence. Nevertheless, Badiou's thinking of the event – as a manifestation of what will, retroactively, be seen as having not existed, and that topologizes itself as a rupture of the conditions of order – is very suggestive, particularly in the way that it institutes an irrevocable demand even as it disappears. The event is thus a form of transcendental that intrudes into the immanent (whence the significance of mathematics), so that it provides a sense of order while still departing from any discernible meaning, thereby enabling the finite to be a localization of the infinite.

Blanchot's understanding of exteriority, by contrast, does not allow for any such relation of order or any scope for the transcendental as such. In discussing literature Blanchot does not focus on the word or the page, or any generalized notion of writing or the text. Instead, literature is its own irreducible form, however formless or self-negating. Thus literature bears no underlying constituent, since it eventuates as a formal-material complex of concrete emptiness, or 'imaginary'. Insofar as it occurs at once, as a fiction that changes everything but yields no order, it is an event that is also a disaster. Any understanding of Blanchot's thought of the event has to take account of the fact that it is formulated as a disaster, a global rupture of sense that is nevertheless inapparent. Literature does not take place phenomenally but negatively, through what it exposes and displaces, and it is thus that it is opaque and elusive to any thought. In *Qu'est-ce que la philosophie?* Deleuze attempts to recruit Blanchot to his own thought of the event as the actualization of a purely virtual immanence, by suggesting that Blanchot (along with Charles Péguy) has gone furthest into its thinking as he has recognized the two incompatible aspects of the event: that which is actualized and that which is not.[11] But in saying this Deleuze retreats from what he had noted much earlier, in *Logique du sens*, where the thought of the event ascribed to Blanchot is articulated in terms of the encounter with death. On the one hand there is a thought of the event as grounded in the present, as the moment of its actualization, in which case

> the future and the past of the event are judged only according to this definitive present, from the point of view of that which embodies it. But on the other hand there is the future and the past of the event taken in itself, which evades every present, because it is free of the limitations of a state of affairs, being impersonal and pre-individual, neutral, neither

general nor particular ... this ambiguity is essentially that of the wound and of death, of the mortal wound, no one has shown this like Maurice Blanchot: death is at once that which is in an extreme or definite relation with myself and with my body, that which is grounded in me, but also that which is without relation to me, incorporeal and infinitive, impersonal, that which is only grounded in itself.[12]

Such a reading had also appeared the year before, when Deleuze considered the way that the death drive bears its own repetitive mode of time, but it is only in *Logique du sens* that he begins to view death in terms of the temporality of the event. What is important about this reading is the manner in which it exposes a different relation of time, an opening that is not onto the inexistent transcendental of a pure multiplicity but something more formless, a mere exteriority without order or coherence.

In order to draw out this point a little more clearly it is useful to turn to a very different model. In the transition between one year and the next there is a movement of time that encompasses both continuity and discontinuity, there is a rupture and re-beginning, and traditionally this point is marked by a festival. The New Year's festival effectively and ostentatiously covers over this transition and the potential disorientation of returning to zero while also adding one. Time has passed through a revolution in which everything has changed and yet all is as it was, and the fact that this occurs without explicit political activism does not reduce its significance. Instead, the rituals involved with the New Year indicate the awareness of the dangers of any changes in the transcendental order of the political, which is also reflected in the changes found in the transition from one ruling entity to another. Such changes derive from the *passing* of time as such, which the yearly order has granted its own mythical and abstract sequence in passing from one period to the next. What is notable is the fact that this transition is marked in Roman rituals by the figure of Janus, the two-faced god who faces both forwards and backwards. Janus is unusual as he has no counterpart in Greek myths, which is to say that his necessity only arose with the Roman ritual calendar, there being no abstract revolution of time in Greek thought. More importantly, his appearance as a figure that marks beginnings and endings places him not only in a pre-eminently critical role, but also before all other figures in the pantheon, even Jove. Janus appears to mark and to cover over the transition, the very change that allows for the new and thus for beginning as such, as well as ending. There is an intrinsic ambivalence to his role that enables the difficult move from one to the next, and so the very possibility of there being 'one' and 'the next'. But this is not all, for as Ovid makes clear in the *Fasti* Janus was originally known by the name of chaos, the ancient thing (*res prisca*), for between and below the closing and opening that he marks there is simply the gaping or yawning (*hiare*) of an untethered, unhinged hiatus. What is encountered in the revolution of the new is not a re-beginning but the risk of an interval that opens onto an inane and shapeless form (*sine imagine moles*) (1: 103–11).[13] There is no simple transition between one and the next but a rupture and loss of sense. It is as such that Blanchot comes to speak of this change as the disaster, rather than the event, and that it is articulated in terms of mortality as well as literature. But within this articulation there remains the relation between what is ambivalent and what is irrevocable, between the effects of a negation that includes the middle space between truth and falsity and the contradiction of the true and the not true. Any fidelity to the event of literature that Blanchot may articulate is thus towards its untethered errancy as that which more critically unravels the rule of order, as well as more openly exposing its underside.

A particularly acute illustration of this kind of disruption can be found in a short film by the Austrian experimental filmmaker Martin Arnold, *pièce touchée* (1989), which takes an eighteen-second sequence from *The Human Jungle* (Joseph M. Newman, 1954) and stretches it out to sixteen minutes. The sequence begins in a domestic setting with a woman (Paula Raymond) sitting in an armchair reading a newspaper; behind her the front door of the house opens and a man (Gary Merrill) comes in and bends over the back of the chair to kiss her; she then gets up and they both leave the shot to the left. But in stretching this sequence out Arnold has stuttered its progression so that each frame advances only by repeating itself.[14] Any humour this film may have evaporates in the face of the unease of seeing the microstructure of temporality exposed as a chaos of discontinuity. Through a complex pattern of repetitions each action is iterated across waves of variations, and by making use of lateral and vertical inversions Arnold is able to indicate something like the autonomy of each of these steps. When a movement from left to right is iterated with its inversion it creates a circular reflection or echo, but through their repetition these cycles are found to be incomplete and only create empty hollows of action, singular vortices without meaning or purpose. While this may appear to be an exercise in revealing absurd patterns of gender or sexuality, it also reveals moments of profound vertigo, as in the movement of the woman rising from the chair that becomes wholly deformed, and her subsequent abandonment as an isolated figure of mechanism. But the transformation of these steps also leaves them uncertain, as there is a lack of clarity over the relation between what proceeds or succeeds and thus of whether movement as such is even possible.

The sequence starts with a still image but gradually the woman's lips and fingers move, and then there is a sudden explosion of interlinked movements as the door opens behind her, the hall light goes on and off and her head turns towards the doorway as the man comes in. Through its obsessive repetition the sequence exposes linkages between these movements that are causally, and thus, temporally, undecidable. It is significant that this part of the sequence revolves around the opening of the door as it is stuttered back and forth – along with the flickering of the hall light, and the grinding, distorted loop of the sound of the door opening that extends across the whole film – for in this way the door opening and closing marks the film as a whole, insofar as its movement is extrapolated to reveal more than just the gender dynamics of a 1950s B-movie but the spatiotemporal construction of movement and sense as such. This means that, in revealing the construction of sense in this sequence, its Janus-like destruction is also found. There is no certainty to action when it is examined in such a way, only the anguish of its frustration, which is repeated over and over again. There is a nightmarish sense of the fastidiousness associated with extreme obsessive-compulsive disorders here, where any action can proceed only if it is conducted perfectly, and if not, it has to be repeated. But it is not certain whether the individual suffering under such conditions is attempting to counter the chaotic microstructure of discontinuity or is provoking it. Either way, it indicates how the process of activity appears when the sense of continuity and causality is removed, when there is no certainty about the movement from one moment to the next, when each point needs to be restarted as if it were each time a re-beginning.

While the iterated manipulation of frames may seem to reside within a digital schema, it is more akin to an inherent and irresolvable gamble. And in this perspective there is an alternative to the modes of declination, like weariness or waiting, commonly associated with Blanchot's writing, as this stuttered sense of obsession bears a defiance, a deliberate rejection of the causality and finality of ordinary activity, a defiance more often found in the protagonists of Kafka's stories. In this obsession the moment appears to be without end, which suspends its movement of consequence, for with each question or doubt that K. raises he defies the worldly order of progression. His interrogations are attempts to seek out and extend these ruptures, possibilities that have somehow not been accounted, and that surface under the pressure of this contestation. There is an element of the revolutionary to this discovery, since the danger and risk is an index of its impossibility, the fear (precisely) of the unknown as the mark of a life where every moment is not subordinated to its end. But, equally, this is a course of action in which, as with the movement of writing, each moment is a question that must be posed again and again. Thus it is possible to reconsider the figure of Gracchus, for example (or the film noir protagonist, as will be seen), not as one sunk into passive melancholy, but as immersed in the sober chutzpah of the gambler; not exultant, for there is still everything to play for and this will always remain so, but calm and determined, ready to continue to put themselves on the line as they are sure in the knowledge that they have nothing to lose, but also that they are condemned to this pursuit.

To explore this point in relation to the rupture of literary order it is necessary to look at the formal exposure that occurs within Blanchot's writings as they begin to fragment in the 1960s. The first text to do so is *L'Attente l'oubli*, which is concerned with a man and a woman who attempt to make contact with each other. Early on in the text, which is broken up into fragments of speaking, narrative description and speculative meditation, there occurs this piece:

> ❖ The pressure of the city: from all parts. The houses are not there for people to dwell in [*demeure*], but rather so that there can be streets and, in the streets, the incessant movement of the city.[15]

This fragment is unusual as the city is not mentioned anywhere else in the text, indeed; there are hardly any references to the exterior of the hotel room in which everything takes place. Instead, it almost seems to anticipate, or to have been misplaced from, Blanchot's later work, *Le Pas au-delà*, which deals extensively with the activity of the streets. Anthony Abiragi has provided an extensive and illuminating analysis of this fragment, but in doing so he relates it to the general thematics of the voice, and its lack of expectation. While this may integrate it within the text, its anomalous status should first be addressed, for in standing out from the other fragments it is remarking on their arrangement.

It cannot be ignored that the pressure being discussed, which leads to incessant movement, is also that of the tension between the fragments in the text and the space between them. Thus the suggestion that the houses are not abodes to remain (*demeure*) in refers to the necessity to avoid thinking that meaning 'resides' in the fragments of the text. Instead, Blanchot seems to be hinting at a diacritical relation between the fragments and the spaces between them, where the pressure comes from all sides. A diacritical pressure would both constitute and destabilize the text insofar as it operates laterally through it, which suggests that we should be more concerned with the relations between the spaces and the fragments for in themselves they mean less than their (negatively) iterated elaboration. This emphasis on the negativity of relation echoes that within the text between the man and the woman, and between the modes of waiting and forgetting and speech and thinking, by showing that the space that unfolds as a result of this diacritical tension is formed by its suspended relations. As a 'whole' the text is then formed not by the meaningful entities that it may contain but by the negative space that arises between its parts by virtue of their lateral differentiations. The way that form, rather than just sense, is diacritically constituted (and destabilized) indicates that Blanchot is seeking to understand how the text as such becomes (de)formed by its (suspended) relations, especially when the opening of the text relies on this negative iteration. It is as such that the work can have no beginning but only unfolds according to its own fragmentation, and in doing so exposes the space of this absence and errancy.

A text operating under such a pressure is one that has not covered over its opening transition but has stepped aside into its interstitial space, which is necessarily as formless as it is constitutive, and thus is not merely negative but neutral. As such, this space would be profoundly abyssal in that it is not just ungrounded but in its bottomlessness gives rise to a vertigo that comes from the gaps between, since this is a space without form or sense, a sheer gaping of a relation without end. Blanchot's contemporary announcement (that we are at a turning point only if there is no certainty of that being the case) derives its pressure from this space as a result of its ambivalent resistance to certainty, which is thus the most forceful evidence of its occurrence as a turning but also prohibits any straightforward decision or fidelity in relation to it. Instead, what imposes itself on the reader is a reversal in which the fragile material contingency of relation is exposed, without its articulation. This is the reversal that is marked in the fragment above in the movement from focusing positively on the houses, to one that sees them negatively in terms of the streets. This reversal then illuminates the previous paratactic statement about pressure from all parts, which means that there can be no privileged perspective. In concise terms, the negativity that enables reason to be reason, insofar as it permeates it as its determinative function, perpetually presents it with its own annihilation. This is because negativity has no natural limits, so there is always a risk that it will unravel to excess, thereby exposing reason to its own destruction. It is this endless destruction that is then endured in literature as a space without order or consistency.

But as the figure of Janus indicated this schism also occurs in the other direction, as it were. Rather than there being a re-beginning that exposes a caesura, there is also a caesura that brings about a re-beginning. Blanchot speaks in these terms about the poem and the way that it calls for its poet, who will bring it to realization. That is, the poem only exists negatively, in a state of expectation, but this means that 'it is, in a way, because there is the poem that the future is possible' [PF: 108/103]. Language makes possible this reversal from the merely accidental exposure of the abyss to its provocation, and, in poetry in particular, by virtue of its temporal reflexivity, this caesura is called forth in the awareness of the absence that marks its situation. This negativity or constitutive incompleteness not only provokes the poet but unfolds the very possibility of the future as that which may fulfil it. Like the revolution, the poem is nothing in itself but in calling for its lover it makes its occurrence retroactively possible. Blanchot is discussing the poetry of Char here, whose writings, as I will show in the next chapter, are especially sensitive to this movement, in that their dense and fragmentary appearance impedes a linear reading and instead generates a complex of partial rereadings that in going back and forth to its moment of rupture draw out its excess, without ever making it present.[16] In this way the poem, like the revolution, gives itself in its absence as that which will, in disappearing, make possible the future. To take two non-poetic examples first, in a devastating account of the failed revolution in Egypt in 2011 the cycle of events exposes its demeaning in a very specific way. The author, Omar Robert Hamilton, structures his account in three parts: the period of excitement within the revolution, the violence that followed the election of Mohamed Morsi and the return to the status quo ante with the military coup. Each of the sections has its own style and tenor but Hamilton provides a telling insight by marking their sequence with the titles, Tomorrow, Today, Yesterday.[17] This is not just to show the cycle of demeaning but also to indicate the specific temporal index of the moments, which is not simply counter-intuitive but real and forceful: The revolution realizes itself under the banner of Tomorrow; it is never there, it is only the expectation and demand for what is not present, but, like the poem, the caesura of this moment cannot be sustained and its passage leads into what is merely now, and then only what was. There may be an inevitability to this cycle, but this is because the revolution cannot substantiate itself as that which is present without sacrificing its call for what is not present.

The second example is much older and is the apparent explication of nihilism provided by Gorgias:

1. Nothing exists.
2. Even if something exists, it would be unknowable and inconceivable.
3. Even if it could be apprehended, it would be inexpressible to someone else.

As a model of philosophical logic this falls very short, but in its anxious hypotheticals it presents a parody of Hegelian logic that is more interesting in its poetic formulation.[18] For Gorgias conveys the movement from being to thought to language through a retreat from negativity, while still remaining within its negation. A counter-world of negativity is thus exposed, which nevertheless bears its own forms and structures, thereby indicating that it is still possible to unfold this extreme starting point. But in doing so the claim of this emptiness is betrayed into existence, as existence, even if this remains apophatic. The poetic tension of Gorgias's thought, which makes it difficult to ascertain its status and position, makes it a key moment in the sceptical suspension of ontology, of any thought of being as presence, but also shows how the movement of nothing animates thought with another tendency. The temporal opening exposed in this thinking is complex partly because of its hypothetical positioning, but also because these hypotheses depend on nothing, which leaves their opening indefinite and undetermined, for what kind of thought could follow in the wake of this, to what does it call?

It is evidence of the pervasive effects of the modernity that Hölderlin announced that in two different but parallel œuvres, film noir and Blanchot's writings, there is a considered response to this rupture of emptiness, a response that moves from a faux pas to *désastre* by way of fatelessness, ambivalence and errancy. This makes their contemporaneous emergence highly significant in that both are explorations of the peculiarity of the times (which have not passed), and of the contingency that permeates the historical and yields a different mode of experience that takes place through a persistent negation of negation, which displaces any sense of its event.

2

Ruptures and deviations

II. The desire of form

If the caesura is a rupture of form in which there is an opening or rebeginning, then this is because its negativity bears a force that occurs as a peculiar mode of time. This rupture is focused in literature, and especially poetry, because, as Herder was one of the first to show, poetry operates through time to a much greater extent than painting or sculpture. This is the case because poetry manifests itself as a particular conjugation of temporal movements (anticipation and recollection, waiting and forgetting) that are both material and signifying and that engage the reader of the poem as well as its writer.[1] The force of poetry takes place through time, which is thus the dimension of its actualization in thought and language, thereby exposing each to the temporality of the poem as the possibility of formation that the caesura brings to a profound degree of acuteness. So, when the caesura occurs in poetry, for example, it brings with it a temporal rupture that is also a critical (un)founding of sense. Music may do this on a more abstract level, and cinema perhaps operates in a more structured register, but within the poem, due to the concrete negativity of language, there is scope for thought to experience possibility as such, the sheer exposure of thought to what is not (yet, or anymore). To the degree that poetry is denser and more fragmentary than prose, it opens a temporal schism that is itself denser and more fragmentary, a moment or rupture that could be called a turning point if such a designation can be made: 'the poem is this movement towards what is not and, even more, the enjoyment [*jouissance*] of what has not been granted, the appropriation, in the most substantial presence, of a This is not yet there, This will be there only if I myself have disappeared' [PF: 108/103]. Consequently, as Blanchot explains, the poem 'escapes us because it is our absence rather than our presence and because it begins by making emptiness, and takes things from themselves, and substitutes endlessly what cannot be shown for what it shows, what cannot be said for what it says' [PF: 107/

103]. The sacrificial and appropriative aspects of this movement should not divert us from the manner in which the claim of nothingness asserts itself in the poem as that which exposes the future but affords no certainty or clarity. It is not surprising then that Char's poetry should involve a convergence between violence and eroticism, 'this exalted encounter of contraries, this orgasm of "for and against animated by an equal and murderous violence" (of which Artine speaks in the *Marteau sans maître*)', since this reveals the extreme refusal of the poem to be accommodated to any easy operation of thought as well as the passion of its response [PF: 107/102]. These contraries are its temporal dimensions of rupture and provocation, in which is found the sovereign demand of the poem to reconstruct reality on the basis of what is not there and what remains impossible, insofar as it cannot be realized, such that the poem exists as the impossible, in place of the world.

However, Blanchot has misquoted Char here, since the line from *Artine* does not speak of an opposition of for and against but rather, and quite emphatically, of a struggle between for and for:

> The appearances of Artine went beyond the border of those countries of sleep, where the *for* and the *for* are animated by an equal and murderous violence.
>
> OC: 18/321 (emphases in the original)

He would also seem to have read this line against the grain, as Char's sense seems to be more closely grasped as Artine's avoidance of those places that bear this equal and murderous violence. Considering the large number of quotations that mark Blanchot's essay, it seems unlikely that this error can be put down to poor memory, as he would appear to be writing with Char's works at hand, and it is notably the only quotation that is incorrect (while there are other minor lapses, this is the only instance of a serious change of sense). Thus it would seem that this is simply, but unusually, an instance of misreading. While Char's poems make much of a Heraclitean play of opposites, it is evident that he sees the poet's role as one of surpassing such disputes by short-circuiting them. In this way the poet moves beyond the unavoidability of position and affirmation and also its inadequacy, so that it is no longer a case of holding to a position either for or against but of departing from both. As will be seen, there is a sense that Blanchot is struggling to fathom Char's poetry because of its richness and variety, but he is also encountering something that is quite different from what he finds in the poems of Mallarmé or Hölderlin. This singularity can be found in the poetic thoughts entitled *Partage formel* (1945), which is the locus for much of Blanchot's discussion and which he explicates thus: 'The poetic imagination distances itself from reality in order to join this very movement of self-distancing to it, to make interior to what is that which is not as its principle, the absence that makes presence desirable' [PF: 108/104].

Poetry takes on the form of desire, but in doing so makes reality that which desires by activating this constitutive lack within things. It thus 'realizes the imaginary by rediscovering the imaginary in the real' [PF: 109/104]. What is intriguing is the emphasis on the actual transformation of reality by way of desire as this gives evidence that Char is not operating like Mallarmé, by thinking and working through language, but is concerned with the 'free distribution of the totality of things' and their communication, 'for it is in the poem that the complete and completely free presence of beings and things is realized' [OC: 160/113; PF: 109/105]. This sense of realization achieves its full range in the poem because the poem, uniquely, is, in Char's words, 'the realized love of desire that remains desire' [OC: 162/117].

The earthiness of Char's poetry may present something of a challenge for Blanchot, but it also allows him to break new ground by introducing a thought of poetic language as density traversed by desire, and thus as bearing an enigmatic violence as it realizes the longing of things. Conversely, some of the ontological language used by Char will be resisted by Blanchot as he comes to move away from the notion of presence in relation to language in his later works, but at this time, unlike in his essay on Heidegger's reading of Hölderlin that will follow shortly after the Char essay, he seems to commit himself to an image of the poet as articulating the unveiling of being. It even seems that Blanchot is willing to admit of a 'common presence', as Char terms it, that unites and supports things and their communication, which he will otherwise later reject. But Char's language of fragmentation allows for this admission as it makes possible a thought of the common as that which is 'pulverized', just as the medium of light exists as particles and waves, radiation and combustion, which is the Heraclitean sense of the formal sharing and division (*partager*) of things in their free distribution.[2] Char's language thus asserts a pressure on Blanchot's thought as he comes to think together the notions of the fragmentary and the *neutre* (that will only later be given names) as converging-diverging:

> Horrible, exquisite, moving earth and heterogeneous human condition seize and qualify themselves mutually. Poetry draws itself from the exalted summit of their moiré.
>
> OC: 162/117

Such is the tectonic vision of ontology that Char conveys: fiery, material, obscure and unpredictable. It is as such that he will also be drawn to the cave paintings at Lascaux, where the exposure of this chasm will be to the incomprehensible and unnameable. The timelessness of this vision derives from the fact that it does not form part of any temporal sequence but simply yawns onto its convulsions and turmoil. Poetry makes it possible for linearity to be obliterated, literally, to be overwritten, again and again, to the point of its destruction, leaving neither negativity nor its other, neither affirmation nor its other, neither position nor tendency but density and volatility. It is as such that it is also a literature of resistance.

Indeed, it is perhaps this combination of an ontological language with a volcanic tension that leads Blanchot to reconsider the possibility of language operating with notions of presence and unity. While this combination is worked out in Char's poetry through their mutual instability, for Blanchot it will become more and more apparent over the subsequent years that this pressure on language will need to be worked through on an abstract or formal level. The use of fragmentation and parataxis in Char's language will offer guides to this change, but it will also be necessary to grasp the way that these formal changes bring about a change to the very possibility of thinking through language, to the kinds of thought that this different form of language will make possible or impossible. In much the same way that Blanchot will find with Heidegger's reading of Hölderlin, the pressure exerted on thought by poetic language does not fully contest it, but nor does it confirm it; rather there is a demand to think through its particular resistance to thought with all of the contradictions that this involves. It is significant that Char's works are then articulated through an engagement with worldly activity while desisting from the time of the world, just as, in different terms, Hölderlin's thought was also led to negotiate its own time. This point is explicated by the note that prefaces *Feuillets d'Hypnos*, his fragments from the maquis, where Char makes clear that they were not written from the point of view of the self or of the work but only insofar as 'they were affected by the event'. The distance between this form of writing and any Sartrean mode of engagement becomes all too apparent, and shows in advance of Blanchot's later response to Sartre how far the ambivalent tension and materiality of language will unsettle any straightforward translation of word and action.[3] For although these notes are slight and impersonal, mere 'nothing' in comparison to the gravity of the circumstances, nevertheless the event finds in them that which will become lasting [OC: 173/133]. This is the case because 'poetry is revealed to itself, not only when it reflects itself, but when it decides itself and can thus speak of everything, exactly because it is itself in everything' [PF: 111/106]. But for poetry to decide itself even as it reflects itself is for it to engage the movement of ambivalence in materiality, the gravity and lightness of the roll of the dice, by which it becomes part of not only the movement of events but also their thought:

> Boldness of being for an instant oneself the accomplished form of the poem. Well-being of having glimpsed the sparkle of matter-emotion instantly queen.
>
> OC: 62

The mode of time in the fragment both initiates and unravels movement; by folding it back against itself it evades progress or evolution and instead finds a movement that neither negates nor affirms but remains grammatically, and logically, *neutre*. Blanchot sees this condensed form of language as one of a sovereign presence because it demands and expresses itself to an absolute degree, and so the 'presence' at issue is one in which 'the smallest possible unit of time contains the strongest reality of images' [PF: 111/107]. This explosion of thought and reality is such that what is lasting and what is passing are both marked and exceeded by a point that cannot be reduced to either, as there is a negation of syntax by form and a negation of form by syntax, without either becoming stable.

The images that might be understood to be inside the poem are no more inside it than they are outside it, since they do not appear as descriptions or indications but rather as a specific articulation of things and thoughts that is opened up in the poem for the first time. This is the basis for the enigmatic and oracular quality that Blanchot perceives in Char's works, and that links him to the writings of Heraclitus, for the opening that occurs in the poem exposes a time without, which is neither past, present nor future but simply gapes, a time of absence or waiting that simply is not. It is at this point that Blanchot's analysis starts to approach the consideration of negation that Badiou had discussed, by way of a very interesting reading of the nature of poetic images. The image does not merely negate the object, nor indeed is it negated by it, since this would follow the logic of substitution found in the understanding of images as signs or illustrations. Instead of an image working metaphorically, by taking up a certain association with an object and then supplanting it by translating it into another form, which in its arbitrariness lacks necessity or force, the image takes up the object through its own absence, which thereby allows for its coupled completion and destruction. The image, as Blanchot writes, is first an image, the absence of what it gives, which introduces it as the presence of an absence. But, in this absence, the image exposes the 'underside' of the object, 'its reality of earth', or matter-emotion, in Char's words. Thus the image is not the object but nor is it not the object; instead, it is both the object and not, thereby breaking the rules of the excluded middle and non-contradiction. Both image and object are changed by the exposure of their materiality and absence, for in doing so they are exposed to their own transformation, to a fragile and unforeseeable series of changes:

> In this new presence, the thing loses its individuality of object closed by use, it strives to be metamorphosed into a completely other thing and into all things, in such a way that the first image is also led to change and, carried away in the cycle of metamorphoses, becomes an endlessly stronger and more complex power of transforming the world into a whole by the appropriation of desire.
>
> PF: 112–13/108

The movement from use to desire, by way of a transformation that is fierce and endless, brings a different tenor to Blanchot's reading of poetic language, which is transformed through material desire into a power of radical and total change. The negativity of the image takes on the material ambivalence of transience and density, the thickness of things and the movement of becoming. Neither presence nor absence, and yet also both presence and absence, a force that is not of language but is rather that which supports and undermines it; space as plenum and void, time as breach and rebeginning, and their undecidable life death.

The sense of this Heraclitean formula is not just to be found in the manner in which it reconfigures life and death but also in the pressure that it places on the nature of conjunction and antagonism [EI: 122–3/87].[4] Language makes possible this formulation, but it is drawn from the ambivalence in things themselves and, as Blanchot goes on to suggest, this *neutre* formulation, insofar as it neither posits nor negates, affirms nor denies, is that which the entire history of philosophy has sought to domesticate 'by substituting for it the law of the impersonal and the reign of the universal'. While we might associate this suppression with that of materiality by the concept, he also (rather unusually) aligns it with the repression of the drives, and together these provide for a powerful focus in understanding the role of desire in Char's writings [EI: 441/299].[5] For, although writing is the speech of the dead, of an absent voice, as Socrates insisted (*Phaedrus*, 275d), it is also the voice of this absence that marks it as the past or future in its intrinsically unknowable opening. So, in exposing ourselves to this voice through reading or writing, we are exposed to its time as a gaping of sense, an opening that is irrational in that it depends on nothing and has no reason. It is as this incompletely self-negating form that writing speaks and is endured in the experience of literature. The poem, like the revolution, is thus no more than a promise of happiness, which is to say that it is an experience, here, of what is not here, and so is a sensual experience of both pleasure and pain, which is its erotic sense: 'This pain and suffering is, in a sense, the only form in which we, as conditioned creatures in the face of beauty, can think, feel, or experience utopia at all' [A: 147/92]. Beauty thereby exists as a tension between the subjective and objective and, as Adorno's reading of the *Phaedrus* shows, this tension becomes the basis for any aesthetics that would discuss it, an aesthetics that cannot be considered disinterested as it is grounded in desire, a desire that never fully sublimates itself, and so remains riven by this tension and its erotic suffering: 'the concept of beauty is simply incompatible [*unvereinbar*] with the concept of health and essentially no beauty can be thought that, as such suffering, does not have a certain kind of affinity with death' [A: 162/101]. Thus Adorno can go on to say that

> art captures utopia as something present [*eine gegenwärtige*] among us, albeit at the cost of its reality. And herein lies the double-sidedness

[*Doppelte*] of art: insofar as it is critical and does not as it were betray the absolute it opposes reality; yet at the same time, insofar as it declines [*verzichtet*] from realizing that absolute, it becomes embroiled with reality – not to say, degraded by it – and then in turn becomes a part of the merely existing, of mere reality.

A: 163/102

In doing so, he not only finds the entire history of aesthetics in Socrates' palinode on the erotic nature of beauty (*Phaedrus*, 249d-252b), but also finds that Plato goes further than Kant or Hegel in drawing out the desire, or sensual madness, that is central to the experience of beauty, which means that it is materially complex and dynamic as 'there is nothing spiritual in a work of art that is not also sensual, and there is nothing sensual in a work of art that is not also spiritual, though without the spiritual and the sensual ever simply subsuming each other' [A: 166/103].[6]

Although there is no necessary (or etymological) relation between the yawning and yearning of this opening, there remains a resonance between them insofar as they refer to an opening without natural limit or closure that simply gapes. The desire that emerges across this opening is singular as it evades both its Kantian and Hegelian versions. While it may appear dialectical, as there is a relation between the desire to submit to the material opening and a desire to subsume it formally, in which each mediates the other, there is no resolution because the opening knows no limits and so there is no point at which the dialectic can complete itself. The same is true in relation to the Kantian version, as the attraction and repulsion felt within the oscillations of desire is not recouped in any sublime notion as the awareness of a harmony between the freedom and nature of the human mind. As a sheer yawning the opening does not offer any respite; instead the tension between attraction and repulsion gives rise to a profound and irresolvable vertigo. As its caesura is temporal and logical the force of this vertigo is to be found in thought even as it is experienced as a sensual, material abandon, for the body is cut loose from order and oriented towards the rupture that provokes and disturbs its thinking. As with the poem or the revolution, desire is not responding to anything in particular but instead to the possibility of utter transformation, a possibility that is not given or revealed but only indicated by the negation of what is and what is not.

The description of *eros* given by Diotima in the *Symposium* depends on this interstitial situation. As she points out, *eros* is neither mortal nor immortal, good nor bad, beautiful nor ugly, but takes up a position between (*metaxu*) that enables the humans and the gods to communicate. This is usually taken to mean that *eros* provides the medium through which the harmony of the cosmos is maintained, as well as allowing for a communication between the world of forms and the material world without which there would be no possibility of knowledge. But the place between is also that which separates, and that which reveals the lack of fit between the two aspects, for *eros* desires the beautiful and the good because it lacks these things (*Symposium*, 202d). In this way, the interstitial site is that which exposes the extremes, through its yearning for that which it lacks. Diotima's argument about this between-space derives from the fact that a lack of wisdom (*sophia*) is not necessarily ignorance (*amathia*) as there is that which is neither wisdom nor ignorance, since it is possible to have correct opinions without being able to give an account (*logos*) of them (202a). That is, there is a place here for truth without the philosophical *logos*. The name for this space, which is also a form of communication and thought, is that of the *daimon*, of which *eros* is but one example, and, as Diotima explains, it is through this *daimon* that there exists such things as prophecy and poetry, which are those forms of irrational (ungrounded) knowledge that exist outside philosophy.

This sense of separation has been emphasized by Klossowski in his reading of the story of Diana and Actaeon. Much like Socrates in the *Phaedrus*, Actaeon steps into a space that allows him to experience a different mode of appearance. This step is as much a disaster or faux pas for him as it is for Diana, and the mutual divergence entailed by their combined impossibility arises because each experiences their existence as an image: 'the demon *simulates* Diana in her theophany, and inspires in Actaeon the desire and insane hope of possessing the goddess. It becomes Actaeon's imagination and Diana's mirror' [BD: 46/35; emphasis in the original].[7] This interstitial space is double and it is thus that it communicates: Diana only sees an image of Actaeon insofar as she experiences herself as an image, and Actaeon does the same. Their opening to each other is through the image, or rather, it is the *daimon* that makes this impossible encounter possible in its image-existence, and the nature of the *daimon* is desire as the form and event of change. The moment of the encounter is its own torsion of origin, result and experience, which is how Blanchot describes the singular form of the narrative or *récit*. The encounter takes shape in the narrative as the reflection of its own caesura, which also indicates the anomalous status of the revolution as an entity; since 'the revolution' does not exist or take place, it is not a figure, just as Diana only appears by way of a simulacrum through which Actaeon can encounter her/it. This entails a collision between the modes of linearity and circulation, such that this moment of impossible transgression is 'original', as it is that from which the different orders of history derive.[8] As a result

> the demon, because it is neither god nor man but as it were the *reflection* of the one in the other, itself excluded from the mythic world, inaugurates in its intermediary position the way of seeing and of judging of the theologians and metaphysicians; from this it divides the universe into three regions: that of the gods who it says are impassible and immortal; that of its own immortal and passible fellows [*congénères*]; that of

passible mortals. Its immortality, being for it only endless time, becomes an object of experience; from this it projects into mythic space the time of reflection; it thus recovers mythic space, which is for it the outside, in interior or 'mental' space, and in its role of mediator between the two worlds – that of the gods and that of the mortals, still united in absolute mythic space before its proper mediation – it asks itself what is 'exterior' and 'interior', and finally concludes in favour of the nothingness of pure appearances: thought.

BD: 60–1/45–6 (emphasis in the original)

If the encounter is recognized by the fact that its narrative is its origin, result and experience, then this indicates the manner in which time and language have become distorted by desire so that what occurs and its reflection are integrated into but also separated from what is. It is as such that the event yields to writing and to disaster, since it is intrinsic to its exteriority that its sense and materiality cannot be distinguished – this is its image-existence, which is not to reduce its impact but to show that it is both obtrusive and elusive; *that* it has happened is more certain than *what* it was, which is the sense of its traumatic vertigo. This (mis-)step takes place through desire, which is simply that of wanting something different, of wanting some kind of change, something beyond or outside the norm, because this is desire. It does not recognize any laws or prohibitions any more than the reality principle or the rules of non-contradiction and the excluded middle, which means that it does not concern itself with preserving the self. It seeks only its own satisfaction, which cannot be achieved as it is *only* desire, only yearning, the *schlechten* opening that is also its faux pas. This reading is found by Blanchot without going through Freud, but rather by joining Char with Heraclitus to find the form of desire in the (impossible) desire of form, which is as political as it is literary and philosophical.

As noted earlier, Herder understands the movement of change as force, but it is no more than the relation that enables change to take place in the movement from one thing to another; force does not pre-exist the transformation as its condition or rule, it is simply that through (*per*) which change takes place. As a result, force is part of the movement of desire and infection as both are contingent or contagious and although this means that it is not reducible to language, nor is it separable from it, and this also means that its effects are unlimited as it does not only work on the basis of what is proximal or direct. From this point of view, it is only an arbitrary numerical convention that confines New Year's Day to one day a year, since by virtue of the contingency and materiality of desire each instance of its occurrence is a new historical departure (which is what will become pervasive to film noir). As the possibility of its occurrence is ubiquitous, so is its potential rupture, thereby suspending the possibility of continuity in favour of a universal catastrophe that is ignored only insofar as it is denied and suppressed. Kafka's similar version of history, as seen from the point of view of the disaster, its ubiquity and invisibility, would then make the arrival of post-revolutionary despair meaningless: the revolution is neither there nor not there and so can neither be celebrated nor mourned, there is only the inevitability of universal and perpetual micro-breakdowns. The law and the state are only illusions that attempt to conceal these immanent fractures or confine them to particular events.

Desire is that which occurs between the particular and the universal, with all the lack of fit that this entails such that it is never satisfied (politically, aesthetically, religiously, etc.). This movement between the material and the impersonal is at the heart of Char's thinking of the earth, which forces a reconsideration of the way that Blanchot later subscribes to Levinas's critique of so-called pagan worldviews, as it is in this earthly situation that Char's poetry finds its intrinsic tension.[9] The lover and the poet would seem to inhabit the interstices of this yearning, which is also to inhabit a situation exposed to its ineradicable contingency. Thus the distance that the lover and the poet take to the revolution reveals the imperative of permanent revolution, which bears a fidelity to nothing more than its endless desire; it is not for anything other than the perpetuation of its own vertigo. Is this not simply a dangerous form of anarcho-nihilism? From the position of politics (revolutionary or not), the answer would have to be yes, but what is intriguing is that it is nevertheless ubiquitous and, moreover, the basis of politics. There can be no conversion of the yearning lover into the faithful Leninist cadre as the lover cannot recognize any party, yet they persist and pervade society as its most critical ruptures. The lover, like the criminal (for whom desire becomes emptied into another form, as will be shown), operates on a different, but not non-political, level. They expose the fissures out of which society forms itself through their denial and suppression.

III. Dissembling events

Blanchot returned to Char six years later in his long essay on Heidegger's 'Der Ursprung des Kunstwerkes'. While Heidegger is not mentioned in this essay (he is only referred to as 'a contemporary philosopher'), Blanchot is clearly following his thought very closely even as he marks his own points of emphasis and deviation.[10] Initially this essay was published in *Les Temps modernes* under the title of 'L'art, la littérature et l'expérience originelle', which makes it apparent that Blanchot is not interested in discussing the origin of the artwork in general as much as its particular occurrence in literature. Moreover, it is the experience of the origin that is the focus such that literature *is* this 'original' experience. Hence, and in contrast to Heidegger's essay, Blanchot discusses the work of many poets, especially

Char, and in doing so the image of a 'horrible, exquisite, moving earth' takes on considerable weight.

As is well known, Heidegger's analysis of the work of art centres on the way that it is torn between the two aspects of the world and the earth, roughly speaking: its socio-historical resonance and its material conditions and resistance. Given what has already been sketched out by Blanchot in his earlier reading of Char, such a model evidently has relevance, but Heidegger's essay largely uses the examples of an ancient Greek temple and a painting by Van Gogh to demonstrate this model, so the particular tension in the work of literature remains obscure. Blanchot takes up this point by saying the following:

> The painting is not made from material ingredients added to a canvas, it is the presence of this matter which without it would remain hidden to us. And the poem likewise is not made with ideas, or with words, but it is that from which the words become their appearance and the *elemental depth* upon which this appearance is opened while it closes itself.
>
> EL: 233/223 (emphasis in the original)

Such would seem to be a fairly straightforward rendering of Heidegger's thought, made all the stronger by the use of his vocabulary of appearance and presence. But the tension that is exposed in the poem needs to be examined closely, for if it is 'that from which the words become their appearance', then the poem is not its words but that which enables them to occur in their own light, as it were. However, it is also the depth that is exposed and concealed in this occurrence. The poem is thus, as Blanchot makes clear, a site and its depth, rather than an arrangement of thoughts and meanings, which suggests that it is no more than the site of this depth as it opens and closes, thereby giving it a temporal as well as spatial dimension.

As he goes on to say, this means that the earthly aspect of the work is not simply material but 'elemental', by which he would seem to be associating his thought with the phenomenological analyses of the night conducted by Merleau-Ponty and Levinas, which emphasize the peculiar nature of its depth. But he is also recalling an archaic mode of designation as well, a mode of poetic language that names without defining in that an element is solely that within which something dwells, and, when taken in itself, as 'the elemental', it is that which conveys a certain formless context or milieu. It is as such that Blanchot can turn to Char's line about the horrible, exquisite, moving earth, which conveys this complex of unfolding and disturbing without fully determining it. But in doing so, Blanchot brings to Heidegger's thought a sense that was missed due to the latter's avoidance of a considered discussion of poetry in the artwork essay. If we look to Heidegger's description of the way that the earth is brought forth in the artwork, we find a telling lapse:

The rock comes to bear and rest and so first becomes rock; the metal comes to glitter and shimmer, the colours to glow, the tone to ring, the word to say. All this comes forth as the work sets itself back into the massiveness and heaviness of stones, into the firmness and pliancy of wood, into the hardness and lustre of ores, into the lightening and darkening of colour, into the ringing of tones, and into the naming power of words.[11]

The framing of each aspect of materiality works until the last clause, since the naming power of words is not akin to the heaviness of stone or the pliancy of wood (unless we look at these objects solely in utilitarian terms). Heidegger's predisposition towards approaching poetic language through the notions of saying and naming overlays the elemental dimension of words that Blanchot is seeking to expose. Witness Blanchot's own version of these lines:

The obscurity of this presence that escapes comprehension, which is without certainty but brilliant [*éclatant*], which, at the same time that it is an event, seems the silent repose of a closed thing, all this we try to hold, to arrange comfortably in saying: the work *is* eminently *what* it *is made of* [ce dont elle est faite], it is what makes its nature and its matter visible or present, the glorification of its reality: of verbal rhythm in the poem, of sound in music, of light become colour in painting, of space become stone in the house.

EL: 232/223 (emphases in the original)

Verbal rhythm is very different from the naming power of saying: there is less emphasis on the evocation or annunciation of being and more on the appearance of the poem through its unfolding materiality. Rhythm, as Heidegger had explored elsewhere in relation to Aristotle, traditionally concerns the structured appearance of materiality, an orderly, worldly formation.[12] But for Blanchot the sense of rhythm comes out more forcefully in the work of Mallarmé, who refers to a 'mould that does not take place as any object that exists but borrows all the scattered ores, unknown and floating according to some richness, to quicken there a seal, and to forge them', a concentration that 'attracts no less than disengages for its unfurling [*épanouissement*] ... the thousand elements of beauty'.[13] Rhythm is not so much a unitary gathering but rather an opening that disperses, not to dissipate but to render its obscure materiality visible in its disengagement (*dégagement*). Rhythm is a kind of principle that is nothing (but verse), neither transcendental nor empirical but apparent only through the transparency of its obscure unfurling: *terre mouvante, horrible, exquise* [EL: 235/225].

This movement of unfurling or disengagement (the contrast with Sartre is implicit) is critical as it means that it is not directed towards a goal that would complete or satisfy it; instead, the lack that underlies this movement remains through its expression as its endless elemental resistance to appearance. Although Blanchot makes use of a language of presence and essence in this essay, this will become weakened and qualified in his later works so that any sense of ontology will be lost. And the failure to adhere to a transcendental-empirical order affects the temporality of this movement, as it is neither within the order of worldly time nor is it removed into a timeless sphere of ideals. The poem unfurls its own time in the same way that it disengages its own materiality. It is thus no accident that Blanchot starts to discuss the work of art in terms of the event, but in doing so he is moving as far from Heidegger as he is from Hegel's understanding of history. The unfolding that occurs in Char's description of the earth is not gathered up into a moment of illumination but is materially, temporally and lexically elusive. What is revealed here is the eccentricity of thought and language in the face of this enigmatic elusiveness, the impossibility of circumscription that leads the poem to fall away into opaque, jagged moments (or absences) of disengagement and fragmentation.

Necessarily, this dispersal has its effects on the poet as well as the poem, for, as Blanchot goes on to show, speaking and hearing find their principle in the tearing apart of this unfolding such that the poet 'is held in this divergence [*écart*] where the still wordless rhythm, the voice that says nothing, but does not cease to speak, must become power of naming in the one alone who hears it' [EL: 236/226]. While Blanchot's use of *écart* resembles the notion of *Riß* in Heidegger's thought, the modulation of this notion as a rhythm without words and an empty voice marks it as a force of deformation as much as formation and, further, indicates how the poet (and reader) results from it as its mere possibility (I will return to this use of *écart* shortly). The realization of this possibility is not inevitable, the poet or reader is always to come, which is why their existence is marked by an inescapable absence, a lack that can never be fulfilled and that entails that the poem is always incomplete. Such is the nature of its event, which is less an occurrence than a slippage of absence, an exposure to the outside of sense. As evidence of this fragmentation Blanchot shows how the poem, despite its indifference, gives rise to a distinction between the author and the reader. It is only the latter who is able to bring out the words of the poem anew each time, while the former is dispossessed by the work; being no more than a trace of its actualization the poet only survives this moment of creation by dying into it [EL: 237/227]. (This movement will become key to Blanchot's understanding of the event of the *récit*, as will be found in Chapter 4.) Although both author and reader are equal in their singular relation to the work, and can in fact be the same person, they do not share this relation for there is an irreducible deviation of sense between them, so that there can be no privileged or given relation to the work. Intriguingly, there is a moment in Blanchot's writings when this distinction breaks down, which is highly resonant for his early work. This is the scene at the beginning of chapter 4 of *Thomas l'Obscur* where the protagonist, in reading a text, finds himself 'in relation to every sign, in the situation in which the male praying mantis finds itself when the female goes to devour it. They looked at each other. The words, issuing from a book that was taking on a deadly power [*puissance mortelle*], exercised a gentle and peaceful attraction over the gaze that touched them'.[14] This would be the experience of reading in which the reader enters into the author's relation to the text, and is thereby exposed to its mortality, and it is this interrelation that is loosened or displaced as Blanchot begins to move away from the concentration of the *récit* in the 1950s towards a more fragmentary and dispersive textual relation.

Hence, the temporality of this other relation is extraordinary, for if the work is an event, then it 'does not come to pass outside of time, any more than the work would be simply spiritual, but, through it, another time comes into time, and into the world of beings that exist and of things that subsist comes, as presence, not another world, but the other of all worlds, that which is always other than the world' [EL: 238/228].[15] Such a thought of the event is no closer to Badiou than it is to Heidegger, for here the event is neither within the world nor without, neither immanent nor transcendent, but is rather a *lapsus* or parapraxis, 'the slip [*glissement*] that brushes the outside', which is later called the disaster [PAD: 86/60]. It is thus that Blanchot can discuss the work of art in terms of an excessive refusal that is at the same time a beginning or opening, which is to say that it is a departure: both affirmation and negation. A departure not only from the world but also from truth and meaning, becoming mere deviation, constant errancy: 'it is not only in relation to truths already known and certain that it seems strange, the scandal of the monstrous and of the non-true, but it always refutes the true: whatever it may be, even if it is drawn from it, it overturns it' [EL: 239/229].

The ontological language that Blanchot uses in this essay, and in *L'Espace littéraire* as a whole, is unusual. It is not used to the same degree in any of his other works, early or late, and to that extent it is clearly brought about by his reading of Heidegger, but it is also a language that is being drawn into a set of thoughts and perspectives that Blanchot has been developing himself. However, the disparity between these discussions of essence and presence and the deviations from these terms is not fully negotiated. As I have shown elsewhere, the impetus for this negotiation will arise through the changes in his fictional writings in the 1950s, where this disparity will become more explicit and critical.[16] The notions of presence and essence in relation to the work of art are very powerful, as they indicate how the artwork exists in its own factical state, its own singular appearance, which is intrinsically different in kind to other objects. But the errancy of language that Blanchot has explored undermines this notion by exposing it to a disunity and fragmentation. That this disparity is not fully thematized here presents a potential trap for readers, but it is not necessary to advert to Blanchot's later qualifications of this kind of language to understand the problem as the evidence is already there in his earlier thought, which is slowly and discreetly coming to contaminate the language of ontology. Where 'La littérature et le droit à la mort' had been a deliberate if tacit critique of Hegel's thoughts on the language of the work, the critique of Heidegger in the 1952 essay is more indirect (especially considering the comments in his earlier essay on Heidegger's reading of Hölderlin) and thus harder to recognize. However, careful reading shows that Blanchot is developing the points of his understanding that diverge from Heidegger (as well as from Hegel and Sartre), for in discussing the historical changes by which art has become distanced from the sacred, it becomes apparent that the work is no more than a ruinous hollow whose transparency does not indicate the sacred but only its absence, and thus its own appearance as this ruin. This transformation is also reflected in the worldly relation of art to history and politics, where the impossibility of art acceding to a model of work or action reveals that it is not the voice of the human that appears in it, for the work only makes the absence of such a voice appear: 'the work gives voice in man to what does not speak: to the unnameable, the inhuman, to what is without truth, without justice, without rights, here man does not recognize himself, he does not feel justified, where he is no longer present, where he is not man for himself, nor man before god, nor god before himself' [EL: 242/232]. And so, destitute of all other concerns, the work becomes an experience and search for its origin, of beginning as such, of that which says *commencer* without responsibility or aim, as Beckett would later examine, but a beginning that is also a breach or departure.

It is thus of considerable interest that although this is an essay on Heidegger and not Char, it is Char who is referred to rather than Heidegger, and who forms the constant counterpoint to the latter's thoughts on the work of art. Furthermore, this is before Char's own relation to Heidegger had developed, as well as before his own thoughts on the origin of the work of art, which would arise in the cycle of poems he would write after viewing the cave paintings at Lascaux. Thus Blanchot has seen the profound philosophical basis of Char's poetry and linked it to Heidegger's thought, yet without assimilating them. Instead, the contingency and materiality of Char's works is emphasized in contrast to the grander ontological vision of Heidegger, and the evanescence of this position gives rise to a thought of the poem as much more obscure and transient, the hollow, invisible shell of emptiness that passes for its event and repeats itself, even within the reader's reception, by way of its inexhaustible errancy. While Char's sense of materiality may resemble the notion of the earth in Heidegger's descriptions, this sense is put in doubt by the fact that there is no way of rendering Char's poems in terms of the worlding of the world, for what comes out in its place is the partiality and elusiveness of his thought of the world, particularly in *Feuillets d'Hypnos*. And, crucially, for Heidegger the earth is earth *for* the world and vice versa, the interrelation between the two is fundamental and thereby constitutes their essence. Hence, without their prior unity (even in division) the sense of what world and earth might be is radically altered. Also, and as was the case in Blanchot's reading of Hölderlin, the power of the word in Char's poetry is less concerned with the naming and unconcealing of being than with its own resistance and fragmentation, which is not part of the unifying *polemos* of being but the eccentricity of the word. That Char's later poems should move towards a more Heideggerian evocation of being does not affect Blanchot's reading, since this has more to do with Char's changed position after the war and his changing understanding of poetry.[17]

Blanchot's own interest is in the nature of the 'work' and the 'art' in an artwork, where the work (as a noun and a verb) is oriented towards the question of art, not as an idea that can be realized but as an impossible point that is both beyond the work and not beyond it, like an asymptotic drive. This distinction separates Blanchot's understanding of the relation of the work of art to time from the epochal models developed by Hegel and Heidegger, for through its microscopic deviations the work exposes the endless break-up of sense that accompanies any notion of its historical opening. The poet submits to this uncertainty in submitting to the work of the poem: the uncertainty of what does not lie within the realm of the possible and thus is impossible. Thus the poet is 'deprived of a steady presence and a true abode. And this must be understood in the gravest sense: the artist does not belong to truth, because the work is itself that which escapes the movement of the true' [EL: 249/237]. The work does not happen, as it does not take place, but nor does it not happen; as an event that does not occur in the sphere of possibility it also cannot pass away but repeats itself interminably as its own opening and deviation. This uncertainty also has an effect on the experience of the work, since thought and language are exposed to the dissimulation of meaning and appearance to such a degree that language and being are put in doubt: If the work does not happen, then it is not, and if it does, then it does not reveal or convey anything, and between the two there is an instability in which nothing is affirmed, an abyss that is undecidably both ground and groundlessness [EL: 250/239]. This complex of iterated negation resembles the thinking of nothing that Gorgias developed, but renders it reflexively rather than serially, that is, each iteration of the effects of negation are overlaid on each other, which is the obliteration and dissimulation of the work instead of a series of ontological postulates.

The exposure experienced in the work of art thus starts to encroach upon the space of death in its combined possibility and impossibility, which indicates the degree to which the work puts the very existence of the artist in question. It also allows Blanchot to address Heidegger's thought of death as the utmost possibility of existence, and with the same degree of qualification that he has shown in relation to the possibility of the work of art. Blanchot makes this point quite explicit by asking whether, if we have art, in all its evasion and resistance, this does not mean that the relation with death can also never be authentic or harmonious as it can never be part of a relation of possibility. Instead of any kind of relation of assumption, in which death is incorporated and mastered as part of the appropriation of the movement and finitude of time, death, like the artwork, brings about a reversal in the relation of time, exposing the impossibility of a time that does not and cannot be brought to any end, voiding any capacity or possibility that might seek to overcome it. Although the transition from a discussion of the groundlessness of the work of art to that of existence may not appear to be given, the experience of the artwork is one that undermines any secure relation to history or language, and so exposes thought to this groundlessness, to the absence of the event. This rupture then enables Blanchot to make the stronger case that it also leads to an exposure of subjectivity to its endless mortal disruption. In effect, the artwork demonstrates or indicates this more fundamental disturbance; in his words, there is a profound disparity between the experience of art, which is that of impossibility, and the thought of the human as a creature of possibility (after Heidegger's understanding of *Dasein* as *Seinkönnen*):

> How, if he is altogether possibility, can man be given something like art? Does this not mean that, contrary to his supposed authentic demand, that which is in harmony with the law of the day, he has a relation with death that is not that of possibility, which does not lead to mastery, or to understanding, or to the labour of time, but to the exposure to a radical reversal. Would not *this reversal* then be *the original experience* that the work must touch, upon which it closes itself and that constantly threatens to close in upon it and withhold it?
> EL: 252–3/240–1 (emphases in the original)

In itself this is a surprisingly simple but quite devastating challenge, but Blanchot is not seeking to establish a hierarchy between death and the artwork; rather he is indicating the manifold nature of the disruption of possibility, which occurs through language, thought and existence. It is not just that this rupture cannot be appropriated as a possibility but rather, its extreme reversal: that it undermines all that might be considered possible or proper or one's own.

The encounter with death is linked to the encounter with the work of art only insofar as they both involve an experience of endlessness, of the fact that the end (in whatever form it may take) does not end, which thus exposes the human to utter impotence and insignificance. The artwork, like death, irrupts as a force of dissembling, undermining truth and meaning, and exposing thought to an exteriority that neither is nor is not, and so evades the circuits of being: 'Whoever experiences this suffers an anonymous, impersonal force [*puissance*], that of an event that, being the dissolution of every event, is not only now, but its beginning is already a beginning again, and under whose horizon everything that comes, comes back' [EL: 253/241]. This rupture gives onto a time outside regular or possible time, a time without distinction or moment, a nondescript, neutral form of time, 'n'importe quelle date', which also affects the existence marked by it, rendering it without qualities in and through the instant (that is not an instant) of death. These lines are a reflection of what takes place in many of Blanchot's narratives, particularly in the temporal uncertainty that occludes the moment of death in *L'Arrêt de mort*, as will be seen later, and also in *Le Très-Haut*, which begins from the point of the narrator announcing that he is just such an impersonal, anonymous figure, and whose effects the novel then proceeds to unfold. The event of this exposure is not an event but a disreputable (*sournoise*) error, 'in the wake of which indeterminacy condemns time to the halting exhaustion [*piétinement harassant*] of repetition', the characterization of which is more closely found in Sisyphus than Orpheus, as Blanchot will come to find [EL: 254/241]. But as such an event, as Adorno also recognized, art cannot secure itself from its own compromise or reification, just as death, conversely, cannot be appropriated in any form that would grant it a meaningful status, since both aspects are merely dissembling affirmations.

The relation between death and the artwork remains pivotal but necessarily unfixed, since it is not as if one encounter produces the other; hence the association that Blanchot considers in these pages remains unfocused. Each sphere is an original experience without there being any requirement to make either primordial, and it is precisely because their interrelation is not subject to any order that it persists in being problematic, for it is in each case an encounter with endless uncertainty. For the human, such aporias demonstrate the range of ruptures that can arise and punctuate existence, thought and language, ruptures that, *pace* Heidegger, do not form part of any order or truth of being, and that lead to multiple, eccentric fragmentations, as the work, having 'turned us towards the outside without intimacy, without site and without rest, [is] engaged in the infinite migration of error' [EL: 256/244]. Blanchot thus marks out the distance between his thought and that of the presence or essence of being, which also means that, in the period since Hegel announced that art was a thing of the past and that it was now history that had become absolute, it is in relation to this departure from history that art finds its own question and origin. It is in this impoverished or destitute time that art finds its absolute, and thus Hölderlin's question becomes its own answer, but instead of finding in this absence a call for its return, Blanchot states the opposite: that the deeper the forgetting that occurs in this loss, 'the more the deep speaks in this language' [EL: 258/246]. For Blanchot it is Char who is the poet most worthy in our time to answer Hölderlin, as his writings indicate that it is the poet who 'lives' this empty time of absence, even if this is as the intimacy of distress, and in whom its error becomes a profundity of deviation (*égarement*)

[EL: 222/214, 259/246]. Rather than claiming that Hegel and Heidegger are wrong in their estimations of art, Blanchot shows that the complexity and ambiguity of the artwork prevent us from finding answers to the questions it poses, and that the philosophical structures that are erected around these questions cannot be substantiated. These structures do not simply become undermined but are permanently suspended in this uncertainty, which may at times support them and at other times not, but which nevertheless remains unresolved in its negativity.

IV. Falling into error

It is this expanse that is explored in *L'Espace littéraire*, which from its title onwards removes itself from being and from time. The nature of literary space for Blanchot lies in this sense of removal, of gaping and divergence, of the *écart* exposed by literature and the spacing that this brings to being and time. While Heidegger's project was concerned with being-in-the-world and the question of our existence, Blanchot distances himself from this ontological concern by turning to the question of literature, which is concerned with itself, and away from our place and relation to the world towards the practice and work of literature. In a sense, this distance is its exteriority to philosophy and ontology, as the question of literature diverts the concern with existence and the world into another relation of the work with itself. Literary space emerges between the generality of the world and the singularity of *Dasein* as another arena, a neutral one, neither lost in the confusions of *Gerede* nor disclosing itself in the dialogue of *Sage*, this language is other as it is simply the language of literature. Thus Blanchot begins and ends *L'Espace littéraire* with a focus on the essential solitude of the literary, picking up a concern that goes back to the opening essay of *Faux pas* but sharpening his account considerably by contrasting it with Heidegger's account of the work of art, which was less interested in the question of its practice than its self-positing *Ur-Sprung*.

When *L'Espace littéraire* appeared in the summer of 1955 it was Blanchot's thirteenth book, and although his fictional writings had consistently changed since the publication of *Thomas l'Obscur* in 1941, with each work breaking new ground formally and thematically, his critical writings had remained more or less within the general current of conventional literary criticism. *L'Espace littéraire* was a profound departure and an experiment in trying to broach the distance between his fictional and critical writings. Arising out of an intense period of work it sought to bring critique into the space of literature, and thereby bring this space to its own critical voice. The work was thus sui generis in a highly reflexive way that was only prefigured by works like Bataille's *L'Expérience intérieure*, of which it can be seen as a literary extension. In doing so Blanchot finds not merely a new space or form of writing but a discourse that is unique, being neither philosophical nor literary-critical but, in recollection of Bataille, an experience of its own exploration and vice versa. Such a project risks solipsism, and there is a sense that Blanchot reached a certain impasse in writing this work, except that in the appendices of the book a point of departure arises that casts everything before it into relief, since the last chapter draws out a moment of reversal, a turning away (apparently) from the disorienting remove of literature. This should not be understood as a movement of resolution or revelation, as Heidegger found in the depths of profound boredom, for example, but rather a more radical suspension of everything that had been raised so far through a movement that cannot assert itself as it suspends the very certainty of assertion. Hölderlin's categorical reversal that fuels Blanchot's discussion in these last pages of the book is not about a simple turning back from theology to the earth but a much more destabilizing rupture of turning as such [EL: 286/271–2]. Hence, the movement into literature of critique and its reverse, which the book as a whole has pursued, is placed under a greater problematization that does not indicate an aporia as much as a rupture of movement that is also a movement of rupture, thereby alluding to the fragmentation of relation that will take on more significance in the following years. Such a reading benefits from hindsight and is perhaps more buried in Blanchot's writings at this time than he was himself aware, and certainly it escaped the attention of even his most careful contemporary readers.[18]

While much of the work was written in the years 1952–3, the appendix on Hölderlin was written later and was first published under the title of 'Le tournant', before being renamed 'L'itinéraire de Hölderlin' in the final book, making clear the change in emphasis from the space that had been discussed thus far to a turning or wandering that is aimless and eccentric. The focus of much of the book had been on the approach to death or the work, and its impossible asymptote, but now this movement is even further undermined by becoming wholly detached from any centre or origin, and it is thus that it is rendered remote from any approach to the other, any ethical or onto-theological centre of gravity. Hölderlin's significance lies in his commentaries on Sophocles, in which he uncovers the movement of the tragic and its radical caesura, a breach that affects thought and language as much as time. In his reading of *Antigone* Hölderlin wants to establish how the modern world differs from that of Ancient Greece, for in the time of Sophocles the word truly kills and thereby enables a movement from this world into another. By contrast, for us moderns the word does not end in murder or death but attacks the spirit, as our fate is precisely to lack a fate, which is to say a relation to history and the gods, and so the inimical force of nature is turned away from a movement to the other world and back to the earth, as the doom of the fateless. Despite associating the earth with the fatherland and the patriotic it is these latter terms that are reformulated under the pressure of the earth, which is now considered as the mode of infinite and absolute reversal, an endless turning away of time and relation. It is thus that Hölderlin comes to think the earth not in terms of stability and identity but as Hesperia, the irresolvable indeterminacy of the crepuscular and its unending errancy.[19] These thoughts had arisen in Blanchot's reading of Heidegger's essay on the work of art but had not been extended to examine their broader effect on history, which alters how the site of dissembling is construed, as these thoughts not only bear a sense of endless reversal without centre or goal, and thus without any form of truth or work, but also convey a reversal of history. The reflexive focus of Blanchot's understanding of *L'Espace littéraire*, as that which seeks an approach to its own hidden centre, is thus placed under pressure, leading to a need for his writing to remove itself from any residual ontological gravity of presence or essence.

While Beda Allemann's dissertation brought Hölderlin's writings on tragedy to Blanchot's attention, the revision of history that they contained only brought into focus a number of points that were already emerging within his thinking at this time. For during the 1950s Blanchot not only found himself prompted by a disaffection with the approach of ontology but was also driven to reconsider the relation of his thought to issues in history and politics, which was drawn out in his reaction to the works of Camus and Mascolo. From this perspective a better understanding of the key issues in the Hölderlin article can be gained, as Blanchot speaks at length of a 'double infidelity' to which the poet must be faithful, an infidelity to both the gods and the earth, a turning away from that which has turned away, which opens a space between. This space is the space of literature as a void or hiatus of history as much as of language or thought, a space that is not opened by the desire for transcendence or the urgency of exile but is a gaping without beginning or end. This is not a yearning for anything, either for elsewhere or for return, but a yearning to remain yearning, without immediacy, that is, not a bridge between the gods and the earth but a persistent turning away or revolution, a permanent breach: 'the poet must no longer stand between gods and men as their intermediary, but should hold himself between this double infidelity to maintain the intersection of this double, divine, human, reversal, double and reciprocal movement, through which is opened a hiatus, a void, that from now on must constitute the essential relation of the two worlds' [EL: 288–9/274].

This essential relation is clearly still open to confusion, so Blanchot goes on to specify that it is a breach in which time itself turns back, essentially, and this reversal is, as Hölderlin noted, terrible, as it is the terrible idleness (*Muße*) of tragic time itself:

> It is terrible not only because it deprives us of the benevolent presence of the gods, of the familiarity of inspired words, not only because it throws

us back on ourselves in the destitution and distress of an empty time, but because it substitutes for the measured favour of divine forms ... a relation that threatens to tear and divert us without end.

EL: 290/275

Thus the essential rhythm, the regular formation of things, is torn asunder and cast into a formlessness without rule or order, a perverted essence, poisoning time, as he had remarked earlier [EL: 272/260]. Desire here is not concerned with its consummation but with the refusal of such, not with the light of realization or the darkness of its simple rejection but with a much more profound contestation of phenomenology, as poetic language 'belongs neither to the day nor to the night but always is spoken between night and day, one single time speaks the truth and leaves it unspoken' [EL: 291/276]. This is the time of the crepuscular, twilight, that moment described in French as *entre chiens et loups*, which had been Blanchot's initial title for the collection later given the more Bataillean name of *La Part du feu*.[20] This expression is used by Blanchot to translate a line from Hölderlin's hymn 'Germanien', and is referred to repeatedly in *La Part du feu*, showing how his earlier readings of this breaching of sense have exposed their temporal ramifications as a reversal of history. It is thus that he has come to his own revision of being and time by way of the space of literature, and in doing so uncovered that which is neither space nor time, material nor formal but a merely neutral rupture.

Consider how this point changes what was developed in his earlier reading of Hölderlin, where he had made clear that the poet's word cannot be associated with chaos or the night but is rather the day 'anterior to the day, and always anterior to itself, it is a before-day, a clarity before clarity to which we are closest when we grasp the dawn, the distance infinitely remote from daybreak' [PF: 124/121]. Although the dawn bears the same uncertainty as twilight, its phenomenological resonance is amended in the later text to draw out the radical reversibility of its historical sense; its ruptures and deviations (*écarts*) rather than its place as the site of an originary appearing of appearance. So, while the reading of Hölderlin that Blanchot develops in *L'Espace littéraire* is not that different from that which he had made earlier in terms of the nature of the poetic word, the emphasis on its groundless and endless turning not only strengthens his resistance to the Heideggerian reading but also introduces a critical-historical turning. Furthermore, throughout *L'Espace littéraire* he has taken up writers whose works he finds particularly significant and indicated how the intrinsic movement of their works comes up against an aporetic pressure that they seem to avoid. Thus, for Mallarmé, Kafka and Rilke, the impossible and enigmatic approach of the work is passed over, even by such persistent writers, in favour of the work itself. This problem prompts the examination of the origin of the work, for which Char's poetry is crucial insofar as it situates itself precisely in the opening of this approach and finds a form that relays this tension without reducing or converting it. But it is the significance of Hölderlin's historical experience of this tension that allows for this situating of Char, who, as Blanchot noted, is the poet most worthy in our time of responding to Hölderlin. Thus the reading of Char and Hölderlin is chiasmic to some degree as each comes to inflect the other and thereby provides the means to read them, which only puts more pressure on Heidegger's epochal reading of Hölderlin.

Although it does not become a key term for Blanchot, *écart* is used often enough to take on a distinctive role. Because of its multivalency it can encompass the differing aspects of 'work' as both a verb and a noun, and it is useful to compare two statements where these aspects are held up for closer analysis. In the essays on Mallarmé and Paulhan in *La Part du feu* the notion of *écart* is developed as a way of understanding the removal of the word from the thing, and the distance that is then exposed, so that in the final essay of the collection Blanchot can emphasize this point by saying that literature

> believes that it stands apart [*à l'écart*] from everyday realities and actual events but it has precisely removed itself from them [*s'en est écartée*], it is that remove [*écart*], that recoil [*recul*] before the everyday that necessarily takes it into account and that describes it as distancing [*éloignement*], as pure strangeness. What is more, it makes this putting at a remove [*à l'écart*] into an absolute value, and then this distancing seems to be a source of general understanding.
>
> PF: 307/316

Five years later it is not the work that is understood by way of this remove but the experience of the writer, which brings a different tenor to the notion. As was mentioned earlier, Blanchot finds that in the experience of the work, particularly poetic works, the poet 'is held in this *écart* where the still wordless rhythm, the voice that says nothing, but does not cease to speak, must become power of naming in the one alone who hears it' [EL: 236/226]. The distance thus becomes a space of error, since the poet who belongs to the poem as this non-space 'is always outside himself, outside his birthplace, he belongs to the foreign, to that which is the outside without intimacy and without limit, that separation [*écart*] Hölderlin names, in his madness, when he sees the infinite space of rhythm' [EL: 249/237]. As a result, the 'wanderer [*errant*] does not have his homeland in truth but in exile, he stands outside, *on the other side*, at a distance [*en deçà, à l'écart*], where the depth of dissimulation reigns, that elemental obscurity that lets nothing pass through [*frayer*] it and, because of this, is terrifying [*effrayant*]' [EL: 250/238].[21] The *écart* is both a separation and a deviation, and the two are interwoven such that each leads to the other without assimilating it, precisely because the space of rhythm is endless. It is thus that *écart* becomes the term for the work in both its verbal and nominal aspects, and that its labour becomes inseparable from alienation. There is a gap, and there is a divergence; there is a slip, and there is an opening. The relation to the work is not that of subject and object but rather one of mutual estrangement and interruption. Equally, there is no origin or event that is not already displaced by this removal and errancy, and in doing so ontology and politics are dislodged just as much as being and the revolution. The notion of *écart* captures much of the ambivalence of Blanchot's thinking of literature, and in doing so he perhaps goes further than Merleau-Ponty or Derrida in realizing the effects that this literary ambivalence has on the possibility of history and philosophy as discourses by indicating how thought in this *écart* of language is exposed to sheer dissembling and permanent revolution.

If the deviation or swerve (clinamen) is primary, then it is neither towards nor away from a norm. Hence, it is not simply a flaw but an opening of space, a contingent spacing out, which yields both a gap and a new pathway. It is as such that this spacing can be understood in terms of errancy, as that which is both a wandering and a falling, where falling is not moralistically considered from the point of view of that which it has fallen away from, but merely as ungrounded, unguided motion. There still remains a sense in which deviation is a breaking away from a previous path, with all the risks and potentials that this may bring, but it is also the exposure of a spacing. The two aspects of a deviation and a rupture are clearly linked but bear different resonances and do not support any hierarchical ordering, making each primary and yet separate. This sense of an anomalous and para-originary disparity is to be found in the notion of *écart* as it is used by Merleau-Ponty and Derrida, which is also taken up by Michel Serres in his reading of Lucretius. This notion is not the same as the clinamen, but their imbrication can be seen in the way that an *écart* is a difference *between* or a divergence *from*, indicating an opening that is either between x and y, or away from x. But by rendering this form originary, in a way, it becomes detached from any norm or rule and is simply a gaping without an exterior or interior limit. Crucially, of course, the clinamen in Lucretius's thought is identical to matter, and in doing so he does not speak of discrete and indivisible atoms but of *corpora*, which deviate, accidentally but intrinsically: 'at uncertain times and uncertain places they pull away [*depellere*] a little'. This is a movement that has always been part of their motion, without beginning or end, and it inevitably leads to encounters, interactions, for 'unless they were accustomed to turning aside [*declinare*], all would fall downwards like drops of rain through the deep void, nor would a collision occur'.[22]

These accidents are prior to space or time insofar as they make these possible, and as Althusser emphasized, this also means that they are prior to being or language, to any ontology. Althusser's discussion of this transformation of materialism, in which matter is rethought on the basis of its random collisions, begins with a recollection of Heidegger's discussion of the event as it is exemplified in the impersonal phrase 'it is raining'.[23] This formulation of the anonymity and groundlessness of the event also refers to its bland contingency, which begins to draw its thought away from the destinal donation of being. Rain falls and in doing so brings cold and damp, impeding visibility and mobility and making life uncomfortable, treacherous, as everything becomes slippery. But rain does not just fall; it is blown by the wind, strikes objects and bounces off surfaces, making noise alongside its other disturbances. Rain never just falls, which has its effects on any understanding of the event, for, as Lucretius stated, it is never without errancy. There can never be a truth or measure to the event; it is not available to the *logos* or to history, as it is not part of the course of things even as it is banal and everyday, which says much about those discourses that have constructed themselves by suppressing the persistent errancy of the event.

Rain is one of the distinguishing marks of film noir (in which Hölderlin's understanding of tragedy – with its formal reflexivity, meaningless deaths and narrative ruptures – finds its most compelling modern form) precisely because of its blandly disruptive effects, which thus renders the accident primary in its thematics. In many classic films noir society does not exist; there are only individuals falling through the void that coincide solely by virtue of their contingent deviations. These accidents lead not just to the major forces of lust, greed, fear and anger but also to the absurdity and clumsiness that pervade their milieus. If the accident is primary, contra Aristotle but also Freud, then this renders the world of film noir intrinsically unclear and pointless. When there is only deviation, there is only alienation, and vice versa; there is no stable subsequent or prior state to the accident that can be construed as more substantial; it is not *for* anything but simply unfolds. This deviation radically reconfigures the relations of past and future, as the nature of fate in film noir so often makes clear where the apparent dead end of the future is overlaid with an endless rewriting of the past, and also reveals the transformation in the ontological dimensions of the event, since the accident occurs as and only leads to (evermore) disorientated and deteriorated situations, which is ably expressed by the fact of being in the wrong place at the wrong time. The doom of the characters in film noir is that they have no fate other than the implications of the accident; there is nothing but a *pas de chance*.

3

Chiaroscuro

V. The shadow of events

French critics were already calling films like *Le Quai des brumes* dark or 'noir' in 1938, but at this time the term simply referred to the darkness of the world that these films depicted, and as such it was largely used in a negative manner, as Rebatet demonstrated. It was only later that the term would be taken up more explicitly in order to understand why it appeared to have become the defining feature of the American crime films that began to be released in France in 1946 after the wartime embargo was lifted. Although *Le Quai des brumes* was condemned by critics on both the left and the right, and would be banned by the French military and the Vichy regime, there were some writers who were fascinated by its mysterious combination of violence and despair as it seemed to mark a new understanding of the pitilessness of a world without justice or order, where there is no longer any scope for heroism or moral certainties. This indeed was the view of Nino Frank in reviewing the film in 1938, and it would have been with these thoughts in mind that he would start discussing American 'noir' films eight years later. As such, the notion of 'noir' would become reconsidered in response to this new kind of crime film that was stranger and more violent than its French predecessors, but was also more realistic and less poetic.

It is useful to look a little more closely at how this early reading was developed in order to grasp the manner of its later transformation, which also reveals much about the changing times. For Frank, Carné's film is set on the borderlands between life and death, where the merging of land and sea and the ubiquitous mist and decay indicate the collapse of these boundaries. The characters that congregate at Panama's bar seem to be lost and doomed, marked by fate but also by caprice, and it is in these terms that Frank unfolds the scenario of the film, since Panama's is not so much a last chance saloon for 'there is never a last chance, and even love no longer counts when one is really at the end of the road'.[1] What is seen is thus the random configurations of a few worn-out figures, and, as Frank insists, 'no one will ever be saved, as hope is only an illusion'; consequently, the story does not involve morality, or even destiny, but only chance, chance as an accident or by-product (*sous-produit*) of fatality, into whose murky and bottomless depths everything slides. Frank was given to such poetic evocations of the films he had watched, but it is also evident that he is seeking to go beyond a mere reiteration of the mood of *Le Quai des brumes* to understand its basis and its implications. As a result, it is possible to see how this mood would prove to be so overwhelming, and how viewers would seek to counter its influence in some way. For what Frank has seen is the effect of its corrupting atmosphere, which unavoidably seeps into all forms and values and leads to a lethargic nihilism or violent rejection. But underneath this mood lies another understanding of the place of fate in human lives, and its transformation by the corrosive effects of chance, which becomes the distinctive trace of its modernity. And, in a remark that would become more significant in the later readings of American noir, he writes that 'these stories always go quickly, as violent death is very fast when it is a matter of arriving before life [*avant la vie*]'. This is not just to comment upon the random and sudden acts of brutality that come to distinguish later noir films, but to perceive death as that which somehow precedes any event or possibility of life, not as a doom but as that which always already marks life with its priority and preponderance.

So, when French writers came to discuss the new American crime films that appeared after the war their responses would be attuned to a reading that American audiences may not have recognized. Frank's reviews were perhaps more suggestive than others, but what many critics began to see in these new crime films was a world that was not just concerned with greed or revenge but one that was riddled with a pervasive loss of meaning and hope. And, critically, what these films conveyed was an experience of a world of alienation that was as distinctive aesthetically as it was socially, and they did so by manifesting their own forms of style and narrative. It is as such that they appeared as a thoroughly integrated worldview that was also intrinsically cinematic. Indeed, film noir became a specifically American art form in that it arose from and directed itself towards the milieu of American life and provided a distinctive perspective not just on modernism or urbanism but on the American experience of these phenomena, with all their sexual, linguistic, legal and commercial aspects. This is why the classic period of American noir, from the early 1940s to the late 1950s, remains richer in its implications than any of its subsequent variations and reformulations. It was not just the experience of war and depression that laid the ground for film noir but everything that went along with this: the violence and poverty, immigration and paranoia, corruption and cynicism, which marked the massive changes in American society between 1920 and 1960 and in which the modern urban world of capital realized itself in all its contradictions and deceptions. Furthermore, film noir arose from a particular combination of European directors and American crime writers, the Hollywood studio system and the strictures and demands of wartime production, which created a unique blend of the mundane and the stylized that would pass as soon as these influences had become assimilated into the artistic mainstream and displaced by the new post-war generation. In this way film noir is as important an emblem of its times and their experience as baroque drama or Gothic fiction.[2]

While Adorno and Godard, among others, may have decried the passing of silent film as the end of the first truly artistic period of cinematic production, talkies introduced it to a new phase where, in film noir particularly, word and image, sound and vision, came together in such a way that they made a novel and fully integrated form, even if these elements occurred discordantly. For what is peculiar about film noir is not just its jarring visual effects and moral uncertainties but the disparity between the world of desolation it presents and the manner in which its characters persist in this world. In a world that is bereft of trust, luck and hope, there would seem to be no point or means for carrying on with life, and yet that is precisely what these films so remorselessly draw out – the experience of living on when there is so little reason for doing so. It is here that the cadence of the language becomes important with its repetitions and slang, as it is here that some form of defiance occurs in the face of this lack of reason, a defiance that is based on nothing and yields nothing as it makes no difference.

It is not my intention to make any kind of comparison between Blanchot's writings and film noir but to understand the conditions that made their respective investigations of alienation possible, and the ways that living appears to carry on in this world of alienation. It is significant that the two worlds of Blanchot's fiction and film noir are chronologically parallel as this indicates how they may have arisen, at least in part, out of shared responses to the circumstances of the changing world order, and while there may be some superficial stylistic similarity to these different worlds, what is more intriguing is the way that French critics came to discuss film noir. The earliest book to develop a reading of film noir (Borde and Chaumeton's *Panorama du film noir américain*) came out at the same time as Blanchot's *L'Espace littéraire*, and like Blanchot its authors sought to come to terms with the discordant perspective and experience of a new art form, to understand what the alienation of the work entails, and what this implies about our place in the world. This is not to advert to a reading in which both the literary and filmic worlds of noir are simply studies of existential angst and confusion as this would be to remain at the level of individual psychology, but rather to understand the logic and ramifications of these worlds in terms of their transformation of relation and identity. Film noir, like Blanchot's writings, conveys an experience of the world under the sign of an extreme disaster of meaning and possibility, and, in its own way, which differs from that of Blanchot, it also seeks to convey something of what can still be done within the endless terms of this experience.³ To discuss this complex tension I will focus on Borde and Chaumeton's work before looking at the films themselves, as they were the first writers to take this experience seriously and to try to formulate its dimensions.

It is not insignificant that 'film noir' is a creation of the page rather than the screen, and that its supplementary, *nachträglich*, estranged appearance in another language is intrinsic to this experience. Much has been made of the anomalous nature of noir, in that it is not entirely a genre or a style (and the same can be said for the notion of 'poetic realism'), and that it was not fully recognized as a phenomenon until critics writing in another country started to discuss it and, in doing so, provided its name. But what these points imply is that, empirically, film noir does not exist as a thing, a unitary entity or object; rather, there are only exemplars, as has been demonstrated by list after list. Thus, it is beyond the unifying approach of a theoretical analysis as it is estranged from any essential identity or form, but it is also as such that it materially, and obscurely, derives from the times. Moreover, film noir is not just about alienation in that it is of the times but, as Borde and Chaumeton emphasize, it also seeks to convey this mood: 'The vocation of film noir was to create *a specific malaise*' [PFN: 24/13; emphasis in the original].

From the beginning of their study Borde and Chaumeton lay out the tensions within film noir, which, on the one hand, 'responds to a certain type of emotional resonance as singular in time as it is in space' but, on the other hand, it is 'the presence of crime that gives film noir its most constant mark', such that, in 'all senses of the word, film noir is a film of death' [PFN: 15–16/5]. It is this concrete manifestation of a universal that intrigues the writers, a specific experience (American, urban, mid-twentieth century) of that which is entirely bland and meaningless, and yet this experience is mediated by the slippage between the initial mention of crime and its later appearance as death. Film noir is intensely concerned with crime but, as they say, all the various instances of crime simply 'weave the plot of an adventure for which death is the stakes [*l'enjeu*]' [PFN: 16/5]. But if the stakes of the plot lie in death, then no one can win, there can be no happy resolution and equally each pursuit of the plot will become escalated to this absolute degree; the stakes are raised immediately and irrevocably so that there can be no way back. The situation is not merely desperate but fatal and this is why it becomes (in 'all senses of the word') a film of death, of a world where death is the only reality and in which, as a result, death is made filmic, pervading the film as its inevitability even when it is not directly present. It is the mark of death that makes itself felt throughout the film, in its characters, dialogue and plot, as well as in the random irruptions of violence and emphatic lack of hope, for in being a film of death everything that is presented becomes evacuated by its lack of reason.

It is then critical that film noir pursues this plot from the point of view of the criminal, for in doing so the fatal journey is seen from within, as Borde and Chaumeton write, as opposed to the view from outside that characterizes the police procedural film [PFN: 17/6]. Indeed, in film noir, there is no outside; there is no other point of view to which we can turn for a consoling alternative, while the police procedural, conversely, takes up its objective perspective by way of its systematic accumulation of details, the deceptive reality of empiricism and the positivism of undeniable evidence. This teleology of justice is unravelled in film noir by its constant intimacy with death, which means that it is not the aim or meaning of the film but its milieu, that in which it is immersed, and as a result the culmination of the film becomes less significant, which is why flashbacks feature so prominently, to such a degree that the film can even occur from the point of view of the dead as in *Sunset Boulevard* (Billy Wilder, 1950) or *D.O.A.* (Rudolph Maté, 1949). Consequently, the fundamental difference between film noir and the police procedural for Borde and Chaumeton is moral, for the characters in film noir are as compromised and ambivalent as the situations in which they find themselves, as opposed to the relatively simple morality of procedurals.

In film noir the characters occupy a space between ('le milieu', as the criminal underworld is called in French), a space of corrupt police and honourable criminals, of rules of conduct that are arbitrarily imposed and lifted, and where professions are ambivalent or irregular, like that of the private detective or hired killer. All this indicates the middle ground between the supposed natural states of law and crime, while revealing the inevitable lack of a basis to such a distinction and the difficulties of trying to maintain it. In such situations trust can only be a temporary occlusion of an underlying and impending betrayal, and so the intentions of the characters in the changing ambiguities of these situations are often concealed, if not altogether muted, and replaced by a passivity or 'morbid curiosity'; like Jeff (Robert Mitchum) in *Out of the Past* (Jacques Tourneur, 1947) they bear a desire to see things through that appears more idle than committed [PFN: 20/9]. These are not characters who are *engagé*, since even if they do commit themselves, for the sake of nothing other than the plot, as it were, then it is only to the emptiness and pointlessness that comes from having nothing better to do, which is the state that occurs in the absence of any transcendental goals or reasons.

Is this alienation a result of capitalism, urbanism or the antinomies of the American dream, as it is called, or is it that the materialistic outlook of the secular world, with its mercenary venality and inane commercialism, comes to converge on the philosophical understanding of materialism, its contingency and facticity, the sheer obtrusiveness of the material that voids all meaning and value? The dialectic of this movement is often barely perceptible, as it is a case of distinguishing between the meaninglessness of an empty existence and that of an existence stripped of all transcendental goals and reasons, between film as a product of commercial compromises and as a comment on them, however slight. Are the characters passive and compromised because the world has rendered them thus, or is it because this is the only way of existing within this world, as their compromises bear as many possible sources of resistance to reification as manifestations? Thus, it is in the dialogue of these films (as in the opening scene of *The Killers* (Robert Siodmak, 1946), or throughout *Double Indemnity* (Wilder, 1944) as will be shown later) that there can be found both the banality of a language reduced to repetition and stock phrases, and the resistance of a language open to the vibrant expressiveness of repetition and stock phrases. These equivocations are as erotic as they are moral, as dangerous as they are absurd, and as such they expose different relations of thought and identity, as well as of fatality. The double ending of *The Woman in the Window* (Fritz Lang, 1944) demonstrates this issue quite starkly as it is a question of deciding, impossibly, between a happy but entirely unconvincing ending and one that bears all the truth of the foregoing story, which leaves the place of death unresolved.[4]

These equivocations arise through the characters' own contradictions, with which they are more involved than with each other. The tensions between activity and passivity, knowledge and intention, desire and caution, place each character in their own web of confusion and uncertainty, and it is in this way that they become drawn into violence and the complex inversions of the dialogue and plot. Thus the solution to the crime is often less important than the realization of the contingency of these situations and their worldly negligence, which is its modern form of tragedy. Film noir does not concern itself with the conflict between freedom and necessity so much as with contingency in its absolute form, which is both gratuitous and inescapable. Not only are individuals distorted by their characters and situations, but this becomes more complicated by their contingent reactions to the characters and situations with which they come into contact. (There are many examples here but *Deadline at Dawn* (Harold Clurman, 1946), *Somewhere in the Night* (Joseph Mankiewicz, 1946), *Hollow Triumph* (Steve Sekely, 1948) and *Woman on the Run* (Norman Foster, 1950) are particularly worthwhile because each are focused on how this disorientation is lived.) This is why relations and circumstances change so quickly and unpredictably and violence, when it comes, is often brutal or bizarre. There is no fair or sophisticated use of weapons here, as Borde and Chaumeton note, and as a result, violence itself emerges as a new form in the history of cinema, as the terrifying rupture of the contingent. For in a film that navigates 'the ambiguity of a criminal milieu in which the power relations ceaselessly change', the mutability of killers and victims and deception and betrayal is ever present [PFN: 19/8]. If the underworld is itself the milieu, then, conversely, this says much about the stakes of that space between where values are endlessly compromised. And, if 'film noir has renewed [*renouvelé*]

... the theme of violence', by showing how it is random and ruthless, then it is the characters themselves who become displaced by this new form, as 'an unknown race rises up before our eyes with its tics, its stigmata', that of the hired and motiveless killer, the complete realization of the capitalist contract and a fetish of decisiveness in an uncertain world [PFN: 20–1/9–10].

Hence, there is 'in this incoherent brutality, something of the dream' [PFN: 22/10–11]. The plot unfolds unclearly and almost without order, based on the merest of premises, and as a result, in the words of Sadoul, reviewing *The Big Sleep* (Howard Hawks, 1946), 'the story remains fuzzy [*pâteuse*], like a nightmare, or the ramblings of a drunk'.[5] But, as Borges wrote in response to *Citizen Kane*, 'nothing is so frightening as a labyrinth with no centre'. This unease reveals something important about the nature of such rambling, for it is indicative of 'the error of the infinite', in Blanchot's words, in which he finds the truth of literature.[6] This is not simply the secular or irrational world of modernity, in which there is no ground of reason, but rather its underlying field of contingency, which has no limit. Such a sense of aimlessness led Sartre to dismiss *Citizen Kane* for its lack of historical positivism, but he had also used this charge to dismiss the 'absolute pessimism' that he saw in Blanchot's novels, which 'take place in an entirely imaginary world, and whose heroes *only remotely* resemble men; the events which take place in them *appear* to be symbolic, but are actually not' (emphases in the original).[7] But it was in precisely these terms that French critics a year later would begin to praise the new crime films then emerging from Hollywood. For, in contrast to this emphasis on historical agency, the arbitrary nature of the plot in film noir is made explicit in that it very often begins with an accident or a mistake, or a contrivance so obvious as to be negligible. The actual impetus is unimportant; there is only its contingent necessity and its unravelling, which is itself contingent, as it reverberates from one accident or mistake to another so that it has no more of an end than a beginning. The plot simply derives from the collision of the characters and the situations, but this does not offer any greater insight:

> In real film noir, the strangeness [*insolite*] is inseparable from what could be called the *uncertainty of motives* ... All the strangeness of the œuvre is there: these shapeless [*larvaires*] and mysterious creatures who only make their play in death. Elsewhere, will a figure glimpsed in some nightclub finger an accomplice or an enemy? This enigmatic killer, is he to be executioner or victim? The complexity of criminal relations, the multiple networks of blackmail, the mystery of motives – all this converges in incoherence.
>
> PFN: 22–3/11

But describing this appearance as dreamlike only restates its enigma, since if the plot of film noir resembles a dream – and it is from this point that its allegorical (sociological, psychoanalytical, mythical) readings arise – then this is because it does not find a satisfactory empirical explanation, either in the circumstances or in the characters. As Sartre noted, the distance of the characters from humanity does not render them symbolic, for while the plot may be driven by material situations, it is not reducible to them and so cannot be resolved or explained by them: 'the departure is realist and each scene on its own could pass for a fragment of a documentary. It is the accumulation of these realist shots on a bizarre theme that creates a nightmarish atmosphere' [PFN: 23/11–12]. What is in excess of the material are the relations (or non-relations) between them, which are opaque, if not inaccessible or nonexistent. In a world of complete alienation, there can be no final or lasting meaning.

Thus, film noir can also be said to be exposing something of the material-historical specificity of its medium, so that it is as intrinsically cinematic as the narratives that Blanchot is contemporaneously exploring are of literature. This would explain how noir comes to present itself in such an integrated and enigmatic form as an examination of the open-ended contingency of cinema itself, a form without inherent rationale or structure but created through multiple and conflicting material circumstances, its desires corrupted by its means and finding only the chiaroscuro (visual and narrative) of an endless decline. Consequently, Borde and Chaumeton conclude that 'all the components of noir style lead to the same result: to disorient the spectators, who no longer find their customary points of reference' [PFN: 23/12]. But, as with other areas of modern art, these disorienting factors quickly became clichés, and it is precisely to the degree that they were unfamiliar that they became assimilated, which is why it is much harder to appreciate the strangeness of these films now. However, Borde and Chaumeton go further, by claiming that 'the moral ambivalence, criminal violence, and contradictory complexity of the situations and motives all combine to give the public a shared feeling of anguish or insecurity' [PFN: 24/13]. This disorientation is not developed in order to shock or to edify but to draw the viewer into the actuality of the world, which takes place in the inhibition of its resolution into specific reasons. As these films are of the world, it is as such that they convey its obscurities and contradictions, since they lack the possibility of gaining a place outside the world from which to judge and resolve its flaws.

American film noir was not 'influenced' by French poetic realism or German expressionism for, as Borde and Chaumeton made clear, what it names is not just a sphere of films but also the experience of its audiences during the confusion and degradation of the post-war period. So, any connection to the stark designs and moral disorder of German films of the 1920s lies more in their common experience of a society in decline, than in any direct or shared lineage of auteurs. Evidence for the misreading of this overlap between film and society can be found in Lotte Eisner's *L'Écran démoniaque*, which appeared in 1952 and gave a tendentious account of expressionist cinema that grounded it in a model of German 'character' drawn from Spengler's vision of a decaying society plagued by irrational and apocalyptic elements. While she usefully shows how expressionist literature provides many of the images for its cinema from Caligari to Mabuse, she also follows Kracauer's thesis (whose book on German film would not appear in French until 1973) that Weimar cinema was a transparent display of the apparently mystical ideology of the German character. In doing so she focuses on the visual elements of expressionism, particularly the use of twilight and chiaroscuro effects, in order to ascertain what this might say about German cinema and character and finds that their meaning lies in Spengler's enthusiastic nihilism. Expressionism is thus the expression of a pathological vision, a metaphysics of sickness, in which the real and the unreal become inverted and give rise to a tortured experience of contradictions. It is this focus on visual effects that allows for a comparable response to film noir, which also arose in a society seemingly experiencing its own decline. However, contrary to the national psychologism of Eisner's reading, this connection is made apparent materially in these films by the fact that chiaroscuro lighting effects often arose not through direct influence or conscious desire, but simply out of necessity as a result of limited budgets and poor resources, which was experienced in Germany in the 1920s as much as it was in America in the 1940s, and that thereby gives material expression to exactly this level of degraded aesthetic possibilities.[8] The stark appearance of these films is partly a manifestation of their own impoverished experience, an experience that is a microcosm of the world from which they have arisen with all the senseless compromises that this entails. The significance of Spengler is instead less direct, as it comes from the fact that he was able to analyse how this social decline takes place and how individuals become invested in its degradation, which casts light on the way that film noir is a reflexive examination of this world only insofar as it is also its expression; it is only able to show this disintegration by conveying it, since it is part of it.

While film noir found itself becoming familiar to the point of cliché within a few years, a parallel but inverted fate befell the work of Spengler, which seemed to be forgotten as soon as it became actualized. The fate of film noir is highly revealing as it indicates something of its appearance and reception: that it arose with all the coherence and boldness of a specific vision, and that this vision became a cliché as soon as the times changed and its sphere of reception could no longer respond to it in its concreteness, for cliché arises where the connection with reality has slipped away and it is only the connection to other images that is apparent. With Spengler a seemingly similar trajectory took place as his work was instantly popular and then just as quickly fell into oblivion, but at just the same speed his thoughts seemed to become concrete, as Adorno wrote: 'His oblivion in the midst of confirmation lends the threat of blind fatality, which emerges from his conception, an objective moment' [P: 48/54].[9] His work, despite its poor conceptualization, weak grounding and extreme pessimism, took on an objective character almost by virtue of its own oblivion, thus confirming itself in the same manner of invisibility as film noir, which is why they are both so difficult to discuss evenly. Nevertheless, the two spheres are mutually illuminating in their vision of a world removed from any possibility of hope or justice. It is clear that Adorno is fascinated by Spengler's power, since he fills his essay with many lengthy quotations and goes out of his way to show the importance of his work, despite its considerable intellectual failings, almost as if it were a popular version of his own thought.

In the second volume of the *Untergang*, which, as Adorno points out, is where the thesis is most fully worked out, Spengler's speculative history of culture culminates in a discussion of the modern metropolis, from which he diagnoses the problems of contemporary society. After denouncing the loss of connection to the land and the concomitant loss of faith and piety, Spengler goes on to warn that when 'the mass of tenants and overnight guests in this sea of houses leads a vagrant existence [*irrendes Dasein*] from shelter to shelter, like the hunters and shepherds of primeval times, then the intellectual nomad is fully formed'. For 'each of these splendid mass cities houses terrible misery, a neglect [*Verwilderung*] of all customs that even now, between attics and garrets, in cellars and backyards, is breeding a new primitive man [*Urmenschen*]'.[10] Such provincial fears seem easy to dismiss but, as Adorno explains, this image of the city-dweller as a second nomad, that is, a nomad of our second nature, deserves special emphasis: 'It expresses not merely anxiety and estrangement but rather the dawning lack of historicality [*Geschichtslosigkeit*] of a condition in which men experience themselves merely as objects of non-transparent processes and, between sudden shock and sudden forgetfulness, are no longer capable of any experience of temporal continuity' [P: 50/55]. Adorno wrote this article shortly after discovering Benjamin's theses on history and although it largely deals with the dialectics of bourgeois pessimism, it also demonstrates something of the temporality of alienation to be found in the spaces of film noir. Thus, 'modern art can be regarded as an attempt to magically keep the dynamic of history alive, or to increase the horror at the stasis [*Erstarrung*] to shock, to catastrophe, in which the ahistorical [*Geschichtslose*] suddenly takes on the expression of the long past'. The difficulty of this procedure is intense, for 'history seems to have been extinguished. Everything that happens, happens to men, not through them'. In this age of universal accidents, 'events play themselves out between oligarchs and their assassins; they do not arise from the dynamic of society but rather subject it to an administration intensified to the point of annihilation' [P: 54/58–9]. It is at this point that Spengler's diagnosis of the iniquity of civilization leads to a craven submission to its few domineering forces, after which the force of his diagnosis becomes muted. But up until this point his analyses of democracy, urbanism, economics, warfare, journalism and popular culture focus astutely on the corruption and alienation that have ensued in the modern age.

The purpose of this contrast with film noir is to indicate that the apparent fixation on shadowy lighting effects that Eisner sees as representative of the German character can be understood only by way of Spengler's pessimism if we recall the materialist principle that aesthetic or stylistic forms are derived from concrete circumstances. That is, the prevalence of chiaroscuro in expressionist and noir films comes from the fact that this form arises from the world it is seeking to convey, in other words, it is the chiaroscuro of morality and situation that gives rise to its appearance in the style of the film. These are not arbitrary effects but come about because the material at hand manifests itself in such changeable forms and so the style is a further point of manifestation of this world of disorientation and alienation, which thereby displays it in its own form. The style of these films is just as much a symptomatic expression as is their violence and deception, absurdity and eroticism, which means that chiaroscuro is more than simply being a kind of lighting but is the material form of an entire world of heightened and confusing contrasts. Chiaroscuro is a mode of ambivalence that is not concerned with the simple blurring of distinctions but with sudden and drastic changes of tone and sense. It is thus that it can be found in the narrative and characters of film noir through their changes in direction and mood so that it becomes difficult to determine the status or position of the drama (which indicates how the counter-rhythmic interruption that Hölderlin found to be central to tragedy has become immanent to the world of noir). Coming to understand what this chiaroscuro of meaning might imply is not easy, as it is not grounded in anything other than its changes, which themselves do not bear any intrinsic direction.

VI. Universal accidents

In *Double Indemnity*, the character of Walter Neff (Fred MacMurray) works as a salesman for an insurance company, which means that he sells policies designed to provide cover in the event of an accident. It is the job of the company as a whole to emphasize accidents in order to sell policies, but also to minimize their liability so as to reduce their losses. Thus the company seeks to establish a comprehensive assessment of the probabilities of all types of accident. It cannot, of course, prevent them, but through the use of statistics it seeks to predict their likelihood when assessing the cost of the policy, and then through subsequent investigation it seeks to determine their actuality. Sales and claims thus work on opposing sides of the incident and with differing aims, but in doing so they attempt to cover all its eventualities, whether this means protecting the company or the client. Accidents can never be wholly avoided so all the insurance can do is to provide compensation after the fact, which may help minimize its effects but at a loss for the company. Hence, although the company may appear to be providing support for the client, albeit belatedly, it only does so to the degree that it can keep these expenditures to a minimum. Ultimately, its aim is to make money for itself, based on the fact that accidents generally do not occur very often; it thus seeks to develop a science of accidents to assess the likelihood of that which is intrinsically unpredictable and thereby 'manage' risk. Under cover of its bureaucracy insurance makes profits by treating individuals as statistics within a field of probabilities, which in effect merely extends the relation already found in unofficial insurance. In a basic protection racket, 'insurance' guarantees that one would avoid 'accidents', while in the official world of actuarial charts risk to the individual is displaced across the entire field of other individuals. The larger the organization the more it is able to conceal its machinations, but in both cases the individual becomes a number and a source of profit as long as their behaviour is carefully monitored. The individual plays the same role as the customer in a gambling house, the naïve mark who does not know the odds and is easily played for the benefits of the house. The insurance company thus bridges the gap between official and unofficial risk management, and in becoming part of (Western) society during the early twentieth century it provides an example of how such enterprises became legitimized through bureaucracy. This change had a huge effect on the management of life on an individual and a social level, which was particularly felt in American society during the 1930s under the expansion of a wide range of New Deal systems of social support, and it is in this period of transition that the tensions between the legitimate and illegitimate aspects of the accident became most obvious.

Thus the role of the claims investigator in *Double Indemnity*, Barton Keyes (Edward G. Robinson), is that of an enforcer, which is complicated by Keyes's apparently paternal feelings for Neff. However, these feelings are as much of a charade as Neff's own salesman's patter, as Keyes's only interest is in the company: he may express affection for Neff but this is only insofar as he sees him as a recruit, a talented student; otherwise he is just as cynically self-interested as Neff himself. The dialogue of the film is a trap, a series of manipulations in which the viewer is the first victim, as we are led to feel that there is a bond between Keyes and Neff, and that the characters have some control over the events in which they find themselves by virtue of their verbal dexterity. But the innuendos and slang are only further deceptions masking their own self-deception, in which Neff is the most tragic figure. It is the irony of his role that he fails to recognize the significance of the accidents that surround him – the first meeting with Phyllis (Barbara Stanwyck), the meeting with Lola (Jean Heather) in the car, the actual accident in which Dietrichson (Tom Powers) breaks his leg, the meeting with Jackson (Porter

Hall) on the train – all these elements lead to his undoing because he is not able to see them for what they are: encounters that force him off course. Far from finding the smooth efficiency of going 'straight down the line', to which he aspires, Neff is bounced from one encounter to another, at the mercy of these accidents rather than managing them, as the first image of his careering car makes clear [DI: 38].

Neff is, as he says himself, a dead man walking, as much a narrative figure from beyond the grave as Joe Gillis (William Holden) in *Sunset Boulevard*, his story caught in the netherworld of his dying moments that is relived as he speaks into his office dictaphone [DI: 73]. Equally, the oppressive music that marks his descent is, as has been pointed out, an unresolved dirge, its notes counting out his decline but failing to lead to either a conclusion or a culmination.[11] While the narrative is structured through the voiceover and flashback, this attempt at control is punctured by two blind spots where we see Phyllis on her own, outside of Neff's perspective. These moments break through the layers of artifice and indicate the nature of their relationship, which is ultimately not based on lust or greed but on the death that each sees in the other as a way of escape. Although it would seem that they use each other as tools to break out of their current situations, this escape becomes synonymous with death in that it is both the means and the end of their plans. It is evidence of the immanence of the system that the only path out of it is through death, and even this does not lead to anywhere else; like Keyes, Neff has no real life outside the office and his attempts to leave it only lead to ruin and return.

The closed world of the film is quite apparent as it only features the figures in the insurance office and the Dietrichson family and a few extra characters. For a film involving such ruthless criminals there are no representatives of the law present, everything is dealt with through the operations of the insurance business, which appears all-powerful. It would seem that the traditional agencies of the police and judiciary are incapable of responding to the uncertain world between official and unofficial enforcement, and so insurance investigators come to operate in the same milieu as the journalists and private detectives in other films noir. Hence, the pursuit of these unofficial investigations is often littered with their own paraphernalia in order to substantiate their legitimacy, however contingent. One of the most obvious demonstrations of this milieu, and its conflict between regularity and eccentricity, is to be found in the excessive systems of timekeeping and irrelevant clues in *The Big Clock* (John Farrow, 1948), where the closed world of tabloid journalism is forced to investigate itself. However, the discussions of claims and policies, percentages and probabilities within *Double Indemnity* also demonstrate the airlessness of this environment, to the same degree that the businesses in the films of Cain's other works, *The Postman Always Rings Twice* (Tay Garnett, 1946) and *Mildred Pierce* (Michael Curtiz, 1945), also suffocate the movements of their characters.

If actuarial tables attempt to account for all types of incident, then they are profoundly ambivalent as they simply mark the occurrence of an incident for which its aetiology is left absent. This means that fraud becomes coextensive with insurance: the risk that the tables seek to encompass is both that of the event's occurrence and that of its possible deception, so that it is impossible to assess one side without the other. Insurance becomes a system of paranoia in which every incident is suspect until proven otherwise, and where numbers indicating likelihood only lead to further numbers marking likely fraud. The accident is precisely contingent, as it could always have been otherwise, which works in both directions as Neff discovers in finding that real accidents come to disrupt his fake ones. This means that the world of noir is not entirely fatalistic, despite this pervasive sense of doom, for the nature of this doom is that it is never experienced as such but is inhabited as if there were an alternative, as if escape were possible. And if the senses of omnipresent alienation and cynicism appear to belie this feeling of escape, they also fuel it, since they mean that nothing can be trusted, nothing is certain. Thus, Neff's attempt to 'crook the house' is his attempt to find the slight deviation that would let him escape, and although the end of the line might be the cemetery this does not necessarily mean that death itself is an end, or that it negates his escape [DI: 37]. The two paths may be interlinked but they are not the same; instead it is the contingency of the accident that separates and connects them.

An indemnity refers to compensation paid in relation to certain kinds of accidents. The life insurance policy that Dietrichson unknowingly takes out contains a double indemnity clause, which means that the insurance company will pay out twice the normal amount if the accident is unusual. It is this possibility that drives the couple to kill Dietrichson and stage his murder as an accident, although it is Neff who plays the most active role. Hence, the characters are taking advantage of the fact that accidents are both likely and unlikely, in that there is such a provision in the policy in the first place and that it is heavily compensated as it does not happen often. The plot thus revolves around a conundrum that is intrinsic to insurance as a whole; that it attempts to manage the unmanageable, to incorporate contingency and unpredictability into a system. Equally, their plot incorporates the gambler's logic in which greater risk implies greater profit and this sense of doubling up, of raising the stakes, permeates the script, nothing is done for only one reason, actions are repeated and relations duplicated. In doing so, and in common with more widespread noir motifs, these acts of mirroring or shadowing do not provide greater security but only greater uncertainty, since they make it impossible to perceive any single cause or purpose; nothing has a fixed meaning as it is always marked by duplicity. That there is a double indemnity means that there is greater compensation, but only under conditions of greater improbability, a heightened risk that, paradoxically, has become the norm and the exception in this world of statistical immanence, insofar as each implies the other.

In the world as seen by the insurance company there is no distinction between good and bad acts but rather an intimate linking of risk and cover in which greater risk involves greater cover and, as a result, greater compensation. Thus individuals are not only considered as risk types but as costs; as soon as Dietrichson has been covered by his life policy he is no more than a potential dividend waiting to be realized. This is the effect that insurance starts to introduce into social relations, which helps to explain the most problematic part of the film: the motivation of the characters. Neff may state at the beginning of the film that he committed the murder for money and for a woman, but the rest of the film puts this statement in doubt as neither he nor Phyllis appear to be strongly motivated by either greed or lust. While they desire escape, and need to use each other, the performances of MacMurray and Stanwyck do not support any stronger characterizations. Indeed, perhaps the most disturbing aspect of the film, which was recognized by contemporary reviews, is that the two characters appear simply amoral as they do not commit the crime with any passion at all.[12] Equally, Neff's acts in his last encounter with Phyllis are just as cold: he does not care whether she actually killed the first Mrs Dietrichson, or whether she is actually seeing Zachette (Byron Barr); he has simply decided that she must die as it is getting too risky with her still around. The crime is thus superseded by a more profound problem, which is the lack of motivation in the criminals, and it is this that makes the film so dark. For if there is only risk and compensation, then there is only a system in which one is constantly testing these limits, knowing full well that at some point the odds will come out against you.

Decisions are made without much difficulty, actions are carried out with little emphasis and the mechanics of the crime, while explicit, remain in darkness (literally and metaphorically). The contrast with the similarly muted characters of the criminals only reveals that this darkness is unrelieved by any real purpose or motive. (It is one of the key aspects of noir, which *Double Indemnity* was one of the first to fully exploit, that darkness is always both literal and metaphorical, and that the sense of this darkness is precisely that these two aspects cannot be clearly separated.) This might suggest a certain fatalistic necessity to their trajectory, in that they are condemned to play out a role that has no reason, but this reading is complicated by the fact that they have chosen to go along with this course, and that it remains gratuitous not just because it lacks any rationale but also because it remains marked by its chance encounters.[13] Neff's last encounter with Phyllis seems almost arbitrary; it might not have turned out like this but she has become a liability, and Keyes's suspicions about Zachette only make his decision easier. Again, it is more a question of risk and cover, the risk to Neff being greater if Phyllis remains alive, and without any dividend in the form of their relation. But this is not inevitable; it is more like a passing calculation, which could have come out differently under different circumstances.

Consider how the crime develops: It is a Tuesday afternoon towards the end of May 1938, and Neff is driving back to the office from Glendale when he remembers that there is a car insurance policy in Los Feliz that needs renewing (not a person, but a policy drives the plot).[14] When he arrives at the house Mr Dietrichson is out but his wife is there, and Neff happens to surprise her in a state of undress as she has been sunbathing. Their subsequent conversation is filled with innuendo, establishing the point that both are happy to take risks with each other despite the fact that she is married. They arrange for him to come back the following night to see Mr Dietrichson, but when Neff gets back to the office there is a message from Phyllis to say that it would be better to come on Thursday afternoon. When he arrives then it is obvious the mood has changed, the house is purposely empty and Phyllis introduces the idea of taking out a life insurance policy on her husband without him knowing about it (thus raising the stakes on their risk-taking). Neff rejects the idea and leaves, but that night Phyllis come to his apartment and, after having sex, Neff declares that they will go ahead with it as he has a plan (the risk is now worth taking, and is also less purely risky). Two days have passed from the first meeting and it is only the third time they have met, and yet everything has now taken place, almost imperceptibly. Admittedly, relationships are always truncated in film plots, but nevertheless, aside from the flirtations, there is little here to build upon to determine their course of action; their attraction to each other is both obvious and yet oddly empty, just as the talk about money seems rather false. Dietrichson is merely an obstacle, not to anything in particular, just an obstacle (we have not actually seen him yet). Instead, it is more about each of them seizing the chance that the other happens to suggest.

The transitional sequence here is key because until this point Neff has behaved in an ordinary (if sleazy) way, but when he leaves the Dietrichson house the second time something has happened. Phyllis has just spoken about the life insurance policy and Neff has walked out; as he does so his voiceover begins:

> So I let her have it straight between the eyes. She didn't fool me for a minute, not this time. I knew I had hold of a red-hot poker and the time to drop it was before it burned my hand off. I stopped at a drive-in for a bottle of beer, the one I had wanted all along, only I wanted it worse now, to get rid of the sour taste of her iced tea, and everything that went with it. I didn't want to go back to the office, so I dropped by a bowling alley at Third and Western and rolled a few lines to get my mind thinking about something else for a while. I didn't feel like eating dinner when I left, and I didn't feel like a show, so I drove home, put the car away and went up to my apartment. It had begun to rain outside and I watched it get dark and didn't even turn on the light. That didn't help me either. I was all twisted up inside, and I was still holding on to that red-hot poker. And right then it came over me that I hadn't walked out on anything at all, that the hook

was too strong, that this wasn't the end between me and her. It was only the beginning. So at eight o'clock the bell would ring and I would know who it was without even having to think, as if it was the most natural thing in the world.

DI: 30–1

The sense of inevitability seems almost tragic, just as the agency remains opaque. The voiceover is spoken from a point much later in the plot, but the thoughts expressed do not indicate any greater retrospective awareness, the tense of the words remaining caught in their moment as they slowly unfold.[15] There is no positive desire or will, only the negative residue that remains when everything else that is not desired is removed. The decision occurs almost out of idleness, rather than sheer passivity, as if that was all that was left when there was nothing else. This point is emphasized in the next lines when the bell rings, just as he had expected:

Neff goes to the door and opens it.
PHYLLIS: Hello.
Neff just looks at her.
PHYLLIS: You forgot your hat this afternoon.
She has nothing in her hands but her bag.
NEFF: Did I?
He looks down at her hands.
PHYLLIS: Don't you want me to bring it in?
NEFF: Sure. Put it on the chair.
She comes in. He closes the door.

DI: 31

In a different scenario, at a different tempo, this could be quite absurd, or nightmarish. Instead, the bland insolence of the exchange indicates the strangely empty form of eroticism that brings them together, as if they were no more than ghosts, except that their movements have become the most natural thing in the world, as Neff had said. What this scene demonstrates is the sublation of desire into dialogue, and its concomitant material evacuation, which is partly what is meant by the designation of hard-boiled. Direct expressions of feeling are lost so that dialogue becomes detached from action, and this then frees action to become separate from thought or intention. Sound and vision start to move in parallel tracks, and it is a compelling virtue of the film that it still makes sense if the sound is muted, or if one only listens to the soundtrack, but each time a slightly different film emerges. In combination the two tracks create a density that to some degree overpowers their differences, the variations and deviations of each individual track, which provide its points of transition. More precisely, the ambient elements of the mise en scène, the music, lighting and sets, generate a more sombre atmosphere, while the active elements of dialogue, voiceover and characterization operate in a more heightened register, as if they were trying to remove themselves from the stagnation of their milieu. Thus it makes sense that the first sign of trouble arises in relation to Phyllis's anklet, as this is not just a mark of her sexuality but also draws the eye downwards:

NEFF: Accident insurance? Sure, Mrs Dietrichson.
His eyes fall on the anklet again.

DI: 17

What is interesting about *Double Indemnity* is that these moments do not so much mark points of seduction and deviation that lead to disaster, but are rather emblems of an already-present deviation in both characters and situation. So although there is a disparity between the tone of the milieu and that of its active elements, these are still of a piece. Hence, it makes no difference when Neff leaves the house after rejecting Phyllis's idea, as he has already been veering in that direction. Equally, it does not actually matter what name is inscribed on the anklet as Neff rarely calls Phyllis by her name.[16] The name, like the hat, is a contingent detail, in that it could always have been otherwise; it is a material accident that leads to a slight change of course that only brings out the underlying lack of any intrinsic direction. As with Diana and Actaeon, Walter and Phyllis have both stepped into a different and dangerous milieu in which they do not appear to each other, as much as they appear as the idle images of their own empty desires.

This tension between what Phyllis and Walter say and what they do becomes very apparent in the sequence at his apartment, and, more discreetly, between what Neff does and what is said in his voiceover after he leaves the Dietrichson house, where the sense of distraction is looming through and despite his material attempts to remove it. In a way the absent hat says everything that we need to know about the lack of rationale for the crime, an absence that is only apparent through the combination of the visual and audio tracks, which together carry the momentum of these incidents that make it all seem so natural. This absence could be construed in psychoanalytic or symbolic terms, but this is unnecessary as its meaning is obvious; the characters make no attempt to conceal their motivations (or lack thereof) from each other. She turns up at his apartment empty-handed because that is precisely what she has to offer, and he lets her in because that is the most natural thing to do. In other circumstances, this could be deeply romantic, or indeed, tragic, in that neither character is able to deviate from their assigned paths, but the series of accidental encounters that have led to this meeting, and the lack of persuasiveness in the characterization of their feelings for each other, instead seem to phrase this meeting as one that only happens because they have nothing better to do. This seems to be a form of recidivist inertia, in which there is the constant risk of falling back into bad ways through the failure to adhere to what is required and expected, leading to a criminal type that is not merely prone to accidents but is almost entirely constituted by them as it lacks any essence that would enable it to keep a distance from them, leaving it prey to every evil influence.

This amoral lack is what makes the film disturbing, as is emphasized in the opening voiceover where Neff explicitly rejects the idea that his account is a confession. He takes responsibility for the murder, and declares that he did it for money and for a woman but as he then says, 'I didn't get the money and I didn't get the woman', rendering the whole account gratuitous [DI: 11]. Responsibility is thereby unravelled as Neff may be materially responsible for the act, but as he seems to lack any real motive, his character comes into question. The law needs to condemn the act but also the agent, to show that he or she was criminally responsible for breaking the law. However, Neff returns to the office (rather than fleeing to Mexico) not to make a confession and thereby take on the responsibility of the act but to set the record straight for Keyes, to close the file by showing Keyes that what he had overlooked was not just that the crime was committed by someone close to him, but that it could be committed by such a person, and that it was done simply because it was possible. This position is not the same as that found in Camus's *L'Étranger*, despite Camus's desire to take up the plain or blank style of Cain's novels, because there is no attempt to make a moral discussion out of the story; Neff is not trying to claim any existential freedom from theodicy like Meursault. Instead, he tries to cast the story as a tale of twisted love and fate, but this is only the polish that he, as a salesman, is trying to give it by presenting it 'all wrapped up in tissue paper, with pink ribbons' [DI: 10]. Lust and greed are only proximal causes; beneath them is the curiosity prompted by idleness, as his actual account shows:

> Maybe she had stopped thinking about it, but I hadn't. I couldn't. Because it all tied up with something I had been thinking about for years, since long before I ever ran into Phyllis Dietrichson. Because, in this business you can't sleep for trying to figure out the tricks they could pull on you. You're like the guy behind the roulette wheel, watching the customers to make sure they don't crook the house. And then one night, you get to thinking how you could crook the house yourself. And do it smart. Because you've got that wheel right under your hands. And you know every notch in it by heart. And you figure all you need is a plant out in front, a shill to put down the bet. And suddenly the doorbell rings and the whole set-up is right there in the room with you ... Look, Keyes, I'm not trying to whitewash myself. I fought it, only maybe I didn't fight it hard enough. The stakes were fifty thousand dollars, but they were the life of a man, too, a man who'd never done me any dirt. Except he was married to a woman he didn't care anything about, and I did.
>
> DI: 36–7

Neff's rationale is just as empty as Phyllis's hands; an idle thought, an opportunity, not the love he may feel for Phyllis but merely that insomniac itch that asks to be scratched and won't go away, an itch made possible by the equation between a life and a sum of money, an exchange that incurs no responsibility as it arises out of no fault but by accident. In the universe of insurance there is no transcendental theodicy, only the materiality of bodies engaging in limited relations of cause and effect, a universe of contingency that leaves no room, and has no need, for moral responsibility. The sleight of hand is almost perfect: first Neff (fraudulently) sells Dietrichson a policy, then he kills Dietrichson, the money that was made to appear in the policy (as a potential) is then realized and Dietrichson is entirely unaware of what has happened. Money that did not exist is brought about through murder but for it to continue to exist this exchange must be perpetuated; therefore further substitutes are recruited (Lola and Zachette) to allow this realization to take place. The getaway is always flawed, not because of any moral retribution, but because it relies on the *schlechten* infinity of capitalist criminality, the endless exchange of bodies for money.

In a lecture from 1977 Foucault discussed the development of insurance and the notion of risk in an analysis of criminal responsibility, and in doing so quoted from the pioneering French legal scholar and jurist Raymond Saleilles, who in 1897 described the results of this understanding of accidents:

> Next to a relation of causality attached to personal fault, a fault having been the demonstrable cause of the accident, there is a relation of causality attached to a purely objective fault, that is to say, to a material fact that in itself appears as a chance fact [*fait aventureux*], not irregular in itself, nor contrary to the customs of modern life, but disdainful of the extreme caution that paralyzes action, in harmony with the activity that imposes itself today and as a result braving hazards and accepting risks; that is the law of life today, that is the common rule; and the law is made to reflect this current conception of life, as it goes through its successive evolutions, if not it is nothing but a construction of rationalizations idly linked together, but empty of reality.[17]

If the structure of the law and of insurance in particular is there to smooth out these ever-present possibilities of accidental disruption, then the actions of the criminal are merely deviations that can neither be prevented nor assimilated as they are its contingent conditions of possibility. As Foucault goes on to explain, this idea led to the notion that there are criminal types that are themselves sources of risk, regardless of any actual fault, as these individuals constitute a risk because their personality bears a high probability of criminality, which means that these individuals are not necessarily to be punished, since they are not in themselves at fault, but rather that their activity is to be curtailed (and not eradicated). Thus the law comes to assign responsibility even in the absence of actual fault, and the insurance business comes to be at the forefront of this process of diagnosis and categorization since it is able to develop detailed accounts of potential liability. As Keyes makes clear, a claims investigator 'is a doctor and a blood-hound and a cop and a judge and a jury and a father confessor, all in one' [DI: 54]. All the medical, legal and religious accounts of causality and responsibility are contained in the insurance assessment, which becomes immanent to public life and withdraws any possibility of finding an exterior court to which one could appeal. So, as the law moves from sanctioning what one does to what one is, according to this model of personal liability, there then emerges a problem when one does not provide an account of one's actions that goes beyond their facts, as Foucault concludes:

> When a man comes before his judges with nothing but his crimes, when he has nothing else to say but 'this is what I have done', when he has nothing to say about himself, when he does not do the tribunal the favour of confiding to them something like the secret of his own being, then the judicial machine ceases to function.[18]

While the last point may seem excessive, it nevertheless provides an understanding of Keyes's blind spot, and why the characters of Walter and Phyllis offer so little moral traction. For it almost seems as if their criminality is generated by the attempt to establish an all-encompassing system of risk and compensation, so that they emerge out of the inability of this system to eliminate motiveless acts. In the words of Isidore Ducasse, which Borde and Chaumeton cite to describe the consequences of this systemic breakdown, these are the 'bloody channels through which logic at bay [*aux abois*] is made to pass' [PFN: 15/5].[19] This is to point out not just that, in its passage through the contingent, thought cannot be secured from its most mortal consequences but also that this passage is the inevitable result of the move by which logic is brought to a halt, thereby eliminating any possibility of its immaculate and transcendent separation from the world, so that the movement by which thought becomes entangled in the world is the same as the one in which its fragility and finitude emerge most forcefully.

VII. The negation of negation

Double Indemnity was released in France in 1946 and was one of the films that went to form the new category of 'film noir' as it was discussed by Frank in *L'Écran français*.[20] The other films he mentioned were *The Maltese Falcon* (John Huston, 1941), *Laura* (Otto Preminger, 1944) and *Murder, My Sweet* (Edward Dmytryk, 1944), and a few months later the discussion was picked up by Jean-Pierre Chartier in *La Révue du cinéma*, who also included *The Postman Always Rings Twice* and *The Lost Weekend* (Wilder, 1945). These essays have been widely discussed, but it is worth recalling that they made the important observation that the significance of these films was both thematic and formal. On the one hand, they introduced a new form of crime drama in which the (lack of) motivations of the characters was foregrounded, which made the films more sordid and immoral. On the other hand, new stylistic elements like voiceovers and flashbacks, as well as the emphatically dark milieu with its claustrophobic or nightmarish effects, led to a fragmentation of the narrative that paradoxically enabled it to slide over conventional plot transitions, as Frank wrote, to accentuate the 'lived' (*vécue*) aspect of the story. It is clear that, for Frank, *Double Indemnity* represents the key film in this group as its combined innovations generated an awareness of the social and cinematic displacement that had occurred as Hollywood was drawn away from the previous genre highlights of the Western 'by the dynamism of violent death and unravelled enigmas, as well as from the decor of a vast novelistic nature to that of a "social fantastic" ["*fantastique social*"]'.[21] And it was for this same combination of reasons that *Double Indemnity* was condemned by Hollywood's censor board, the Production Code Administration (PCA), which disapproved of the adulterous and murderous behaviour of its protagonists, the fact that the planning and execution of the act is shown in considerable detail, and that the couple die by their own hands rather than being brought to justice. When the novel appeared in 1935 the PCA had banned its adaptation into a film, but in 1943 circumstances had not only changed as a result of the war but much had been done to cloak the more unsavoury aspects of the story.[22] This occurred quite literally with the use of night-for-night shooting due to blackout restrictions, and the innuendos that masked the sexual and criminal aspects of the intrigue. It is all the more interesting that the ending remained the same as the alternative proved too gruesome, which is to say that it was too explicit.[23]

These points are important because they show that these films were understood from the beginning as having an impact on the social as well as the filmic order. This reading is taken up in Kracauer's article on Hollywood's 'terror films', as he called them, which came out at the same time, and in which he discussed whether these films (extending the theses of *From Caligari to Hitler*, which was published the following year) were broader reflections of American culture. Although this article is hampered by Kracauer's insistence that the cruelty and violence found in these crime dramas is in continuity with that found in Nazi ideology, he nevertheless makes some valuable comments. His argument begins by claiming that the sadistic atmosphere of these new films arose as a way of conveying the horrors of Nazi Germany to American audiences but that this mood, once introduced, then proliferated and began to appear for its own sake. Consequently, the 'weird, veiled insecurity of life under the Nazis is transferred to the American scene', such that 'everyday life itself breeds anguish and destruction'.[24] The terror that Kracauer sees is drawn from the fact that these films (along with *The Lost Weekend*, he focuses on *The Dark Corner* (Henry Hathaway, 1946), *Shock* (Alfred Werker, 1946) and *The Spiral Staircase* (Siodmak, 1946)) depict a world saturated by apprehension and unpredictable brutality, and as this violence is often meaningless it leads to uncertainty over what is rational and what is not. Like Frank, he concludes that the study of psychological aberrations has become the mark of these films, to such a degree that their all-pervasive fear and lack of hope, which undermines individual integrity, is not only inevitable but inscrutable. But, in Kracauer's eyes, this pessimism gives way to gratuitous indulgence, since these films are uncoupled from any social or political critique and so can only offer an empty and vicarious experience of cruelty and morbidity. This reaction was not uncommon among contemporary reviewers, but Kracauer also recognizes the singular physical environment that distinguishes film noir in which 'chance arrangements of inanimate objects are made conspicuous, sombre backgrounds assert themselves'. The sense of this discovery is unavoidable: 'People emotionally out of joint inhabit a realm ruled by bodily sensations and material stimulants, a realm in which dumb objects loom monstrously high and become signal posts or stumbling blocks, enemies or allies. This obtrusiveness of inanimate objects is infallible evidence of an inherent concern with mental disintegration.' And it is here that Kracauer finds that there is a broader social significance to this mood, for these 'horrors are never incorporated in a meaningful pattern that would neutralize them. This would indicate that real life itself fails to suggest such a pattern. Whether society be a spiritual vacuum or a battlefield of irreconcilable beliefs, it seems no longer to provide a shelter for the individual, or principles that would compel his integrity'.[25]

It may seem odd to find Kracauer making moral and psychological judgements about the relation between obtrusive objects and mental disintegration when this relation is exactly what many of these films are addressing, and where the destabilization of the borders between the interior and exterior is a critical focus. Rather than complaining that such horrors are not assimilated into socially meaningful patterns that would enable political change, which risks being as naïve artistically as it is politically, these films operate by drawing attention to the way that film itself gives expression to this breakdown between the material and the mental, and thereby gives sense to it, albeit in its own material form. As one small example, consider a moment in *Detour* (Edgar Ulmer, 1945) where Al (Tom Neal) complains about a saxophone player who had seemed to be part of the soundtrack rather than the scenario. This breakdown between the diegetic and non-diegetic is a strikingly reflexive moment, which offers a critical foothold for the viewer as it gives form to the sense of breakdown as such. So, while audiences at the time were often disoriented by the confusing and violent narratives of these films, they were also offered ways of recognizing the form and nature of this confusion.[26] Thus, if we are to see how these films were not just expressing their world but also providing a commentary upon it, however slight, it is necessary to look at these formal disjunctions between music and scenario, dialogue and acting, that give evidence of a reflection upon these tensions. It is intriguing to find Adorno tacitly working in exactly this area, for although he was often dismissive of popular film he was acutely aware of the interactions between ideology and aesthetics, and of the material fragmentation that can betray these interactions. Even a brief look at his concerns while he was living in Los Angeles makes it all too apparent that the potential for a more astute reading of film noir was latent within his thoughts (the development of this potential will occur in Chapter 5 in relation to Tarr's *Damnation*).

Adorno moved to Los Angeles in November 1941 and remained there until October 1949. During this time he was involved in collaborative projects with Max Horkheimer on *Dialektik der Aufklärung*, Hanns Eisler on *Komposition für den Film* and Thomas Mann on *Doktor Faustus*. He also directed sociological studies at Berkeley on the origins and varieties of authoritarianism, fascism and anti-Semitism. Parallel to these works he wrote *Philosophie der neuen Musik* and *Minima Moralia*, as well as articles on Huxley and Kafka that would later appear in *Prismen*, and studies of psychoanalysis and radio theory. The range of these works is interesting for the way that it indicates a landscape in which the interlinking of music, fascism and popular culture sketches out the movements of disintegration and alienation. In effect, Adorno was developing a formal version of the same investigation that was already ongoing within film noir. Evidence for this comes from the fact that he and Horkheimer tried to produce a short film of their own in 1945 (amply demonstrating their awareness of the importance and possibilities of the medium) that was originally called *The Accident* and then later, *Below the Surface*, which sought to analyse how racial prejudice operates. Despite spending considerable time on this project it was dropped because the process of developing the script ended up pushing it too far from their own concerns, and yet not far enough towards a product that the studios would accept, although it may have helped lay the ground for larger-scale projects like *Crossfire* (Dmytryk, 1947), which covers many of the same issues.[27] Adorno's abiding interest in these years appears to have been in the social and cultural mechanisms that enable prejudices to take root, and it is perhaps for this reason that his responses to popular culture can seem one-sided. (It is notable that both Sartre and Brecht were also very disillusioned by seeing how Hollywood operated on industrial lines, with all the aesthetic and commercial implications that this holds.) But his friendship with directors like Fritz Lang and William Dieterle would have meant that he could not have been unaware of the emergence of a new kind of crime drama, although it is to be imagined that he may have seen in these no more than the mechanisms of corruption by which people become subject to forces of violence and discrimination. These films are harsh in their remorseless venality and, as has been emphasized, they not only sought to depict but to convey these forces. While Adorno may have noticed this latter aspect in the conventionality of character and plot, he seems not to have recognized that the aesthetic form of these films led to an entirely different experience (even if his other writings showed awareness of this point), one that not only conveys corruption but also enables its examination, its own subtle critique.

It is this reflexive critique, however subtle, that marks film noir out as symptomatic of the tensions of its times, as opposed to some of the other films that were appearing during this period.[28] It is the coherence of its aesthetic form, within which this reflexive critique appears, that makes this singularity apparent, as these films appeared fully formed from the outset with their own distinctive form of discourse, which is why they have become so widely, if belatedly, discussed, a delay that is also evidence of their embeddedness within the times. The boldness and simplicity of the noir image is seemingly lost in the density of its formal presentation, but in combination these two aspects allow for its image to be inserted into its historical milieu while indicating the singularity of its material features. Consider the most emblematic of noir images, that of a figure on the run, which becomes changed once it is placed on a rainy street at night, with subdued or high contrast lighting, low camera angles, brooding music, obsessive voiceover and so on. The idea of the image thus appears to be overwhelmed by its presentation, but instead 'syntax and material [*Stoff*] lose themselves and the material affirms its superiority by belying the syntactic form that attempts to encompass it'.[29] With these lines Adorno is discussing epic poetry, particularly the way that minimal syntactic elements, like transitions and conjunctions, seem to disrupt the poetic form with their apparent meaninglessness but actually make it possible for the material singularity of the content to present itself more forcefully, which is also found in the disruptive transitions in many noir films (as Frank had pointed out). The comparison with the epic form is not so remote when it is recalled that film noir is an exploration of the visual and verbal vernacular of urban America, its everyday concerns with the conflict between freedom and destiny given shape in the popular medium of film. In the epic form, as Adorno goes on to explain, the linkages of thought tend to go slack in favour of the image, such that its language, rather than illuminating the image, becomes subsumed into it. As the force of syntax is weakened these images do not become allegories of anything in particular, as they do not bear any judgement:

> It is the objective turning [*Umschlag*] of pure insignificant [*bedeutungsfernen*] representation into the allegory of history that

becomes visible in the logical disintegration of epic language, as in the relieving [*Ablösung*] of metaphor from the course of literal action. It is only by the abandoning of meaning [*Sinnverlassenheit*] that epic discourse resembles the image, a figure of objective meaning arising from the negation of subjective rationalized meaning.[30]

It is thus that the force of the noir image comes to the surface in its historical-material specificity, and leaves behind any particular meaning. This is not to say that all films noir operate in this mode, or that the ones that do are merely historical allegories, but to show how the historical becomes materially visible in their form as sheer contingency, which is why this form is so distinctive and compelling, despite its enigmas. Adorno's approach also shows how such films can exist as artworks, that is, as works that are fully integrated despite their contradictions, by showing how the syntax of their form is consistent with its content. And, by placing film noir and the epic in contrast, it becomes apparent how the latter is transformed in the context of modern urban alienation, where the very sense of community and history, and life and death, as the dimensions of individual action, is disrupted.

While there are films like *Kiss Me Deadly* (Robert Aldrich, 1955), *House of Strangers* (Mankiewicz, 1949) and *Force of Evil* (Abraham Polonsky, 1948) that explicitly explore these epic themes, it is helpful to look at how the structure of the films expresses this situation of alienation, how the figures of the private investigator and the undercover agent reflect the movement between worlds found in the epic, which is also captured in the use of dream sequences and voiceovers, and the formal transitions provided by low-key lighting, which blur boundaries and emphasize ambiguities in such a way that the film's thoroughly integrated form not only depicts but also conveys this alienation. But the problem with an approach that presents events as sheerly contingent in their violence and corruption is that it ignores the Marxist point that all events have their roots in socioeconomic structures. Such is the critique developed by Irving Howe in the wake of Kracauer's article:

> All of life under a decaying capitalist society is increasingly insecure, many pretenses of morality and order are being dropped in political life. This tendency toward open power domination, toward domination of masses by terror and pressure propaganda, is transformed on the screen into images of more personalized insecurity. What is especially noteworthy is that so much of the brutality and horror of these Hollywood pictures is without meaning or purpose beyond the mere accidental existence of some particularly evil individual – this very meaninglessness, incidentally, making it all the more terrifying. Hollywood refrains from associating terror with current social and political life ... Unable or unwilling to connect the feelings of terror which seem so strongly rooted in

contemporary life with their social setting, Hollywood can therefore produce only grotesque portraits of horror, ultimately boring in their viciousness.[31]

Ideology tends to make itself invisible, and in doing so events appear as simply irrational or mindless, thereby preventing an examination of their systemic causes. This is part of the mystique of capitalism, and in making this point in relation to noir films Howe is saying that they are part of the problem in that they merely present images of criminality without examining its origins. However, these films do not, in their best instances, just present such images but are able to show their status and force; even such low-key examples as *Detour* make it clear that its accidents are emblematic of an alienated society. And the more complex of these films, like *Double Indemnity* (not to mention the more socially engaged films of the so-called film gris cycle), go further by showing the nature and extent of such contingent disruptions without indulging in nihilistic pessimism or masochism.[32] Contingency is not thereby explained away but shown to be part of the fabric of modernity, which is to say that capital is itself subject to its chance irruptions. Ideology may seek to hide the sources of events, but those irruptions that are contingent cannot thereby by eliminated; to do so runs the same risk of deception as the attempt to construe social malaise as psychological deviation.

Double Indemnity becomes particularly significant because it shows how the accident is absorbed into the systematization of events as risk, and how it is still able to disrupt this system. That is, the accident itself, if there can be such a thing despite its contingency, operates as part of the expression of social forms and their critique, and the problem of the noir film lies precisely in the attempt to navigate this indeterminacy, which is why it becomes obscure and violent, and also ambiguous. It is apparent that this ambiguity arises in the form of a film like *Double Indemnity* by way of the contrast between the dialogue and the mise en scène, the plot and the characterizations, which are engaged in a complex and subtle movement of incomplete negations that is the source of its disturbing quality. If we recall the problem of negativity that was raised at the beginning of this book, it was found to persist through and beyond the movement of non-contradiction and the excluded middle. In relation to *Double Indemnity* it may seem inappropriate to discuss such logical problems, but it is intrinsic to Hegel's understanding of logic that it is not merely abstract but is the concrete movement of life.

Indeed, in Hegel's words, 'contradiction is the root of all movement and vitality'. As he explains, although it is assumed that contradiction cannot be represented or thought and that it is simply an accident or abnormality that arises only here and there, it is in fact 'the principle of all self-movement, which consists in nothing else than in a display of contradiction', so that 'external, sensuous motion is itself contradiction's immediate existence'. This point bears a significant reversal, for rather than finding (like Zeno) that a consideration of motion leads to the absurd paradox that things do not move, instead it is contradiction that exists, that is itself the existent: 'Something moves, not because now it is here and there at another now, but because in one and the same now it is here and not here; because in this here it is and is not at the same time.' Likewise, inner movement or drive is 'nothing else than that something is, *in itself*, itself and the lack *of itself*', and it is thus that the force of vitality *is* only insofar as it holds and endures this movement of contradiction [WL1: 286–7/439–40; emphases in the original]. In a dialectical fashion Hegel first denies that contradiction is merely accidental, and then raises it to the status of a universal principle, before incorporating it into the very basis of existence, which is of course the speculative operation of upheaval or *aufheben*: to cancel, elevate and preserve. But the accidental nature of contradiction cannot be so easily assimilated, for its universal cannot ever realize itself completely.[33]

It can be seen that Walter and Phyllis are riven by a desire that is both present and not present, and that this contradiction both drives them on and prevents them from finding any way out. Equally, their situation falls into the anomaly of finding that, insofar as this desire is neither present nor not present, it occurs in some other form, which yields its own obscure milieu and tendency. The status of this milieu is amply demonstrated by the questions that proliferate from it: if the nature of desire is problematic, then is Neff responsible or not responsible, since his role as an agent seems to lack real motivation? If the motive force is lacking, then are the events accidents or not accidents? On the night of the murder, is Neff at home or not at home, since a witness attests to his presence there, when he is not, and he appears on the train, but not as himself? In the movement by which the life of Dietrichson is converted into money, what is his status when, alive or dead, he bears a potential value that cannot be actualized? And what is the nature of the relation between Walter and Phyllis when they appear to be working with and against each other, an uncertainty repeated not just in Neff's relation to Keyes but also in the relation between atmosphere and dialogue? This last point seems to become the major point of tension as it marks the relation between the vibrancy of the script and the nonchalance of the acting, in which it is unclear whether the words are seeking to animate characters that are already dead, or whether the characters are drawing the words into their own inevitable decline. There is thus a series of contradictions that run through the characters, narrative and development of the film that are not merely a product of its expression and analysis of alienation but indicate the inability to avoid contradiction, whether in relation to the law, desire or mortality, an inability that in its refusal to be resolved remains a marker of its contingency.

The contradiction does not lie in the relation between positive and negative, which are mutually determining, but rather within each pole, as it were, in the difference between its apparent unity and its contradiction. Thus Hegel's account operates with the same logic as that found in magnetism, which is why the relation between Neff and Keyes is different in kind to that between Phyllis and Walter, and why the latter should in its tensed and mutual repulsion lead to their deaths as an encounter with an irresolvable nullity or blind spot. What lies between poles of the same kind is something that is neither positive nor negative, something that is not thought but real and thus absolutely contradictory, in that it is sheer contingency, counter to all relation or sublation and so without subsistence.

Is it this that Phyllis sees as Dietrichson is killed? It is night and they are parked on an unlit street, and yet she stares into the darkness with an almost frightening intensity. She is not looking at what is happening, indeed, she is precisely not seeing what is going on, to such an extent that she sees and does not see at the same time as she is intently focused elsewhere. There is no sense of excitement or revenge or triumph, only her unblinking gaze into the darkness. She is not viewing the act anymore than its consequences or reasons; she is simply confronting its breach with an empty intensity, neither fearfully nor in a welcoming manner. Her gaze is blind, a vision *of* darkness, as she sees that there is nothing to see.

4

Between deaths

VIII. Frayed edges

In 1948 Blanchot published a short story or novella (*récit*) that marked a departure from his previous works in both its focus and its structure. This was his darkest and most enigmatic work to date, but it was also formally challenging, and in many ways the enigma of this work comes from understanding how these two aspects relate to each other. Was it the case that the thematics gave rise to a particularly condensed and fractured form, or was it the other way around; what is the nature of the relation between the two aspects? Many years later he provided a kind of commentary on this development, which seemed to emerge from the difficulties of following through on a certain form of sentence: '"*I don't know*" has by itself a very gentle attraction; it is the most simple speech; negation collects itself in it to silence itself in making knowledge silent.' This is not to aver to the Socratic profession of ignorance but rather to find a power in the phrase that 'declines the present', for as a response to a specific question it not only declines to adopt the equivocal silence of unknowing but also falls short of its place in conversation: 'It is a response that is no longer really part of dialogue: an interruption from which the abrupt character of cessation is withdrawn' [PAD: 154/112]. In combining the two aspects of knowledge and negation there is a mutual degradation in which the decision of knowing and the sharpness of the negative come up against each other in the doubly serrated and imbricated slopes of a ridge (*arête*) that arrests itself (*s'arrête*). Even if the sentence carries on in the form of 'I don't know but ...', this *but* does not break its declination but prolongs it further:

> 'I don't know', not being able to repeat itself or close itself without running the risk of hardening itself, is indeed the end that does not end. The present that 'I don't know' has put gently in parentheses gives place to a delay ... in which the absence of present dissimulates itself in

knowledge itself in letting another still or already absent present come marginally.

PAD: 155/113

The sentence unfolds into a moment that is not a moment but its absence, and so language and thought encounter their own loss of presence – a mortal, temporal loss.

The *récit* that Blanchot published in 1948 is of this loss, and it is formally and thematically challenging because it exposes itself to the question of what it is to survive, to live on in this ongoing delay and absence, which is 'not to live or, not living, to maintain oneself, without life, in a state of pure supplement, movement of supplementation for life, but rather to arrest dying, arrest that does not arrest, making it on the contrary *last*. "*Speak on the edge* [l'arrête] – *line of instability* – *of speech*"' [PAD: 184/135; emphasis in the original].¹ The question of how to live on in this deterioration of time is also a question of its narration or *histoire*: the 'sense' of life as the possibility of its meaning, and the form that this may take. Blanchot thus comes to an understanding of the peculiar way that the narrative or *récit* operates as a complication and cancellation of its own event. The later description of this node of writing in his 1954 article 'Le chant des sirènes' perhaps renders it too schematically, as *L'Arrêt de mort* conveys much more forcefully the manner in which the event of the narrative is also its dissolution; not just its site and approach but also its absence and delay. As a result this *récit* is an account of death in which, as Derrida noted, its title works in two directions, towards and against its own ridge of speaking, as both the suspension of death and the arrest that is death. That is, there is both negativity and decision, as was remarked by Blanchot (and as Deleuze alluded to in *Logique du sens*), where each counters the other, as one is a cut and the other its lack; one is a cancellation and the other its edge:

> *En arrêtant*, in the sense of suspending, suspends the *arrêt*, in the sense of decision. The *suspensive arrêt* suspends the *decisive arrêt*. The decisive *arrêt* arrests the suspensive *arrêt*. They are ahead of or lag behind one another, and the one marks delay, the other haste. There are not only two senses or two syntaxes of the *arrêt* but, beyond a playful mobility, the *antagony* from one *arrêt* to the other.²

The oscillation or intervention is not between the two senses; rather the indecision occurs within each sense. And it is thus that it is an indecision of death, which marks the narrative with its fatal undoing. Death is not only the impossibility of possibility but also the indecision of decision and its decisive undecidability; what cannot be decided in its decision and what arises from this lack. The narrative is this unresolved antagonism of knowledge and negation: what is decided in its event and what remains outside and evacuates it. Because of this pressure the narrative comprises two parts whose relation is undecided, for even if they are decisively separate it is not decided which is the result of its decision and which is not. Or, as Derrida pointed out, which remains in advance and which behind its event. And as the arrest arrests and suspends itself, so does the *arrêt de mort* arrest and suspend the *arrêt de mort*, destabilizing both its end and its beginning, its movement and its stasis; it can neither start nor halt but trembles on its own ridge of speaking and thinking, the in-decision of its *histoire*.

Thus everything that seems to happen in *L'Arrêt de mort* appears to undermine or be undermined by its narration, such that events not only occur more than once but also do so to a degree that only makes them less certain. For example, the narrative relates the death of a woman that happens twice and that then affects the narrator's relation to other women in increasingly ambiguous ways, which renders its effects more disturbing rather than less. The first part relates the circumstances leading up to the death of a woman named only as J., and it begins with an excess of details (dates, places, characters) as if there were an anxiety about the narrative, about its status and verisimilitude, which these details could somehow alleviate. The narrative seems to be negotiating an approach to what happened with the same ambivalent uncertainty as J.'s own approach to death, for while there is a determination to proceed in this approach, there is also an overdetermination brought about by its circumstances, which risks obstructing the narrative rather than substantiating it, or revealing that it is no more than the array of these details. J. is dying and is apparently pleased with this fact, not through any morbidity or despair but instead because it seems to be an act that she can see through to the end. But in this attempt to approach the end with her eyes open, as it were, she risks losing sight of it and missing the point of death. The medicine she is prescribed is, perversely, more likely to be fatal the weaker she is (which suggests that it simply exacerbates her current condition, like a negative *pharmakon*), and this sense of certainty seems to please her, although she comes to reject its assurance as false. When death happens, it does so seemingly by accident, for although she intends to wait until the narrator is with her before dying she appears to miss the assignation and dies by default. Consequently, when the narrator finally arrives he is able to revive her from this accidental death, only for the actual occasion to catch up with them twenty-four hours later. This time the image of death is replaced by its fact and the first part of the narrative ends.

As the narrator recalls at the beginning of the *récit*, these occurrences happened nine years earlier, in 1938, and he had been haunted by the need to write them down but also by the impossibility of this task. In the second part of the narrative it is the story of these delays and failures that is related as the narrator goes through a series of missed encounters with three women, Colette, Simone and Nathalie. Each time he tries to meet them, either by visiting their rooms or vice versa, these encounters fail to take place. Finally, by a series of accidents he manages to succeed with Nathalie, only to find that she has removed herself, somehow fatally, by having a cast made of her head and hands. J. had also had a cast made of her hands and so the two narratives appear to join up, although Nathalie is not dying and is unwilling to do so, and yet she has had a cast made of her living face and, in staring into its empty eyes, she encounters the same bottomless gaze that J. had found on the night of her first death.

The combination of elements drawn from Poe (M. Valdemar, Ligeia, The Oval Portrait) all converge on the point of death and its uncertainty, of a death that can be arrested or delayed or repeated, and thus of the dreadful anomaly of a moment that is not a moment and so cannot be approached but instead appears as the evacuation of such moments, and its gaze. The two parts of the narrative (leaving aside the epilogue) form the two overlapping sides of a thanatology, of an attempted discourse on death that is also a fatal disruption of narrative, which is why the epilogue then emerges not as a sublation of this tension but as an injunction to look into its null centre, to examine the absence from which it arose. It is thus that *L'Arrêt de mort* emerges as Blanchot's first *récit* and equally emerges from the excess of decay and corruption that had marked *Le Très-Haut*. But it is also the result of the undoing of the narrative in the actual historical events of the Munich accords in the autumn of 1938 and the bombing of Paris in the summer of 1940, a doubled series of events that do not anchor the narrative as much as punctuate it with the impossibility of accommodating them. Hence, it is not just death that proves to be an aporia for the narrative but also history; history as the attempt to relate the passing of moments of time in and to language, which thereby collapses the structure of the narrative. The movement of events is replaced by accidents that, like the blood and poison that percolate through the narrative, move erratically until they scatter entirely, leaving instead a kind of 'living' thought that is no more than its own injunction, the force or gaze of its sheer occurrence, which appears to take on a concrete form, not a presence or agency but simply an independence, like an image. This thought has to be considered in relation to the intense resistance that J. displays in relation to death, which recalls, as Blanchot makes clear, the incredible will of Ligeia in Poe's tale.[3] The resistance is in response to the idea of death as finality, which has to be arrested so that, paradoxically, there is no arrest. But in doing so, the status of the individual who halts the end is put in doubt, for they are now neither living nor dead. If their existence – if it can still be so called – carries on, then it is not as a resurrection or reincarnation but as something more elusive. Equally, this is not the desire to defeat death for the sake of a continued life but rather and simply to realize that dying is not an end. To realize the actuality of death is to realize that it is not final, not in the sense that it yields to a transcendence, which is only to avoid it by displacing it, but that as an ending dying itself cannot end. And so it is against the illusory ending of death that J. places her resistance in order to realize its endlessness, and it is in and as the alien intensity of this resistance that the concrete form of thought takes place.

The uncanny quality of this transfigured existence is reflected in another novel set at the same time, Boileau and Narcejac's *D'Entre les morts*, which although published in 1954 is set quite precisely on the eve of the German invasion of France in May 1940.[4] It is this novel that formed the basis for Hitchcock's *Vertigo* (1958), and the figure of Madeleine (Kim Novak) bears the same enigma as that found in Blanchot's narrative, since her attraction is based in the fact that she is both dead and not dead. First, as she appears to be possessed by the spirit of a dead ancestor, and second, as she herself dies and then reappears in a new form. The repetition of these motifs from Poe to Blanchot to Hitchcock is compelling in the persistence of the enigma of a woman who is neither dead nor alive, neither herself nor someone else, but is the ambivalent image of this persistence. Furthermore, insofar as she is experienced as such, her fascination affects the figure of her companion as well, who becomes drawn into this experience of that which is both dead and not dead, which is thus also an experience of its vertiginous thought, a thought that is terrifying in its uncanny groundlessness. It is for this reason that Flavières in *D'Entre les morts* and Scottie (James Stewart) in *Vertigo* become so insistent in trying to control and define Madeleine, to put a name and form on her existence, which only leads to their undoing. Hence, it does not matter that the figure of Madeleine was a deception as she is not experienced as such, even for herself, until it is too late to make a difference as the thought of her undying persistence has come to corrupt both their existences.

The singular power of these narratives (and Hitchcock's film) lies in the split that occurs midway through them, for in each case the narrative stops in order to start again, as if it were not possible to go on without coming to a halt, a break that in turn only restarts matters. And yet, in each case, the narrative that restarts only dimly repeats what has gone before, creating a sense of repetition that is never fully clarified or explained. The role of this breach is thus critical or pivotal, but because it is not elucidated it also remains a void that ruptures the narrative, or, alternatively, it is a void that seems to join two distinct narratives. As such a blind spot, the rupture cannot be read (marked most emphatically by Scottie's catatonia in *Vertigo*, and by the events of the war in *D'Entre les morts* and *L'Arrêt de mort*), and yet it structures what goes on around it, leading to the suggestion that the rupture is paradoxically but inevitably primary, and the narrative is no more than the reverberations of its breach. But in this way it becomes misleading, as its role of focusing the breaches in the narrative also obscures the pervasive rupturing that goes on throughout the rest of the work. This point is highlighted by the equivocations that introduce Blanchot's narrative, where its beginning is explicitly halting, repetitive and fragmentary. Opening the path into a narrative is a moment of breaching, and so its opening becomes no more than a frayed edge in which the presence and absence of the narrative are equally apparent as it struggles to appear. There is the same diacritical relation between presence and absence here as was remarked in the fragment from *L'Attente l'oubli* mentioned earlier, so that it becomes a question of whether the narrative edge is frayed because of the preceding void, or whether the void arises out of the fraying edge. What is intriguing about these narratives is the way that this rupturing permeates throughout the stories in the uncanny presence of a woman whose identity and status are so uncertain that it causes each of the narratives to stutter obsessively around her absent presence. While this is clearly a form of prosopopoeia for the structural fragility of narrative as such (its lack of grounding), it is also an exploration of the effects of such a vertiginous absence, how the displacements and substitutions that take place do not contain this absence, even as the narratives approach it ever more closely, but rather reveal its lack of subsistence.

Although this rupturing is structural, it is not essential, as the contingencies of space and time so relentlessly indicate, for each of the dates and places becomes arbitrarily significant, no more than passing occasions for the appearance of the absence, which invests them with a structural force but could just as easily have been otherwise or not at all. The desire of Flavières and Scottie may well form the basis of their itineraries, and thus the fraying (and *frayer*) of the narrative, but in Blanchot's *récit* it is more that the narrator is fascinated by the effects of the void itself. It is noteworthy that the sense of fraying and *frayer* work in different directions in French and English, since in French it is a case of a path being formed or broken open, while in English it is the opposite tendency, of a form breaking down. Together they provide a key to the ambivalent status of the narrative in relation to that which it is drawn towards and yet seeks to distinguish itself from, and it is as such that the split in these narratives both precedes and does not precede its formation, and thereby exists neither inside nor outside it. The status of a breach that neither fully separates nor joins, and is not really within or without, is thus left open. To understand the effects of this breach it is necessary to look closely at how it occurs in the different narratives, of which Blanchot's version offers the best starting point:

> These events happened to me in 1938. I feel the greatest difficulty [*gêne*] in speaking of them. Many times already I have tried to give them a written form. If I have written books, it is because I have hoped that these books would put an end to all of it. If I have written novels, these novels were born from the moment that words began to recoil before the truth. I have no fear of the truth. I am not afraid to tell a secret. But words, until now, have been weaker and more cunning than I would have

wanted. This cunning, I know, is a warning. It would be nobler to leave the truth in peace. It would be very worthwhile [*utile*] for the truth not to be uncovered. But now I hope to be done with it [*en finir*] soon. To be done with it is also noble and important.

AM: 7/131

While entertaining some of the tropes of the reticent Gothic narrator, Blanchot's first *récit* begins by remarking the distance that separates its events from its account or *histoire*. Furthermore, the effect of whatever it was that happened is such that writing is in contradistinction to it; writing both negates and is negated by the events, and it is drawn to them to the extent that it fails to respond to them. Indeed, this mutual obliteration is found in the movement of the sentences, where the narrator first states that he has tried to put the events into writing, which is then qualified to a degree that almost undermines this attempt by the conditional comment that follows, and the further twist that his writing was not simply trying to capture the events in an account but to put an end to them, as if they were not already finished. This series of floating negations that are neither fully activated nor relinquished is then granted a stronger significance as the narrator begins to discuss the relation of his writing to truth.

It is key to the development of this work that the opening moves through a sequence of steps, from putting something into writing, to books, and then to novels, for at each stage this transition is one of greater specificity, which then gives way to the relation of words to truth. The latter point skirts the Heideggerian notion of unconcealment but brings to it a greater force, as the equivocal power of words to appear undecidably responsive and unresponsive to the movement of truth is framed in terms of a desire that is paradoxical. It is not just that the narrator wants to speak the truth and also keep it hidden, but he wants to bring the force of this tension to an end, to be done with the demands of this equivocity, whose effects remain so unsettling, and that arises out of his attempts to put his account into words. As a result, when we are told that he had once 'succeeded in giving a form to these events', it follows that this form was only to be found through the 'worklessness' that astonishment imposed on him in the wake of the Paris bombings. Thus, it was only in the idleness of the disaster that he could write the story of what happened, but nevertheless, once he read it, this too had to be destroyed, suggesting that although it could be written in this workless manner, it could not also be read; its history could be one or the other but not both. The challenge is then to find a form for this account that would not lead to it becoming destroyed in being read, and this is the challenge of the *récit* itself. (If we recall what was said earlier about the difference between the writer and the reader, then the necessity for the work in relation to its readers is that it is through them that the work can be experienced anew, which in the current context is to say that the breach of its originary experience can be relieved of the closure of its (historical) end and exposed to the endless rewriting of its future, which is also its void.)

It is disarming to find the narrator then stating that he will write freely, as if he sought a sheer gratuity or negligence of form, which is coupled to his calm declaration that the narrative concerns no one but himself so that it would be without any other relation. But the earlier statement about revealing the truth of what happened would seem to run counter to this isolation, for what kind of truth would concern only one person? Then comes the surprising admission (which perhaps answers this question) that, in truth, it could be done in ten words, *il pourrait tenir en dix mots*. Blanchot is not saying that it could actually be written out in ten words but that it could be covered, wrapped up, as it were, which prompts the subsequent confession: 'this is what makes it so terrifying. There are ten words that I can say' [AM: 8/131]. Not merely the facility to say ten words, but that there is such a possibility, that ten words could be said that could put an end to it all, that such an end could be found in such a way, which is not just a prescription for precision but its finite measure, and the force of its statement. For, as the narrator goes on to say, he has held out against these ten words for nine years (the jarring effect of this numerical disparity is clearly intentional; words and time do not have a natural commensurability and their friction is thus its own historical clinamen), words that would perhaps bring these events, and all that has transpired in their wake, to an end. Words that, he remarks, in the third paragraph of a narrative that has already surpassed ten words, he feels almost sure will now be written, even as they should not, an undecided likelihood to which he seems, finally, to be resolved.

The almost absurd solemnity of this claim is emphasized by the way that the narrator circles around it, in which the simple possibility of expressing ten words is undercut by their immense significance, by the peculiarity of this extremely subtle point. It is not a question of some combinatorial magic that would release the narrator from the hold of these events but of the very fine line that these ten words cast, which separates it from that which it delineates but in doing so also opens it to a breach of this separation. This is the terrifying (*effrayant*) burden of this line or sentence: that it undecidably both evokes and revokes the past, and the events it continues to bear. The confusing proliferation of dates in this narrative has been much remarked upon, especially in its relation and non-relation to actual events, as they are called, in Blanchot's life or in the course of the war. But their effect is of an ahistorical disorientation in which dates become detached from the course of events and form their own rootless discourse, a series of temporal markers rendered meaningless in being uprooted and thereby becoming proper names, even as the events they may or may not name remain wholly removed from such terms.[5] These dates are thus perhaps an indicator of what the ten words might be that the narrator feels would provide the measure of the narrative while allowing its truth to remain unsaid. But in doing so they only expose the gulf that exists between events and their account, which is only rendered more severe when it is the apparent moment of death that is at stake, the moment when the death 'sentence', as it were, can be pronounced and yet when its occurrence undoes any sense of moment insofar as death cannot be arrested at any one point but continues to reverberate. The *récit* attempts to uncover a wholly other form of time, a time without sequence or measure that unfurls from the space between events and their accounts, and is thus neither history nor *histoire* but is the ever-pressing force of the inability to bring its line to term.

Many pages later, after the narrative has followed the extraordinary story of how a woman apparently died and then came back to life, only to die again twenty-four hours later, Blanchot's *récit* abruptly stops. But before it does so, the narrator states that there is nothing important about the fact that this woman died and then came back to life; instead, the miracle (*prodige*), as he calls it, is that she was able, seemingly through nothing more than sheer energy or courage, to make death impotent (*stérile*) as long as she wanted. This point is immediately qualified though as the narrator insists that, events aside, nothing extraordinary or surprising has been said in his narrative: 'What is extraordinary begins at the moment when I stop [*je m'arrête*]. But I am no longer able to speak of it' [AM: 53/151]. Not just incapable but no longer the master (*maître*) of speaking, disempowered just as death itself was, which is captured in the reflexive (and thus duplicitous) sense of the end that has been reached, for the narrator is stopped by the extraordinary, necessarily, as it were. And it is at this point that the narrative breaks off. Consequently, the sense of the extraordinary does not lie in the event of death but in its delaying, not in the facts of the case but in their intervals, their variable and uncertain expanse. The indefinite halting of the end is thus also its deviation, its spacing out or *écart*, an anomalous opening without goal or rule, in and as which the extraordinary arises.

Hence, after the break, the narrative carries on. But as the narrator states, it will now be necessary to take some precautions, not to conceal the truth, for this will be told, but because 'everything has not yet happened'. The possibility that what had happened is still going on means that words will always be inadequate to it, as will any attempt to bring it to an end. In realizing this, the narrator recalls his own death sentence, a phrase written some time before to accommodate the desires of a person who was obsessed by the idea of his death, of having said to this person that he was 'going to write on a piece of paper that if you kill me, you will be acting for the best'. Such a statement seems dangerously irresponsible, but the weight that comes to bear upon it, as a thought to which the narrator is irresistibly drawn, is that of the tension between the act of killing as a negation and as an act for the best, as if the opposite, the absence of killing, would then become the worst. This is not just an invitation to euthanasia but a fascination with the contradiction between the positivity of acting and the negativity of its results, and with the thought that such a powerful negation can be written down, that it can be conditionally committed to paper where it remains active as his own suspended death sentence.[6] This thought is, for the narrator, what brings to an end the years of workless frustration in the face of the demands of the narrative but it also brings its own difficulties, since 'a thought is not exactly a person, even if it lives and acts like it'. Unlike a person, a thought demands a loyalty that makes all cunning difficult, for it cannot simply be deceived even if it is itself sometimes false [AM: 55/152]. The opening out that has occurred in the delaying of the end has seemingly given rise to a thought that reflects this spacing in its internal contradiction, and it is thus that the narrative is able to persist in and as the thought of its own ongoing divergence. This reflexivity may explain why the second part of the narrative is looser and more meandering, staging one missed encounter after another in a series of chance events (much like the second part of Hitchcock's film) that lead to its enigmatic denouement as the thought of this imbrication of activity and passivity, and truth and falsity, is played out. In the face of this thought (of the end?) there is neither memory nor anticipation, neither fear nor tiredness, and it is this singular rectitude (*droiture*) that becomes compelling: the seemingly impossible simplicity of its moment as that which will and will not be, and that will recur endlessly as it cannot be fulfilled without negating itself. Thus the explication of this thought becomes isomorphic with the space and the silence from which it derives, and with which it is in constant reflection and deferral. The nature of such a thought is critical to the second part of the narrative and is taken up in many of Blanchot's later writings, where its insensible force seems to become prominent as if it were a force of language without speech or writing, an imperative without subject or object, which then yields this aimless opening.

At the end of the narrative this thought returns in what would appear to be a kind of summation, but before this point the narrator appears to disavow the basis of his narrative: 'Who could say: this happened because the events had permitted it? This occurred because, at a certain moment, the facts became misleading and, through their strange combination, authorised the truth to take possession of them?' Contingency is not just the sequence of accidental occurrences but their deceptive arrangement that leads one to think that there is a kind of order underlying its appearances. But this doubled contingency appears to be reclaimed as the narrator suggests that its misleading array of facts leads to the eventuation of truth. Affirming this contingency is part of the imperative bearing upon the narrator in relation to the thought to which he has been drawn; as he says, he has not been a mere messenger, plaything or victim of this thought, 'since that thought, if it has conquered me, has only conquered through me, and in the end has always been equal to me [*à ma mesure*]' [AM: 127/186]. Assuming this haphazard fate as one's own is the only means of responding to the demands of the thought that he has encountered, and as such there is a sense in which this is a form of *amor fati*, and, if we recall the relation of this thought to death, of a kind of appropriation of one's end. But Blanchot is neither Nietzsche nor Heidegger because the array of these facts has never stopped being deceptive, and it never yields itself to any assumption of history. Instead, at the end of this narrative of strange events and reversals, there is a simple return to the bareness of the thought itself, whatever it may be, and in doing so the narrative does not end so much as unravel into an openness, which has been prepared by its persistent suspensions of the end.

Except that this is the end, as it is unavoidably (if paradoxically) marked as such by what comes after it. However, this point is immediately complicated by the fact that this short final section of the narrative was removed when it was republished in 1971. The last sentences begin like this: 'These pages can find their end [*terme*] here, and nothing that follows what I have just written will make me add or remove anything from it. This remains, this will remain until the end [*jusqu'au bout*].'[7] By thereby inscribing itself after the end, this paragraph renders the narrative finite, but in doing so its own position and status become uncertain. But the precise point of this end is unclear, for is it the last sentence of the preceding section, the gap before the last section or somewhere in these first ultimate sentences? The deictic *here* is invoked only for it to be displaced straightaway, a point that is rendered more emphatic by the fact that we are told only that the narrative *can* find its end here, rather than necessarily doing so. And this position is then apparently undermined by being removed in the second edition (despite his claims that nothing will make him do so), but the point is subtler insofar as it is marking a site that remains, or will remain, even if it is effaced, until the end. The nature of the end would thereby comprise a self-effacing fold that is neither temporal nor mortal but is simply the narrative term, that from which and to which it is endlessly drawn, which is the point of its own denunciation. On its own, the end of the narrative could not be marked, it would simply come to a close; but by adding this self-dissolving afterword Blanchot is able both to mark the end and unmark it, rendering it definitively unclosed at the very point where it can find its end. Just as the moment of death is both certain and indeterminate, the narrative itself finds the same possible impossibility (and impossible possibility) of ending: it can be found but it cannot be reached, it can be removed but it nevertheless remains, or will remain, until the end. It is this movement of *until* that is being conveyed to the reader in passing through these last lines, such that the narrative is not merely engaging this logic in the denouement of the end but is exposing the reader to it as well. The moment of 'until' is a passing and suspended termination, tending towards but not encountering its term without effacing itself, and hence its own end and possibility. There is no moment when the movement of 'until the end' consummates itself as it simply disappears into its own impossibility. The moment of the end of the narrative does not release the reader but traps them in its own vertiginous return, as Blanchot goes on to write in relation to this end: 'Whoever would remove it from me, in exchange for that end that I vainly seek, would become in his turn the beginning of my own story [*histoire*]'.

As before, where the narrator succumbed to the force of the idea, here the reader finds themselves succumbing to the force of the narrative if they should attempt to remove this ending. A warning, or curse, seems to lie within these words, a claim that would assert itself over any reader (which does not exclude the author himself, as the text's first reader) unwary enough to think themselves able to draw the story to a close, who would then find that it has become their own story: 'My word would be his silence, and he would think he was holding sway over the world, but that sovereignty would still be mine, his nothingness mine, and he too would know that there is no end for a man who wants to end alone.' The end, once invoked in its interminable force, comes to affect those exposed to it so that they are drawn into its never-ending breach. This might seem excessively Gothic in its overtones, but it is more to the point that it draws our attention to the nature of the curse, of words that are not merely literary or allegorical but that bear the actual force of history, words that actualize the terrible movement of 'until', the suspended burden of unrealized time. The death sentence that the narrative bears will never be carried out but will remain hanging over the reader, but this should not lead the reader to think that these pages 'are traversed by the thought of unhappiness'. It is not a morbid or melancholy narrative that has been unfolding but one with a much more demanding task, one that not only tends towards the unfolding of the end to which its pages are drawn but also towards 'the hand that is writing them'. It is not the inevitable course of *histoire* that unravels before the reader but a specific account, with its own material imprint and author that are its actual occasions, which will remain. For, as was developed in the last part of the narrative, Nathalie has a cast made of her head and hands in a strange and disturbing process that appears to render a kind of 'living' proof that, she claims, 'will be alive for all eternity, for yours and for mine!' [AM: 9/ 132, 125/185]. But nothing can be alive for eternity and so for it to survive is precisely for it to live on beyond death, to be not simply living but rather a life that bears itself in death. If the cast is this kind of 'living' proof, then it is a mark of a survival that, in its contingency, is also that of its encounter, and the indeterminate hiatus that yawns open between them. Thus the breach that punctuates the relation between the reader and the text is not the result of a transcendental injunction but a specific concrete experience that deflates literature while also giving it more gravity. Hence, this is not literature as an historical event but as a fateful accident; that which happens to the reader and writer as an exposure to the living suspension of the end and the rootlessness and disorientation that ensues.

The status of this coda is thus uncertain not merely in itself, for it also renders the narrative as such uncertain. Rather than bringing the narrative to a conclusion it undermines this possibility, and in its own position as neither fully inside nor outside the narrative it exists on and as the edge of the text. Without the coda the narrative simply ends but with its metatextual commentary the narrative reaches beyond itself only to withdraw or erase this step. The commentary that would provide a form of transcendental structure to the story, defining its limits and grounding its development, is only essayed. There is a provisional speculative attempt to reach the material basis of the story, but this remains an attempt and not a demonstration. The narrative is left as a series of fragments that are never fully realized, but that are equally not entirely imaginary; instead we find a collection of narrative shards or instances that in their contingency bear a sense of narrative necessity that cannot be said to be either objective or subjective, which is precisely the undecidable imperative or fate that reading encounters, the 'fate' of having no fate, since it would have to wait until the end to be realized.

IX. Historical accidents

Scottie is introduced to a woman, seemingly by chance, who then dies in sudden and mysterious circumstances. Traumatized by this loss he goes into a catatonic withdrawal. Sometime later he meets, seemingly at random, a woman who appears to resemble (at least to him) the first woman. However, the story then repeats itself as the second woman also dies in sudden and mysterious circumstances.[8] The two encounters seem to occur accidentally but then appear to have been intended, just as the woman in the second part only appears to be like the first one but then appears to become her, through a design that is only partly conscious. The second part thus repeats but also seeks to emulate the first part, even though the first is in effect merely the image while the second is its apparent reality. But this image-quality is the basis of the fascination that propels the first part and enables the second part to emerge from it. The two deaths of Madeleine are in some ways the deaths of the image and the body, which would suggest that there is a necessity to their duplication, insofar as death allows for the two parts to come together so that nature and second nature lead into each other. But, as Blanchot remarks in *Celui qui ne m'accompagnait pas*, at the peak of his thinking of the image, 'one can't really disappear when one must die in two separate worlds'.[9] Just as with *L'Arrêt de mort*, the instant of death is dilated to show that what might be thought to take place simply and at once, does not, and that such thinking loses sight of the deviation of death by masking the fact that it is never simple. Whence the anguish of Judy (Kim Novak) and Scottie in the second part of *Vertigo*, for, like Poe's Valdemar, they are caught in the distension of a moment that has become the time of return, a revenant time, where death appears to have taken place but where dying has not ceased as death itself has been interrupted. Neither Scottie nor Judy have allowed death to occur as an event that passes away; instead, it persists, refusing or failing to move on and thereby exposing what remains outside.

Reincarnation involves the movement of a spirit from a dead body to a living one, or, in the words of Elster (Tom Helmore), in describing his wife's illness, a feeling that 'someone out of the past can enter and take possession of a living being'. Madeleine's sickness seems to coincide with the fascination she has developed for the figure of Carlotta Valdes, a distant ancestor who died tragically, although these details are apparently unknown to her. To succumb to such an unconscious fascination is to find a foreign spirit arising within oneself, one associated with a figure now dead. This reincarnation of the dead is both an embodiment of this earlier spirit and an exposure to the dead past, for the two periods and personae appear to live alongside each other, leading to an uncertainty not just about Madeleine's identity but also about her temporal position and status. Does her haunting place her in the past or the present, or, more precisely, is this the past becoming present, or the present becoming past? Thus Madeleine slips between being Carlotta and being herself, in which the two states seem to coincide without fully merging so that past and present, and living and dead, exist together; in Elster's words, she 'goes into that other world', 'somewhere else, away from me, somewhere I don't know', such that she 'is someone else', 'no longer my wife'. Insofar as the living has come under the sway of the past, as the past has itself come to life, there arises an uncanny melancholy, a longing for that which was never held, for a past or a death that is not one's own, and thus can neither be resisted nor explained; as Madeleine says, there is 'someone within me and she says I must die'. So, all that Madeleine seems able to do is to follow an itinerary dominated by the past, and this is the pathway that Judy comes to follow as well, such that the film is split into repetitive cycles of reincarnation and death as she is made to incarnate Madeleine twice over, and also to experience her death, twice over.

However, the sense of these cycles is reversed for her and for Scottie, as for her the first cycle is a charade and the second is real, while for Scottie the opposite is the case. This means that the tense of the reincarnation is different for each of them, not just in its direction but also in its meaning, such that death comes to be in the middle of the cycles and at its ends, to be both its basis and its point, as the narrative folds back on itself. But it is because of Scottie that there is this repetition as it is he who becomes fascinated with the figure of Madeleine (and of Madeleine as Carlotta, as he is unable or unwilling to distinguish between them since it is their strange cohabitation that seems to fascinate him and that appears to coincide with the doom that hangs over her), for like him Madeleine seems marked by a figure of death that cannot be escaped, an anachronism that cannot be surpassed. In the second part this fascination is redoubled into an obsession that instead of freeing them from the grip of the past, merely recapitulates it, and as the past is made to appear again so the figure of death is also recalled. This is not a movement of Orphic recapture; Madeleine is not recalled from the dead so that she might survive, instead her death is recalled alongside her image, like a reverse Pygmalion, as Poe had described in 'The Oval Portrait'. And, importantly, Scottie is also drawn into this movement of errant return, as his catatonic 'death' is followed by his attempt to relive the past by following in the steps of his earlier self, with the same conditions of success.

It is the interplay of chance and necessity that explicates this movement of repetition. As we discover later, the apparently chance meeting by which the plot begins, when Elster contacts Scottie, was not an accident. And, although it seems as if Scottie encounters Judy by chance later in the film, thereby restarting the plot, it is clear that she has not left San Francisco after the murder, just as she has not given up the necklace or the suit, as she too wants to hold on to the past, hoping, as she says in her letter, that she will see him again. Equally, the locations and behaviours that constitute Madeleine's personality seem arbitrarily chosen but quickly take on the status of necessity for Scottie, incontrovertible coordinates that enclose his life but also make possible his release from the same. For each moment seems to be a point from which the story can begin again, such that it has no real beginning or ending as it is caught in an endless iteration. Witness the sequence after Scottie first encounters Madeleine, a sequence often discussed as it develops through a series of scenes without dialogue that could carry on indefinitely. After seeing her in the restaurant, the next day he follows her to a flower shop, a graveyard, a gallery and then to a hotel, where she disappears. At no point does Scottie speak to Madeleine; instead, he watches her from a distance, never making eye contact. And for her part Madeleine engages in a series of actions that appear very ordinary and yet strangely symbolic, everything is imbued with a sense of significance that remains unclear. Mystery has not yet become fate but is tending towards it; each moment and gesture and scene is open-ended and could dissolve into something less interesting (these are still contingencies that could be otherwise), but in retrospect they seem to become points of necessity. What are found are historical accidents, occasions where history itself seems to make a move that could become a faux pas, since an accident of history is not just *by* history but also *of* it; in stepping aside it also makes a different movement of history, an occasion that is neither progressive nor regressive but opens up another space between them. And once it is exposed the mystery draws them both in, for it does not begin with either one of them but between them and by way of their circling around each other. After all, each was hired to play a role in Elster's plan but in coming together a different relation was opened up. Scottie may be following Madeleine through the first part of the film, but in checking on him periodically she is also following him, adjusting herself to his reactions, just as he does to hers. A fascination emerges between them that lacks beginning or end and is without aim or necessity; it simply turns on their own turning around each other, as in the mutual dream that follows Judy's transformation back into Madeleine.

The fascination of this first sequence needs to be explored carefully as the film develops its appearance quite deliberately. After the traumatic end to the chase across the rooftops that opens the film, Scottie is left hanging from a gutter without any apparent means of escape. This is followed by two relatively stable expository scenes in Midge's (Barbara Bel Geddes) apartment and Elster's office (although both have key moments of instability that betray the latent uncertainty that will emerge). The scene at the restaurant that comes next initiates the trailing sequence from the flower shop onwards, but the shock of the encounter with Madeleine in the restaurant seems only to repeat the shock from the opening sequence. Rather than considering the film split between its first and second halves, whose rupture radiates its effects outwards, it is possible to see the initial accident as the flaw that unleashes a series of after-effects that gradually unsettle Scottie's position, just as much as the view from the rooftops that first exposed the abyss. For what occurs in the trailing sequence is a set of encounters or framed movements that in each case triggers a new fissure in his situation, since in each case the encounter is no more than a missed opportunity, a failed meeting. The way that Hitchcock iterates our gaze with that of Scottie as he follows Madeleine may allow for the integration of our gaze with his, so that we are drawn into the mystery with him, but it also underlines the fracturing of this sequence, as the alternation between our perspective of Scottie and our perspective of what he sees only indicates the failure of this reflexivity to close itself. There is only repetition and confusion; thus we only come to share Scottie's gaze to the extent that the latter is emptied out and shown to be made up of nothing but a series of cuts that do not cohere, and that seem capable of reverberating endlessly. The fracturing of the narrative has already started to occur through this exposure to the emptiness of the mystery, as the source of Scottie's vertigo is now not merely a physical height but that of the baseless mystery into which he has stepped, and that necessarily has no end outside of its own rupture. As Madeleine will say later: 'It's as though I were walking down a long corridor that once was mirrored, and fragments of that mirror still hang there and when I come to the end of the corridor there's nothing but darkness. And I know that when I walk into the darkness, that I'll die.'

Thus, the only genuine accident in the film would appear to be that which closes it, Judy's fall from the tower, which however heavily predetermined nevertheless still seems to occur by accident, leaving Scottie stranded without any possibility of moving on. In this way he is returned to the beginning, and although he has now overcome his fear of heights he is left without anything else. He may have brutally pushed Judy and himself into this re-enactment so that he could, in his own words, free himself from the past and have a second chance, but the opposite result takes place. He is now twice as traumatized and with even less hope of finding any escape, and thus is condemned to remain on the brink, outside the present, unable to go on or to go back. Just when he experiences a moment in which the feelings he had for Madeleine seem possible once more, the disaster happens, there can be no return and nor does the second death cancel the first – there is no exchange to be made between them. The negation of the negation (of Madeleine) does not resolve the loss and allow Scottie to start again but only leads further into despair and anguish. Judy's death is tragic not because it is inevitable but because it seems unnecessary, accidental; it could have been otherwise, as if it was not really her death but that of another, in which case its status (and moment) is acutely put in question. So, even though it appears fated and unavoidable, Judy dies by chance, gratuitously, in both senses of the word, which only reasserts the role of contingency in the historical deviations of their lives. At the end there is no reason, Elster has disappeared just as emphatically as Midge, there will be no happy resolution and the extraordinary love that Scottie and Madeleine have shared has only exposed them to a time of utter loss and destitution, moments that are lived over and over and that are neither meaningful nor meaningless, neither real nor fake, but bear the sense of their own senselessness.

And yet, if the second part of the film shows Scottie's attempt to return and recreate the past, then this cannot be done without also repeating the end that closed the first part. Death is built into this attempt not just in its content but also in its form. It is not only because Madeleine died that Judy must die but the very act of trying to recreate the past, of trying to retrieve and repeat what has happened but is now gone, carries with it a tragic fatality. But there is another side to this endeavour, for there is the suggestion that the second death may counteract the first, that with it death itself might be negated. In this way Scottie has not only sought to recreate the past but to escape it entirely by finding a way to defeat death, to live on beyond it. This point brings Hitchcock's film into relation with *L'Arrêt de mort*, and also with Poe's 'Ligeia'. In this story, Poe's narrator describes how his beloved companion Ligeia became ill and, although he tried to save her, she grew weaker until she died. Riven with grief he moves to England where he buys an old abbey and, later, finds a bride, Rowena. In the second part of the story, the narrator decks out the bridal chamber in a fantastic and sombre manner. Concealed in a distant turret of the abbey, the room is hung with thick tapestries of gold with dark arabesques that glitter and shimmer with extraordinary images, while around the room stand huge sarcophagi of black granite. But two months into the marriage Rowena falls ill and is confined to her bed, whereupon she begins to have hallucinations, to hear and see things in the movements of the tapestries. Seeking to revive his bride, the narrator pours her a glass of wine but he seems to feel another presence in the room, and a few drops of something red then appear to fall into the glass. Soon afterwards Rowena goes into a serious decline, and in a few days is dead. Sunk into remorse for a second time he stays by her bed to mourn, but sounds seem to emerge from the corpse, a sigh or a sob, and the body slowly takes on the signs of life again. Finally, and to his horror, she rises from the deathbed and walks towards him, only for him to realize that it is not Rowena but Ligeia, returned from the dead.

As is the way with many of Poe's tales, much of the narrative appears to arise from the narrator's unsettled state of mind, but the development of the second part of the story makes it clear that he is intent on bringing about Rowena's end, as if in some way this could bring about the return of Ligeia. The elaborate arrangement of the bridal chamber is designed to cause anxiety, and it is left unclear whether he actually poisons her or not. The point would seem to be to recreate the deathbed so as to make possible the transformation from one inhabitant to the other, as if by some kind of sleight of hand. It is only through the presence of the dead that this exchange can be made, which is also a way of defeating death. For the narrator, the resuscitation is made possible through his understanding of a line, supposedly drawn from the work of Joseph Glanvill, that man 'doth not yield himself to the angels, nor unto death utterly, save only through the weakness of his feeble will'.[10] Although this recalls *Vertigo* and *L'Arrêt de mort*, it is not clear in Poe's story if this is an exertion of will by the narrator or by Ligeia herself, but in Blanchot's *récit* death is only held at bay by this exertion of will, not defeated entirely. The purpose of this latter exertion was not to eliminate death but to bring it about when the time was right, *au moment voulu*, which would be when the contingency of its occurrence is made a necessity through the act of will, and, conversely, which is not the same thing, when its necessity is found to be contingent.

But this is also to say that death occurs and yet does not, since it cannot fully be the end if there remains that which brought it about or held it at bay. If death itself is stopped, then the end that it was supposed to mark is suspended or ruptured leaving it uncertain as to whether it is still possible, whether it is to come or has passed, whether it can occupy a moment that could be marked as 'when' it occurred. For in being willed to happen when the time is right it is incorporated within life as that which has already taken place as that which is deferred. Hence, 'when' it happens, it has already happened and yet is also still to come. As Blanchot had written in the cover copy for *L'Arrêt de mort*:

> This tale [*récit*] is perhaps strange, but it relates, with complete clarity, events about which everything leads one to believe that they really took place, that they continue, even now, to take place. In a famous tale Poe recounts the dark story of a being who could not resign themselves to die … But what would happen [*arriverait*] if the one who dies did not

abandon themselves entirely to death? What is it that happened, in truth, on the day, when for the greatest and the most serious of reasons, someone who had already entered into death, suddenly, *stopped* death [arrêta *la mort*]? (Emphasis in the original)

The impact of this interruption of death is not merely personal but historical as it affects the very possibility of events taking place. To stop that which is itself a stop, to halt that which is an event par excellence, is to unravel its end and dissipate its moment, so that it continues despite having already occurred, leaving it unclear what or when it might have been or might still be. And with this in mind it is relevant to return to a point Blanchot made some months earlier, where the effects of such a rupturing on language are found, effects that bring together Poe and Hegel by way of Mallarmé:

> So that I can say 'this woman' it is necessary in some way or other that I withdraw her reality of flesh and blood from her, make her absent and annihilate her. The word gives me the being, but it gives me it deprived of being. It is the absence of that being, its nothingness, that which remains of it when it has lost being, that is to say, the sole fact that it is not ... Doubtless, my language kills no one. However, when I say 'this woman', real death is announced and is already present in my language; my language means that this person, who is here now, can be detached from herself, removed from her existence and presence and suddenly plunged into a nothingness of existence and presence; my language essentially signifies the possibility of this destruction; it is, at every moment, a resolute allusion to such an event. My language kills no one. But, if this woman were not really capable of dying, if she were not threatened by death at each moment of her life, bound and united with it by an essential bond, I would not be able to carry out this ideal negation, this deferred assassination that is my language.
>
> PF: 312–13/322–3

It is important not to become too distracted by the gendered manner in which this argument develops, despite its apparent necessity for Blanchot, since for present purposes it is merely helpful in aligning it with the narratives of *L'Arrêt de mort* and *Vertigo*.[11] What is of more significance is the way that the facticity of death underpinning the negativity of language is echoed in the movement of history; it is death that makes (im)possible the possibility of events as that which 'really' occurs.

It is not the case that the sacrifice of one woman allows for the salvation of another, since both narratives do not deal with one death and two women but one woman and two deaths. Death does not allow for the unification of the two women, but rather the same woman experiences both death and the rupture of death, and so dies and does not die, lives on and yet does not live on. Blanchot discusses this issue as that of 'living the event as image [*en image*]', which is not to see the event as imaginary, or to see an image of the event, but to be taken up by the distancing that occurs in the image, to find oneself drawn into the shadow of the event in which there is no scope for 'self'-recognition. Entering this deterioration of the event is an exposure to the ambiguity of meaning as such, that there may be meaning or not, and that this ambiguity cannot be definitively decided but opens a movement of infinite degrees of dissembling [EL: 274–7/261–4]. This is the sense of a language in which death is announced and deferred, in which it is really present and yet suspends such an event, as it is a language that both depends on the actual possibility of dying while also removing this possibility. Hence what occurs 'really' in the event of dying is that which also renders the possibility of it 'really' occurring uncertain: the taking place of dying puts the occurrence of events as such in question.

That is, the rupture of death leads to a rupture of history and *histoire*, as a breakdown in the very possibility of moving on, which may explain why the aporias that punctuate *Vertigo* have led to it being viewed as a dream, at least in part. For example, the point was raised by one of the earliest and still most substantial readings, by Robin Wood in 1965, that the difficulty of imagining how Scottie may have escaped from the position of hanging from the roof gutter at the end of the first scene makes it possible that the rest of the film is a dream that he endures as he hangs and perhaps falls from this height. This reading has been picked up by other critics and alternatives have also been raised, such as that the second half is a dream, as it is difficult to imagine how Scottie may have escaped from his catatonic trauma, and so the rest of the film is his fantasy of resolution and retribution as he unconsciously attempts to make sense of what has happened to him.[12] Each of these readings is feasible but each allegorizes the aporias of these two scenes, since in both cases the film simply cuts to a new scene without any narrative transition or explanation. And while these ruptures appear dreamlike it must be recalled that the film is punctuated throughout by moments of sheer facticity of which nothing more can be said than that they happened. Consider a point from Scottie's first day trailing Madeleine: He has waited outside her apartment block and when she leaves in her car he begins to follow her. She drives down several streets and then pulls into a narrow service alley and gets out of the car. Scottie pulls up behind her and watches as she goes into a deserted basement that leads to a back entrance to a flower shop. This part of the sequence is very odd and never explained: why should Madeleine follow this obscure route to the shop? It would seem that it is, at least partly, the sense of mystery that is being emphasized, for how does Madeleine know about this secret entrance? But what is also odd is Scottie's behaviour, as he pulls into the narrow alley right behind Madeleine's car despite the fact that he is meant to be discreetly following her. There is no way for Madeleine to be unaware of his presence, but bizarrely (as a retired police detective) he is unconcerned by his conspicuousness. Instead of keeping hidden he allows himself to be drawn into her strange behaviour and the mystery that it unfolds. As the previous scene at the restaurant made clear, Scottie is already completely consumed by Madeleine, the fascination was instantaneous and so the subsequent lack of distance needs no further explanation, but its representation shows that it occurs as an occurrence without rationale, for the nature of the mystery is precisely that it suspends the actualization of its status. In a sense, Carlotta is merely a MacGuffin; nothing is really at the root of Madeleine's behaviour.[13]

Looking at the scene in the middle of the film, where Scottie has a nightmare that precedes his catatonia, it becomes possible to assess the relation of these scenes to their irrational aporias. After the inquest Scottie visits Madeleine's grave, and then there is a cut to a shot of San Francisco at night and then another to an overhead shot of Scottie in bed in the dark. The camera looks down on him as he tosses about, and then the colour changes as if a flashing neon sign were nearby, and Scottie suddenly wakes up. The uncertainty of this point is intriguing, as has been widely noted, since the dream begins, apparently, after Scottie has opened his eyes, the suggestion being that he is opening his eyes to the dream (instead of from it), which, albeit obscurely, starts to piece together what has happened to him. However, this collation only occurs through fragmentation, and so if the dream sequence presents a 'key' to the mysteries of the film, then it is only insofar as it is isomorphic to them. The stages of the dream are no less concrete and no more symbolic than the stages of Scottie's first day following Madeleine. They each bear elements of meaning while lacking any coherence or certainty over all. Hence, the undecidability of the narrative is condensed in this sequence without yielding any greater explanation, and so it is not a question of the narrative being either dream or reality since it is both, or something between dream and reality that is neither (thereby picking up again on the flaws in the prohibitions on contradiction). It is not possible to determine the status of the narrative as a whole or in its parts, or how these connect to each other given their apparently insurmountable breaches, just as it is not possible to know how far the enigma of Madeleine is pretence or not, or how far it is Judy's desire or Scottie's that draws them to each other. The fact that these things happened is undermined by how they happened, they may have happened but their interstices or integument, that which would hold them together and provide their ground or reason, remains as obscure and as absent as the deaths that mark them. With Midge and Elster gone from the second part of the film there is nothing left to link Scottie to his previous life, and at the end he reaches a point of complete suspension. The enigmas may have been unravelled but they have not revealed anything but their lack of resolution.

This reading is reinforced by the way that the story does not properly begin, as Scottie and Madeleine appear to behave towards each other in the early sequences as though they had already met. The oddness in Scottie's attempt to trail Madeleine seems to lie in the fact that they do not act as we might expect them to; they seem to share an intimacy as if their secrets bound them to each other (as will be seen). The tragedy of the second part of the film would then be that there is no way they can recreate their relation as it once was, since it had never happened for the first time; it had already prefigured itself and this impression drew them both into its spell. Like Diana and Actaeon, they seem condemned to endlessly iterate their own encounter insofar as they have fallen into a space outside time. It is not that they fall for each other in falling into the bay together; rather their mutual attraction is marked by their first (missed) encounter in the restaurant. When Madeleine walks past Scottie in leaving the restaurant, she stops to wait for Elster, facing to the right; she then turns back to see Elster and so passes her gaze over Scottie as he sits at the bar, turning clockwise across the camera through 180 degrees. At the point of doing so, Scottie, who had turned from the bar to watch Madeleine approach, turns back, reversing her movement by turning anticlockwise away from her. Thus their first encounter is a non-encounter, an exact miss, an accident that (as so often in Hitchcock's films) marks everything that follows. While the accident in *North by Northwest* (1959), for example, occurs when Thornhill (Cary Grant) raises his arm at the moment that Kaplan's name is called, in *Vertigo* the accident is a missed encounter, a mutual occlusion that nevertheless binds the characters together. They are linked by what is not spoken or seen, a blind chance, and so, because it remains hidden, it cannot be plumbed but remains a non-coincident relation.

There is Madeleine and there is Judy – while they are necessarily related they neither merge together nor negate each other. Seemingly, there is no pure Madeleine or Judy in themselves and so neither fully exist on their own terms. Scottie cannot have one without the other, but although they are not the same it is not possible to exactly determine their difference. They cannot occupy the same space at the same time and so their relation remains one of displacement. The difference 'between' Madeleine and Judy, as we say, is, despite appearances, indiscernible, and so Scottie literally does not know who he loves, which has just as much effect on her. For if she does not know who it is that Scottie sees when he looks at her, then she remains undefined by this relation, just as her lack of definition in herself affects Scottie's relation to her. Each finds their relation to the other to be a source of instability and uncertainty, an open-ended non-relation. In their first actual meeting, in Scottie's apartment after he has rescued her from the bay, there is a considerable degree of indirection between them. Scottie is pretending to be an ordinary bystander when he was actually following her, and is concerned that she tried to kill herself when she was not herself, while Madeleine is pretending to be haunted by another woman while concealing her own identity, and is also aware that Scottie is not what he says he is.

Neither is who they pretend to be, but also, and to that extent, neither is who they are either, and so both fail to act towards the other as if this were their first meeting, just as their burgeoning mutual affection also gives the lie to any certainty of self-knowledge that each might assert. And so, as this meeting also fails to be a first encounter, their relation fails to find the establishment that such an encounter could provide. The possibility of a real first meeting has been missed, it is both behind them and ahead of them; they act as if it had already happened, but as it has not, it is still before them. They have missed or side-stepped their own encounter and entered another kind of relation and space where events as such have been evacuated just as much as death has been or will be.

At the end of Scottie's dream, he walks in place against a dark background before coming across an open grave that bears Carlotta's name, and he then seems to fall into the grave. There is a shot of his disembodied head flying towards the screen, which then reverses to a shot down on to the roof of the church, towards which his puppet-like silhouette descends. The background then disappears and the silhouette is left in pure white emptiness. This last sequence begins in darkness and ends in whiteness; moreover, it is characterized by movement without movement, since he walks without changing place and falls without beginning or end. Such would be the logic of dream sequences, but it also indicates something more important, for this untethered movement, which is emphasized in falling, is not merely an intrinsic part of the vertigo experience but also relates to the doctrine of the Fall as such. While this doctrine is concerned with a transgression and the wandering that results from it, it is also found in the noir theme of a flaw that unravels into disaster. What becomes of interest is the possibility of rethinking this notion from a non-theological point of view, as not concerning original sin and the search for redemption but as referring to a clinamen that leads to a movement without beginning or end, a free fall of sorts. Scottie may have fallen in love with another man's wife, or, at least that is what he thinks, but the actual criminal gets away scot free, as it were. But as the details of the scenario unravel (Madeleine is not Madeleine, Elster disappears) it becomes apparent that this is a flaw without origin or resolution, it is a sheer fault, and because it cannot be resolved it persists, leading to further errors, which becomes its mode of temporal development: suspension, repetition and deviation. The vertigo that Scottie suffers from can be gauged by the disorientation encountered when he is unable to manage the distinction between the two expressions, 'I look up, I look down'. It is this that comprises the fear *of* falling, that which belongs to it and is constituted by it as its reflexive mood, both replicating and displacing it.[14] Vertigo is neither movement nor non-movement; equally, it is both movement and non-movement, a movement without movement, in the sense of the disparity between self and world that its dizziness reflects, and the vortical movement of dizziness itself.

X. The disaster

Philosophical discussion of the event, whether it is from such differing points of view as Heidegger, Deleuze or Badiou, is concerned with understanding the origin as a self-grounding, self-unfolding and self-concealing breach, which demonstrates that ontology is not given but *occurs*. Whether in art, love, science, politics or language, what is understood to be an event is the appearance of a world that is unforeseen and irreducible. A new set of terms and dimensions that is strictly irrational becomes manifest, as it lacks any substantiating reason other than itself, and incomprehensible, as it can only be thought on its own terms rather than through any pre-existing categories. Such thinking follows in the tradition of the modernist theology of the new, of the renovation of the world through its own reincarnation, a sudden and explosive transformation that generates its own language and followers. What is compelling about film noir, and is also apparent in Blanchot's thought, is that this notion of reinvention is deteriorated beyond repair by the corrosive effect of contingency, which leads to a very different thought of change, of the accident and the disaster, of material contagion and breakdown. The inevitability that often appears in films noir or in Hitchcock's films as the heavy hand of fate is no more of a reality than the apparently deterministic necessity of Hegel's system of logic. In both cases it is contingency that takes on the appearance of necessity, which becomes necessity, as conditions that could be otherwise become a necessity through the movement of actuality, as Marcuse wrote in 1932:

> The particular factual immediacy in which every actual initially exists and that is only a contingency over and against its possibilities, something that must be overcome [*aufgehoben*] – this contingency is the ground for the fact that the necessity in the movement of the actual is only 'relative', that it can never free itself from this contingency as its inception, its presupposition, but carries this within itself throughout its whole movement. Thus necessity is in itself profoundest contingency! 'Real necessity is *determinate* necessity ... The determinateness of necessity consists in its having its negation, contingency, within it. This is how it has shown itself to be' ... So if we want to define [*bestimmt*] the fully realized [*vollendete*] concrete being, the 'absolute actuality', we must include this contingency in its determination; actuality can only be 'absolute', and only as actuality be necessity, when it has also realized contingency as necessity, when necessity 'determines itself out of itself into contingency'.[15]

Criminality provides an insight into the mechanisms of this movement by which contingency becomes necessity, and in which it exposes a movement of time that is not eventful but accidental, materially deteriorate. Such might be termed the recidivism of history, its permanent declination into a field of persistent loss and alienation, which is what is exposed through the absolute of literature.

The criminal path emphasizes the fact that the real possibilities inherent in any actual situation are contingent, and thus that this actuality is itself contingent, and that recognition of this contingency leads to disquiet. This is not just to be at the mercy of every wind but to find the ever proliferating contingent possibilities that underlie each situation as their own historico-material reverberations. Contingency does not just refer to the fact that it is grounded in nothing but its own possibility that might always be otherwise, but also that, in being so grounded, it is confronted by the ever present possibility of being otherwise. This real possibility explains why contingent situations can only find a ground by continuing in their actualization of further possibilities, for they necessarily give rise to their own displacement. The relation of actuality and possibility, in their '*absolute unrest* of *becoming*', in Hegel's words, is such that the possible, in becoming actual, leads the actual to new possibilities, including the ever present possibility of its complete negation [WL1: 384/545; emphasis in the original]. Hence, just as the contingent is that which grounds, and yet in its lack of grounding also ungrounds any situation, so the necessity of contingency extends to the point of their being a necessity to its completely contingent ungrounding, its utter displacement into what is otherwise. The necessity of contingency lies in the fact that, in that something *is*, it *just* is *as* it is, in its situated occurrence and its ever present possibility of not occurring. If every actuality contains the real possibility of being otherwise, or of not being at all, then it contains its end within itself, and to experience this contingency is to experience its most extreme ruptures and deviations.[16] It is this that would need to be understood as fate, not that what is actual has a fate, but *that there is* fate *in* all its contingencies:

> When we say of things, *they are finite*, we understand by this that they not only have a determinateness, their quality is not only as reality and intrinsic [*ansichseyende*] determination, that they are not merely limited, as such they still have existence outside their limit, – but rather that non-being makes up their nature, their being. Finite things *are*, but their relation to themselves is that they relate to themselves *negatively*, in this very self-relation they send [*hinauszuschicken*] themselves out beyond themselves, beyond their being. They *are*, but the truth of this being is their *end*. The finite not only alters, like something in general, rather it *decays* [*vergeht*], and that it decays is not merely possible, such that it could be without decaying. Rather the being as such of finite things is to have the germ of decay as their in-itselfness [*Insichseyn*], the hour of their birth is the hour of their death.
>
> WL2: 116/129 (emphases in the original)

The word translated as decay, *Vergehen*, is also used for a legal or moral dereliction or delinquency. This is not just a mortal falling apart or fading away, but a falling away from a state assumed to be normative from the perspective of the organism or the state, the bodily or political regime or *politeia*. But considered otherwise, that is, from the perspective of the contingent, there is only falling.

For Blanchot, the place and status of literature in the world seems to echo this position of contingency in its strange paradoxes; on the one hand it is absolute as it relates to nothing but itself, but on the other hand, insofar as it is nothing but this self-relation, it is immanent to the movement of materiality and history. It is this paradox that renders the relation of literature to thought and language, on the one hand, and nature and history, on the other, uncertain and unstable. As this absolute milieu, as he will term it in 1953, literature takes up a place of singular solitude that is neither natural nor non-natural, neither of the world nor beyond it, but rather constitutive of the very possibility of a thought of world or nature in that it is a thought of the whole *through* its materiality and history [EL: 23/32]. It is thus that literature is the thought *of* materiality and history, in both its subjective and objective senses, but this does not lead to the identity of sense and understanding that Hegel sees in language as the externalization of thought because of literature's solitude and contingency. Literature is thought in its accidents. Hence, literature is the means by which thought can pass beyond itself and think the non-thought. Around this time, Hyppolite's *Logique et existence* attempted to develop just such a reading of Hegel by adopting insights from Heidegger to think Hegel's logic without the humanistic anthropology and historicism of Kojève's thought. In doing so he would lay the ground for much of the later considerations of structuralism, in which, combining Hegel and Heidegger, being speaks in language rather than the human, but he would also go beyond it by emphasizing the elements of opacity and alienation that punctuate this speech:

> The Logos is the other of Nature, it is in its determination a negation, it thus refers itself to this other and reflects it in itself ... In this self-negation as Nature, the Logos sublates [*se dépasse*] itself, it is more than itself, it surmounts this negation that is its difference from itself. This is why the Logos is the Whole in the determination of the concept or of sense, it sublates itself in its own limitation; it negates itself, it comprehends Nature in itself, it translates its very opposition with Nature into its determination; *contradiction is the logical translation of this opposition.* The Logos contradicts itself, it is being as nature, but, as the universal determination of being, it is also the nothingness of this determination ... We cannot exit from the Logos, but the Logos exits from itself in remaining itself; as it is the indivisible self, the Absolute, it thinks the non-thought, it thinks sense in its relation to non-sense, to the opaque being

of nature, it reflects this opacity in its contradiction, it raises thought, which would only be thought, over itself in obliging it to contradict itself; it makes of this contradiction the speculative means of reflecting the Absolute itself.[17]

Much like Hyppolite, Blanchot was also engaged in thinking through the mutual articulation and disarticulation of Hegel's and Heidegger's thought, but for him the (contingent) ground for such a thinking was literature rather than logic. Nevertheless, by considering how literature operates as a kind of singular logic (in all the contradictions of this thought) his attempt to extricate himself from Hegel's thinking without diminishing it is not only found to be as far-reaching as that of any of his peers but also leads to the point where he can in his later works write that thought itself is the disaster.

The disaster is not the absolute but its underside or exterior, as it were, that which 'disorients the absolute' through the 'sovereignty of the accidental' [ED: 12/4, 11/3]. Thus 'the idea of totality cannot mark its limits', indeed, insofar as it is thought, it cannot be thought and it is not even concerned with being thought as it is 'the unlimited without regard' [ED: 9/2]. It can be seen that Blanchot is pushing against the line of sense and non-sense that Hyppolite finds to be the essential contradiction and in doing so finds that they diverge radically, leaving a breach without commensurate. The movement by which the contradiction within nature (i.e. the *logos*) is sublated into the absolute does not take account of this breach in its opacity. But if this movement combines sense and non-sense, thought and non-thought, then it also comprises a movement in which there is an underside that deviates from its sublation, a move that is eccentric and resistant. As Foucault explains in 'L'ordre du discours':

> Instead of conceiving philosophy as the totality finally capable of thinking itself and recovering itself in the movement of the concept, Hyppolite made it into a task without end [*terme*] against the background of an infinite horizon: always up early, his philosophy was never ready to complete itself. A task without end, thus a task always recommenced, devoted to the form and paradox of repetition: philosophy, as the inaccessible thought of totality, was for Hyppolite that which could be repeated in the extreme irregularity of experience; that which is given and withdrawn as a question endlessly resumed in life, in death, in memory: thus he transformed the Hegelian theme of the completion of self-consciousness into a theme of repetitive interrogation. But since it was repetition, philosophy was not subsequent to the concept; it did not have to follow the edifice of abstraction, it had to always hold itself back [*en retrait*], break with its acquired generalities and re-establish contact with non-philosophy: it had to approach it as close as possible, not as that which completes it, but as that which precedes it, that which has not

yet awoken to its disquiet; it had to take up the singularity of history, the regional rationalities of science, the depths of memory in consciousness, not to reduce them, but to think them; thus appeared the theme of a philosophy that is present, uneasy [*inquiète*], mobile along the length of its line of contact with non-philosophy, yet existing only for it and revealing the meaning this non-philosophy has for us.[18]

Although Foucault is using Hyppolite as a way to introduce his own turn towards the analysis of specific discursive practices, he is also indicating the role of non-philosophy and its tensed relation with philosophy. This point is of considerable interest in reference to Blanchot's writings, which pursue exactly this line of contact. However, the tensed nature of this relation raises a further question for Foucault, since 'if it is in this repeated contact with non-philosophy, what is the beginning of philosophy?' And, we could add, if its opening is in question, then what is its status? How does philosophy separate itself from non-philosophy, in what is their distinction grounded? Blanchot is especially attuned to the peculiar loss to thinking that such a breach entails, as the contact of thought with the non-philosophy of writing is also its flaw and thus the edge or ridge of its own decision. But, as his later writings attempt to de-scribe (*dé-crire*) – that is, to write by withdrawing or removing from writing, to write from its deterioration – this disaster in thought is also that which undermines its possibility of decision and imposes a distance between it and itself; it is thought's own blind spot and so cannot be experienced. This restless imperative and inability carries no drama or grandeur, it is not pure destruction but rather 'impure loss', but a loss that is itself avoided when we change thoughts and mark their end, and thereby lose contact with what was its non-thought: 'Whence this injunction: do not change your thought, repeat it, if you can' [ED: 16/6, 13/4]. It is thus that the disaster is not of the order of things that happen, it is not an event, it does not come to pass; it is rather the withdrawal of its moment and is related to a form of passivity or forgetfulness, a lapse of thinking.

What becomes necessary at this point is to distinguish such non-thought from mysticism, and its passivity from mere inactivity, which is to indicate how its neutrality is also the absence of work, an extreme singularity of refusal and evasion. This is not to privilege failure and loss; there is no sentimental affect here nor is there any tragic pathos, for there is no purity to be obtained or any sanctity to be reached. There is only the repetition of an empty desire, as the world of noir has made clear, 'repetition as non-power [*non-pouvoir*]' [ED: 20/9]. Notably, Blanchot then proceeds to discuss the later work of Levinas to show his reservations with the latter's thoughts on passivity. But this is also a point of difference in relation to what happens, to the demarcation of events as such and their apparent significance, to the importance of the occurrence rather than its deterioration. For this non-power is the fall of chance, the gratuitous repeated cadence, the fall that is out of time (*contretemps*) and is its decay, which is why Blanchot comes to associate it with writing rather than with ethics, for writing is without ground or purpose and conveys only its own material declination. Writing releases this errancy or default, not in order for it to be recouped in a sacrificial move where the empirical is given up for the sake of the transcendental, but to find the point 'when to write, or not to write, is without importance', when the indistinction and insignificance of writing as material repetition is no longer apparent but persists as its 'un-manifestation of anguish' [ED: 25/ 12, 24/11].

There is a negation of negation of writing, which leaves neither writing nor non-writing, but that which is both writing and non-writing, and it is thus that writing becomes coextensive with its outside in its unresolved self-negation. As it can neither negate itself nor escape its own negativity it exists as the perpetually incomplete negation of its own negation, just as nature is too weak, as Hegel wrote, to comprehend itself or to be fully comprehended and yields to the *logos* only provisionally. Hence the form of this negation of negation is that of a writing that, in this indistinction, converges on that of nature in its own absolute restlessness. Its weakness is the non-power of its repetition as the lapse or fall of its exteriority, its deterioration, not as a drive to repeat but simply as the failure to complete itself or to cease, out of whose disquiet writing arises. It is as such that Blanchot can return to a remark made at the beginning of his career, which is that anxiety converges on writing just as and only insofar as writing converges on anxiety, but there is no 'point' to this convergence, either literally or metaphorically, since, as he had noted, anxiety, like the disaster, 'has nothing to reveal and is itself indifferent to its own revelation'.[19] This 'point' is then transformed in his later works into the equally provisionally named 'primal scene' (that is neither originary nor representational) of encountering 'the sky, the *same* sky, suddenly open, absolutely black and absolutely empty' (emphasis in the original), a breach that is sovereignly accidental, and thereby demonstrates the place and status of literature.

It has been noted that this 'primal scene' is strangely cinematic, in that it involves drawing back a curtain and looking through a window, from which the gaze passes up to 'the ordinary sky', which suddenly opens onto an absence [ED: 117/72].[20] What is important about this perspective is that it emphasizes the way that the gaze is led into a different temporal and material exposure. It is key to Blanchot's description that it takes place in the gaze of a child, who is able to experience this encounter with nothing for the 'first' time, which is a sensation of a time apart that seems to be both impossibly old and intangibly present. But this experience is not held, it is only recalled, and in being recalled it remains elusive since there was literally nothing there (to be recalled, and so no experience or event), and yet it remains as a sensation of absence, which is not yet loss or lack but simply an exposure to a different kind of time and sense. Part of this sensation is recapitulated in the fascination of literature, in the yawning space of its encounter, but it is also to be found in the darkened hall of the cinema and its flickering insubstantial images, images that are not of an absent object as much as they are of their own force of absencing, things that are and are yet not quite things insofar as they foreground their emptiness without letting this become complete. The image, as Blanchot had made clear, is that by which forms are made and unmade, and it is precisely this ambivalence that is brought out in film and literature, in both its temporal and material dimensions, as a time (without time) of hiatus and a formlessness of formation, not yet possibility but rather rupture and suspension. In both film and literature the gaze enters a form of fascination, an empty, endless, gaze, that is opened onto another experience, not onto anything in particular, and even less onto the world of representation, but onto an experience in which 'the image instead of alluding to a figure, becomes an allusion to that which is without figure and, instead of a form drawn upon absence, becomes the formless presence of this absence, the opaque and empty opening onto that which is when there is no more world, when there is no world yet' [EL: 25/33]. This time might be termed plastic or larval in that it is prior to the formation of subjectivity, but it is also a time of death, of a radical deformation of sense and history that can neither be retrieved nor surpassed. As Blanchot had remarked earlier, in living the event as image both the sense of living and of the event are reconfigured.

5

Damnation

XI. The cracks

The French films that were grouped under the title of poetic realism were neither the most numerous nor the most popular, but they became important because of their singular approach, which meant that they become a persistent object of fascination. They were dark, pessimistic dramas about characters on the margins of society trying, and failing, to escape their circumstances, and they came to be discussed under the rubric of poetic realism because they were situated in specific social milieus and dealt with issues of crime and poverty, but were also shot in an expressionist manner and featured scenes and dialogue of an unusually poetic nature. The latter element was the most problematic, as has been shown, as critics disagreed over whether the poetic cast of these films enhanced or undermined their social critique, although this ambivalence is precisely what gave these films such lasting importance, particularly in terms of their role as a precursor of American film noir.[1] Despite appearances, Béla Tarr's *Kárhozat* (*Damnation*, 1987) does not operate in the same mode as poetic realism, although its socio-historical background bears some comparison with France in the late 1930s. Instead, we find a form that is both more poetic and more realistic, and consequently more ambivalent. The importance of looking at *Damnation* is not simply because it allows for an extension of the earlier analysis of noir from 1940s California to Hungary in the 1980s, although this is not a negligible issue, but because Tarr extends the formal problematic of noir much further than any other director by addressing the very heart of its concerns: the aporetic complex of historical and material interaction.

The difference between *Damnation* and poetic realism becomes apparent when we consider how its style emerged out of the internal demands of Tarr's earlier films, which leads it to operate with a different sensibility from that of the poetic realist films of Carné, Chenal, Duvivier, Grémillon, Musso and so on. *Damnation* marks a distinctive change because of a number of factors, perhaps most obviously through the writing of László Krasznahorkai and the camerawork of Gábor Medvigy, as the other major collaborators, composer Mihály Víg and designer Gyula Pauer, had also worked on Tarr's previous film *Autumn Almanac* (1984), and Ágnes Hranitzky, his editor and long-time co-director, had worked with him since his first film. During the early 1980s Tarr was seeking a new form of expression that would take him away from his earlier realist films, which largely used improvised dialogue and non-professional actors, towards a form that would enable a greater exploration of the texture and dynamics of the lives of the marginalized. This possibility was uncovered through a combination of Krasznahorkai's dialogue and characterization with the overt stylization that had already emerged in the mise en scène of *Autumn Almanac*, which created a fully integrated form in *Damnation*, a form that manifested itself through the changes in camerawork. For the most noticeable change that occurs in *Damnation* is the increase in shot length and camera movement that creates a slow meditative format, immersing us in the milieu but also keeping us at a distance from it.

The narrative of *Damnation* can be broken down into a series of repeating scenarios:

> Karrer at home, looking out of the window. He shaves and then leaves, going past a small fire in the stairwell. He watches from beside a pillar as the husband leaves in a car with his daughter and then walks across the waste ground. Talks to the singer through the door to her flat, he wants to come in, she rejects him. Karrer walks to the pub (daylight, no rain, one dog) where the barman offers him a smuggling job, Karrer declines but says he can find someone else to do it (accordion plays).

> Karrer watches the door to the Titanik Bar from across the street (night, heavy rain, four dogs), the husband arrives in the car and runs into the bar, Karrer walks in after him. Listens to the singer, and is then accosted by the husband, warning him off the singer. The cloakroom attendant gives him a further, longer warning about the couple and he then goes upstairs. A man talks to two women about Görgei and Paskevich, and Karrer makes his pitch to the husband and the singer; opportunity in the face of inevitable ruin. Karrer leaves the bar alone (night, rain, one dog). Later at the pub all three are drinking and the husband goes to talk to the barman about the job, the singer then talks to Karrer about her hopes and Karrer's fatal lack of joy (accordion plays).

> Karrer watches from beside a pillar as the husband leaves in the car (daylight, light rain, four dogs), and the cloakroom attendant walks up to him and warns him again (Ezekiel 7: 14–27). When the husband has gone he walks over to the flats, leaving the cloakroom attendant behind.

Karrer and the singer relax after sex in her flat. Karrer leaves. He stands looking out of the window of his flat, chewing. Upstairs at the bar a woman breastfeeds a child next to a television, in the next room Karrer invites the singer out and is rejected (their account is settled), they argue and he leaves (night, no rain, one dog). He sits in the pub after hours, listening to the accordion player.

Karrer watches from beside a pillar as the singer leaves a shop, he talks to her and they walk away together (daylight, no rain, no dogs). Outside her flat he tells her that she means the world to him and he would do anything to be with her. They go in and have sex. He looks out of the window while she bathes. They sit at a table and he tells her about his life, how strong he must be to resist the hopelessness of others. He leaves the flat and hides while the daughter passes him on the stairs. He waits by a pillar outside the police station and then leaves without entering. Later he speaks to the barman at the pub about growing old.

Crowds wait in the hall, staring out into the rain. A man dances on his own in the rain. Inside all four are drinking and the husband warns Karrer that, although there are chances to escape, he'll come to no good. In the toilets the barman tells Karrer that the goods the husband has smuggled in have been tampered with. The singer dances with her husband. A young man recites a poem to a woman. The singer dances with the barman. Karrer watches and the cloakroom attendant comes to talk to him about youth and dancing. The barman settles his account with the singer in the car outside the bar. The dance goes on, forming a large revolving circle, watched by the cloakroom attendant. Later the cloakroom attendant leaves and the young man dances alone.

Karrer speaks to an officer at the police station and then leaves. He meets a dog and walks off (daylight, rain).

The noir aesthetic that operates in the film is, like the words of the song heard in the Titanik Bar, a self-conscious version of the standard that is at times almost parodic in its use of rain and mist, but it is saved from falling into pastiche by virtue of the fact that it operates with a slowness that makes even these hyper-stylized conventions seem naturalistic.[2] After the establishing sequence of shots that introduce us to Karrer (Miklós Székely B.), and his relations to the singer (Vali Kerekes), her husband (György Cserhalmi), the barman (Gyula Pauer) and the world they exist in, we are taken onto a new level of narrative evocation with the scenes in the Titanik. Up until this point the scenario has been presented in an almost straightforward manner with a more or less realistic depiction; indeed, we have a conventional noir set-up: a man down on his luck is trying to change his situation by associating with a woman. To do so he must deceive her husband, and this is made possible by the job he is offered by the barman. The next scene begins with the exterior of the Titanik and Karrer's situation is made clear by the way that he continues to walk normally through the heavy rain while the husband runs, and the decision forces itself upon us: does Karrer walk because that is the kind of person he is, or is this a representation of his world-view, considering that the separation between the two has not been firmly established in the set-up of the film thus far? What then is the nature of the camera's gaze if it is unwilling or unable to make this distinction between subjective and objective? Is it because its gaze operates at a level where these distinctions do not obtain?

Inside the bar we follow the camera around, listening to the song 'It's all over' (Kész az egész), and after a brief altercation in which the husband warns Karrer off his wife we have an enigmatic monologue from the woman in the cloakroom (Hédi Temessy), the first hint that the disparity between the expressionist atmosphere and the concrete milieu is reflected in the characters themselves. To some degree the character of this cloakroom attendant takes on the role of Karrer's conscience but her intentions, like her words, are not entirely clear and to this degree we enter a different sense of atmospheric evocation in which dialogues or, more accurately, monologues are delivered without any awareness of their peculiarity, as if their strangeness was neither unusual nor significant.

At this point, having received three warnings of differing directness (if we include the song), we might expect Karrer to go and, indeed, he leaves the cloakroom with his coat and seems to be heading out via some stairs at the back of a storeroom. There is then an odd move that seems to announce a change of tone, for we hear someone talking about the end of the world, and in the next shot we see two topless women and a man wearing a coat and hat. The man is speaking in very obscure terms about lifting the veil of Maya and the surrender of the Hungarian General Görgei to the Russian Paskevich that marked the end of the Hungarian Revolution in 1849. A nihilistic desperation is suggested here in which the end of the world is embraced as long as it is not witnessed, as if there might be a chance of getting away with it, of arranging some kind of deal. This snatch of conversation then merges with Karrer's own words, who we find in the next room talking to the singer and her husband. There has been a lacuna between this scene and the previous one with the cloakroom attendant but it has been elided as the words of the other man segue straight into the middle of Karrer's speech, broaching its mood for him. Thus far Karrer has listened to other people but has said very little himself, so it is of consequence that his first long speech should come in such strangely mediated terms, ones that appear to reflect his own position within a narrative of disintegration that, despite its final and irrevocable ruin, may still harbour a means to halt it, one that, as Görgei had hinted, would involve money:

MAN:	We'll know what to cling to once this world explodes. Mouth to mouth, heart to heart, star to star. But there'll be no shame any more and the veil comes off. I'm talking about Maya's veil that obscures people's minds. Görgei was some strategist, he told Paskevich: 'Look, if you want to kill Hungarians, do it in an internal war. All I'm asking is a million, for my honour, who would be witness to that? Who would see about it?'
KARRER:	It's true ... I could offer this to someone else but I thought of you. The trip's only three days. You pick up the parcel and bring it home.
SINGER:	How much?
K:	20%
HUSBAND:	All right.
K:	This way, it's a nice family story, but it finishes like any other story, because stories end badly, stories are all stories of disintegration. The heroes always disintegrate and they disintegrate the same way, if they didn't it wouldn't be disintegration but revival, and I'm not talking about revival but disintegration, irrevocable disintegration, so, what's about to happen here is just one form of ruin among the million that exist, so if they put you in jail because of your debts, don't count on temporary ruin, because this ruin is always final, as ruin generally is. At the same time, there might just be a way to stop this ruin, mainly with money, and not by playing the hero. Perhaps a single crack can be covered over.[3]

Before this speech can end the camera has already started to move away, continuing the steady tracking movement from left to right with which the scene started and which was only temporarily halted to allow us to overhear this part of the conversation. These slow tracking movements are characteristic of Tarr's later films and have been widely discussed. Kovács, for example, considers that they bear a kind of material indifference in which everything placed before the camera is treated with the same even disposition since the camera moves independently of the characters [CBT: 57, 63]. But although this captures part of what is underway in *Damnation*, it does not account for the slow but restless pacing back and forth of these tracking movements, which is perhaps impassive but not indifferent, as it follows the movements of the characters even if it also becomes distracted by their backgrounds. There is a sense of generosity to this gaze in which every feature or movement becomes of interest, no matter how banal or wretched, as in the first scene where we pass from a shot of the rough grain of the concrete wall to the equally rough stubble on Karrer's face. This level of observation not only indicates an association between the two but also indicates something of what follows in the sense of a buried richness that the camera will seek to uncover, much like the peculiar dialogue that surfaces out of everyday scenes, out of the cracks in their stories. There is thus a subtle dissonance between what the film shows in terms of the narrative of Karrer's decline and how it shows it in terms of the broad material tenderness that it expresses, in which each aspect refracts the other so that it does not fall into the trap of either glamorizing decay or annihilating difference.

Although the plot is linear insofar as it follows the decline in Karrer's situation, there is a circularity to the way it is represented, with several repeating motifs and circular movements. For instance, the synopsis I have given shows how the first four acts of the story start with Karrer in a position of observation and end with him visiting the pub, and each time he does it is later in the day. In this way the incipient fatalism of Karrer's situation is marked from the outset, just as the mise en scène, with its rain, stray dogs, run-down buildings and pervasive signs of decay, also indicates the inescapable ruination of the environment. What then becomes interesting is the relation between Karrer and his environment, which makes it unclear whether his decline is a symptom of the general decrepitude, or whether the mise en scène is an externalization of what is going on within him, or whether what we see is in some sense operating before, below or between the distinction of subjective and objective. The impossibility of discerning the cause only adds to the sense of entrapment, because it is not possible for the viewer or Karrer to know whether his actions can offer him the chance of escape, or if, as further manifestations of its confusion, they will only perpetuate his decline.

This undecidability is emphasized in the soundtrack where sounds that appear to be diegetic turn out not to be the case, and vice versa. For example, in the very first shot we are given a reverse reveal, in that, rather than hearing a sound and then seeing its source, we instead see an object and are then shown its listener. In doing so it becomes apparent that what we are hearing is not the actual sound of the mining buckets being pulled back and forth but a distorted version thereof, which is to say that what we are hearing is perhaps Karrer's version of the buckets, a subjectively enhanced version of their sounds, which carries over into the subsequent use of music as a low droning noise. Conversely, the first scene in the pub is accompanied by the repetitive notes of an accordion that only later is shown to be diegetic, suggesting a movement of auditory continuity and transformation from object to subjective enhancement and then back to externalization, which exemplifies the mutual distortion of character and environment. This effect can also be found in the blurring of the boundaries between inner and outer, as the floor of the pub appears to be as wet and dirty as it would be if it were exposed to the rain outside, while Karrer walks through the rain as if he were crossing a room. Equally, the disparity between the obscurity of some of the speeches and the acceptance of this obscurity by other characters suggests that internal monologue and conversation are not being distinguished.

This may explain why Karrer spends so much time looking through windows or watching across spaces, as the pillars that he stands beside are not just useful hiding places but are also attempts to mark a difference between his position and that of others; he is the one who looks on. Moreover, Karrer sees this separation as a mark of strength that uniquely distinguishes his situation; indeed, he acts as if he had inverted the dilemma that Kafka enunciated when he spoke of the existence of hope, but not for us. Since the lack of hope is the key to the major speech he makes to the singer after they have sex the second time, where he talks about the way that he has to be strong in order to resist the hopelessness of things that want to attach themselves to him. It is thus that he positions himself by windows in order to mark his distance from the world, which is tellingly removed at the end by the fact that he is no longer looking out over the landscape but has become part of it. For the difference in Karrer's situation is not recognized by the others, as the scene in the dance hall shows: there is a life here that does not respond to him. The discovery of this flaw in his solipsism, which leads him to go to the police, coincides with his fear of children:

> The problem is I'm afraid of children, because those innocent bright blue eyes, those blonde plaits, those tinkling voices, hide a stealthy and ruthless power and its purpose is to maintain the madness of hopelessness, to give a new incentive to the reality beating on our eardrums, to ridicule all resistance without the tiniest chance of salvation. Yet they proclaim a minute chance of salvation – resurrection itself – in such a way that we cannot escape its elemental continuity.

This fear is one that the singer had warned Karrer about earlier when she said that he had killed the love and decency within himself, while she still desires great things. In this way each of the characters that surround Karrer reflect on his situation; even the poem recited by the young man (Péter Breznyik Berg) seems to comment on his thoughts, as if the whole mise en scène was a concrete manifestation of his universe. As such, *Damnation* inflects the noir form with a poetic richness that provides a greater sense of not just psychological but also sociological realism, for the interrelation between individual and environment is as much a political critique as it is an existential one, since figures like Karrer are not only the products of this kind of environment, they also enable it to perpetuate itself. So it is just as possible to see Karrer as a less charismatic version of Irimiás in *Satantango* (Tarr, 1994), or even the Prince in *Werckmeister Harmonies* (Tarr, 2000) – someone who preaches destruction and betrayal as the only way of construing a world in which their own nihilism will not be out of place. Thus, we are presented with the undermining of a central noir cliché; that of the intellectual outsider or brooding antihero who is shown to be craven and self-serving, and the particular fate that such a figure carries: the loss of humanity. Much like Neff, Karrer acts as he does for money and for a woman, and ends up without either, and in doing so, loses everything. But it is still possible to feel sympathy for him as he is perhaps like this because of his environment. Hence, if this is a critique, then its object is unclear, for is it a political critique of a terminally corrupt and mendacious regime, or is it more of an ontological enquiry into the inevitable entropy of all systems, biological, psychological and social?

XII. In the surface

As Rancière points out, the significance of *Damnation*'s opening shot can be shown by comparing it to the standard contextualizing shot used in Hollywood films. The opening he mentions is that of *Psycho* (Hitchcock, 1960), where the camera, positioned atop a high building, pans across a city before zooming in on a half-shuttered window. There is then a cut to the interior of the room where we see two figures in states of undress [BT: 33/ 26–7]. While following the exemplification of the cinematic gaze as that of the voyeur, Hitchcock also gives us a conventional movement from context to focal point: drawing the camera directly into the object of the narrative. A similar movement takes place in the opening of *Damnation*, for again we move from a contextualizing exterior towards the narrative focus, but here the movement is reversed such that the gaze withdraws from an exterior into a room, thereby bringing the camera to a point of discovering, almost incidentally, that this perspective has a subject as well as an object: Karrer, whose view out of the window the camera has seemingly been echoing. Except that there is a disparity between the perspective of the camera and that of its putative subject, which indicates that we are not seeing exactly the same world as him just as the sound of the mining buckets is not presented as we would expect it to be. The uncertainty over whether the stylization of this sequence is a marker of its objective or subjective reality is emphasized in the next shots, where we see Karrer shaving with a blunt razor and then leaving his flat past a small fire that inexplicably burns in the stairwell. On the one hand these images could be indicators of the actual decay of Karrer's environment, but given his complete lack of regard for them, they could also be seen as reflecting his own alienated or disinterested perspective.

In discussing the way that the camera pulls back from the endless line of coal buckets to reveal the figure of Karrer staring out of the window, Rancière goes on to make the point that Tarr has avoided what would have been another convention:

> The moment arrives in which it is necessary to choose: stop the world's movement with a reverse shot of the face that saw it and that must now make an expression that translates what it feels, or continue the movement at the cost of making the person who saw into a mere black mass, obstructing the world instead of reflecting it. There is no consciousness in which the universe is visibly condensed.
>
> BT: 71–2/65

Conventionally, the camera indicates how the narrative will develop by showing us the subject who will be our guide through it, which is what Tarr fails to do. Instead, his camera pulls back to show us the large silhouette of a figure that we see from behind; there is no face-to-face encounter with the apparent subject of this perspective but simply its occlusion. For Rancière this displacement is a marker of the universe that the sequence reveals in which each part is given equal weight, which is also shown by the way that the camera in its long tracking movements seems to pay as much attention to objects as it does to people, with the result that 'the events of the material world become affects' [BT: 71/64]. The significance of this equality for Rancière is that it derives from the fact that the camera is not solely engaged with events but is allowing the actual time of the world to unfold before us, which reveals itself in the tension between the two modes of waiting or expectation (*attente*) that pervade the film: waiting for repetition and also, paradoxically, at the same time, waiting for change.

> There is no story [*histoire*], which is also to say: there is no perceptive centre, only a great continuum made of the conjunction of the two modes of waiting, a continuum of modifications that are miniscule in comparison to normal repetitive movement. The task of the filmmaker is to construct a certain number of scenes that allow for the texture of this continuum to be felt and that bring the play of the two expectations to a maximum of intensity. The sequence shot is the basic unity of this construction because it is that which respects the nature of the continuum, the nature of the lived duration [*durée vécue*] in which expectations come together or fall apart, and in which they bring together and oppose beings.
>
> BT: 72–3/66

Although it is correct to downplay the significance of the story, by discussing the film in terms of a continuum of expectations Rancière nevertheless remains at the level of the plot by only considering the narrative level of the mise en scène; waiting being a central aspect of the narrative. However, these sequence shots are not constructed simply to convey the intensities of this continuum, for this would be to ignore the material presence of the mise en scène, which is what counters its plot or *histoire*. Unfortunately, Rancière has simply assumed that these long sequences exemplify the Bergsonian notion of *durée*, of time as a singular movement of qualitative change, without examining the complex of factors that unsettle their expanse, as the long takes of *Damnation* are marked by the disparity between Karrer and his milieu in which they are not evenly balanced.[4]

In this reading, what we might see as key to the opening shot is the way that the figure of Karrer comes to obscure the view through the window without anchoring it as his point of view, since, as I have noted, his perspective does not coincide with the view that we have just seen. This point is highlighted in the very next shot by a subtle contrast that will become central to the disparity between Karrer and his environment, for after the camera has pulled back from the window to reveal his silhouette there is a cut to a sideways tracking movement that passes from a close up of the wall to a mirror in which we see Karrer shaving. The camera seems to remark on the similarity of roughness between the grain of the concrete and that of Karrer's stubble, but, as was mentioned earlier, Karrer shaves with a blunt razor that he seems not to notice. This lack of attention is confirmed in the next shot as he walks down the stairs and ignores the small fire that burns in the stairwell. What this would suggest is that although Rancière raises a significant point about the equality of the camera's gaze, this equality does not extend to Karrer's own gaze, for in the shot where we see him shaving there is a direct contrast between the attentiveness of the camera as it passes across the wall and the mirror and the inattentiveness of Karrer's gaze. At this point in the film we barely notice this disparity, but it becomes more and more significant as we are given more and more instances of the camera's breadth of interest, which tacitly exposes and draws us away from the narrow focus of Karrer's intrigues.[5] The disparity comes from the fact that Karrer does not realize how deeply enmeshed he is in this world, because he seems to believe that his disinterest keeps him distant from it, and the irony of this trap is that his distance only reduces his chances of escape.

It is only in the dance scene that this distance collapses, which for the first time starts without Karrer. Indeed it is some way into the scene before we see Karrer clearly, as he is forced to confront his change in circumstances in watching the singer dancing with the barman, at which point the cloakroom attendant appears again and offers him a final chance to escape, which he is unable or unwilling to hear. What has taken place here is barely remarked but utterly transforms Karrer's position, for after giving his long speech to the singer in which he tries to persuade her to leave with him, because he is strong enough to resist the hopelessness of others, we next find him speaking to the barman about cowardice and growing old, about the sudden discovery that one is no longer strong. This reversal seems to have come about through the accidental encounter with the singer's daughter on the stairs, an encounter we are not shown but which we can infer by the differing times of their movements, which reveals that Karrer has hidden to avoid the girl. This unrevealed encounter has apparently forced Karrer into engaging with his environment, unlike the fire on the stairs that he had earlier ignored, and it is this discovery that seems to have unsettled him. With the dance scene we are introduced to the world without Karrer: what has been in the background now becomes the focus, a background that is in constant movement in contrast to the mostly static tableaux seen thus far.

But the background has been integral to the way that the reality of the scenario has been developed. If we recall the opening scenes, we can readily see a conventional plot developing around a character whose situation is explicated through several key interactions, but this character is not given any sense of priority in this sequence as the camera spends just as long on the milieu, which seems to absorb him as soon as he leaves his flat, if not before. The substance of the reality we perceive is not constructed through narrative or editing but by slow immersion in a concrete audiovisual milieu, and the more this milieu becomes concrete the more ambivalent it becomes. As the environment intrudes into the camera's gaze it displaces our view of what seems to be going on by suggesting that there is something else here, which is its material profusion. When the scene in the pub at the beginning of the film starts by focusing on a pile of washed beer glasses, obscuring our view of the conversation that we can hear, this introduces a different point of focus. Alongside the negotiations between Karrer and the barman there is another world whose flotsam bears an equal significance on the development of the scenario.

Closer attention needs to be paid to the way that the scenes are constructed if we are to understand how this milieu is developed, for each sequence creates a particular spatiotemporal expanse that operates within strict limits. If we look at the first scene again, we can see how the retreating line of the coal buckets is echoed by the reverse tracking movement of the camera, opening out the space between their opposite movements, a space within which Karrer is found. But there is more, for this space is also opened by the mechanical sounds of the buckets that fill out the space *and* give room for the camera to move back.[6] This interaction of sound and movement plays a central role in the construction of the sequences, which Rancière has failed to notice, and occurs through an echoing effect in which the camera moves within a limited framework by iterating certain tracking movements, which echoes the manner in which the music develops through its own repeating movements. This can be seen by comparing the loose tracking shot around the Titanik as we listen to the lilting chords that introduce the song, as against the oscillating camera movement in the pub as the barman arranges the deal with the husband that is in keeping with the limited range of the accordion's tune. Apparently, Víg wrote the music before the film was shot, according to a sketch of the scenes, and Tarr then played this music while shooting so that it could help 'in creating the exact rhythm of the long and complicated camera movements' [CBT: 18–19].[7] This does not mean that the film is merely the visualization of the music, but rather that its construction takes place according to a non-narrative logic that sees each scene as a specific audiovisual sphere in which the spatiality of the camera's movement is offset by the temporal iterations of the soundtrack, including those scenes where there is only speaking and the camera is mostly static.[8] Karrer's room in the first scene is literally occupied by the sound of the coal buckets being dragged back and forth, which both opens out its closed space and also fills it, providing it with a structure that would otherwise be lacking (which also occurs in the exterior spaces through the presence of the rain), even if this is a structure that does not operate at the level of the human.

But it needs to be recalled that the grating mechanical sound that we hear is unnaturally distorted, which makes it apparent that there is a lack of identity between sound and image. Thus from the first scene we are given images that lack an objective unity and so do not appear as an immediately comprehensible reality. Hence, we cannot say exactly what it is we are being presented with here, as the conventional filmic language in which sound and image are inconspicuously unified is notably absent. The form of this defamiliarization takes place through Víg's orchestration, which reformulates folk rhythms through a repetitive minimalism and subtle electronic distortion. This sense of pervasive estrangement lies behind Adorno and Eisler's response to film, where the emphasis lies on disrupting the immediacy and homogeneity of the form through anomalous or contradictory elements, as was noted in regards to noir: 'It is not a matter of composing in a usual way [*Gebräuchliches*] for unusual [*ungebräuchliche*] instruments. It is more important to write unusually for usual instruments', which could stand as a motto for the distortions found throughout *Damnation* [KF: 103/73].

Everything in the film – the dialogue, camerawork, lighting, soundtrack, acting and sets – operates under a slight distortion from what would be expected given the conventions of film naturalism, which gives it the ambiguity of being neither naturalistic nor non-naturalistic. For while each of the elements of the film bear a strangeness that makes them noticeable they are also natural enough to be followed easily. The key to the integration of *Damnation* is thus the manner in which each of its elements is distorted in a similar way, which enables it to operate as a work while nevertheless estranging each image and thereby putting their status in question, individually and as part of the whole. In this way the viewer is both drawn into the reality of the film but also made aware of its construction, potentially enabling a position to be reached from which the nature of its images can be assessed, how they have arisen as they have, except that such assessment only reveals that the basis of these distortions is unclear, which thus continues to provoke their examination.

This montage-effect in the relation of sound to image displaces the use of montage within the image, which has become naturalized as part of the cinematic gaze. Consequently, the prominent use of the long take in *Damnation* comes from the need to find a form of gaze that is both derived from the material and yet remains strange. By developing this form the film can present sequences that are true to the milieu but that also bring out its internal disparities so that it is not dogmatically representational.[9] For if film were actually left to blindly represent everyday life, Adorno remarks, 'the outcome would be a construction alien to the visual habits of the audience, diffuse, and outwardly unarticulated. Radical naturalism, which the technique of film suggests, would dissolve all surface coherence of meaning and turn into the most extreme antithesis of familiar realism' [MM: 93/ 142]. That *Damnation* does not simply turn into an associative stream of images is due to the disparity between the images and the soundtrack, and also to the temporality of these sequences.[10] Rancière has stated that the time of these shots operates in the mode of waiting, but rather than being part of a lived duration that is essentially a passage of becoming, there is instead a time without issue, since not only are its moments of transition concealed but it also repeats itself without beginning or end. Yet this is not a repetition that is empty; we do not find here the moments of dead time that occur in the films of Antonioni, for instance, as there is movement, albeit one of slow, steady and inevitable decline, but as this is a time that has become untethered from any beginning or end it is necessarily a decline without conclusion. Kovács follows Rancière by speaking of this time as one of slowness that creates a tacit sense of expectancy, that something might change, that there might be some avenue of hope, but this slowness is only apparent to us as the viewers, rather than to the characters for whom the endless cycle of time is simply their Sisyphean medium [CBT: 121].

It would seem inappropriate to describe this as a time of boredom or ennui as it is not a time where nothing at all happens, for although nothing may change a minimal level of occurrence happens at the material level, *things* happen rather than events and it is in the face of this entropy, which is the material form of time, that the characters struggle to configure themselves. For in this time of endless decay the question of whether 'it made sense to speak at all', as Karrer phrases it, has been answered in the negative, while elsewhere, as the cloakroom attendant points out, movements and glances have their own way of speaking. The problem with Karrer, as the barman tells him, is that he sees things from his angle, and thinks that it makes a difference what he thinks, whereas things themselves have their own order that he cannot do anything to upset. It is as if he has seen the cracks in the surface of things and sought either to cover them over or to escape through them, rather than seeing them as the form of things in their concrete disintegration.

XIII. Of things

The disparity between the aesthetics of the film and its narrative is apparent in the fact that, on the one hand, there is, on a literal reading of the plot, a wretched morality play at work in the decline of Karrer, where we see what comes of someone who is manipulative and cynical, which could in turn be a reflection on the kind of environment that has given rise to such a character, a reading that perhaps contextualizes it into the milieu of Eastern Europe in the mid-1980s.[11] On the other hand, the intense stylization of the film provokes a very different reading, which is less concerned with any narrative or *histoire* but is rather focused on directing us towards the peculiarity of a world in which there is an undying eccentricity alongside such ubiquitous decay. Such a reading steers clear of aestheticizing poverty and disintegration through the strict equanimity of its gaze, which instead directs us towards the material vibrancy of the milieu, the joy and beauty as the singer calls it, that inexplicably, stubbornly, remains within the fabric of decay and yields a sense of nameless fascination. This latter aspect is evident at every level of the film and is a deliberate strategy that makes us respond to the narrative as that which is neither realist nor contrary to realism, since everything we see and hear is part of the milieu but is also subtly enhanced to express its own contingent eccentricities.[12] It is as such that Karrer is both of his environment and also estranged from it; that which is produced by it and that which allows us to see how this environment expresses itself. So these differing aspects do not undermine or sublate each other, for they pull in different directions, and it is this ambivalence that gives the film its unique sense; Kovács describes this well when he states that

> one of the functions of the length of the time he dedicated to showing certain sceneries is precisely to let the viewer discover the close cohesion between the characters and the landscape, or their textural similarity. The more the visual analogy is tangible, the more striking is the characters' invisible, interior desire to be detached from this environment. This is what produces tension in the characters, and it is this ambiguity which underlies the ambiguous effect of Tarr's long takes.
>
> CBT: 60–1

As noted earlier, Kovács understands this effect of the long take to be balanced by the apparent independence of the camera in its tracking shots, which in moving independently of the characters provides a perspective that is detached from their own. I would argue for a variation on this reading that modifies the sense of independence Kovács refers to, for the camera is not detached from the movements of the characters entirely, which is his understanding of independence; instead it seems to have difficulty holding itself in a fixed relation to them, which is a significantly different sense of relation. In the scene where Karrer waits for the singer by the shop, Kovács describes the lateral tracking movements that the camera makes that first discover the characters and then leave them. We start with a view of the shop and the camera tracks slowly to the right to discover Karrer, who is also watching it, the camera then moves back to the left until the singer comes into the shot and walks towards the camera where Karrer steps out to meet her. The camera then tracks back to the right as the two walk out onto the road and then stops while they walk away from the camera and out of shot, at which point the camera then continues its rightward trajectory until it comes to rest before a fence. There is then a false match cut to the next scene, which begins with the camera facing a wall in the stairwell of the singer's flat, and then tracks back to the left to reveal the two characters now speaking outside the door of her flat.

As Kovács points out, the actual time the camera spends tracking the movements of the characters in the first part of this scene is small compared to the length of the scene (5 seconds compared to 170 seconds), but however weak their gravitational force they nevertheless form its centre (they are on screen for 102 seconds), for without them there would be little motivation for the camera to move at all. Indeed, it could be the case that the camera is attempting to follow the characters as well as it can, given the constraints of its fixed distance from them. After all, Tarr is not Michael Snow, but is constructing a film with a recognizable plot, and it is in this way that the realism of the work refracts its stylization, just as the reverse is the case. The camera still follows the movements of the characters here, but rather more crudely or more generously than we are perhaps used to, and this difference is significant, as there is a sense that the camera, rather than offering an independent and unfocused survey of the environment, is loosely following the characters but either through some sense of inertia or distraction finds itself moving around them in very broad ambits. Which is to say that the camera, like the characters themselves, is suffering under the same environmental ambivalence that was noted earlier, in which it either finds itself slow and clumsy in its relation to its aims, or is instead caught up in the immense material strangeness of its environment that catches its gaze and leads it away from the characters. This ambivalence cannot be resolved as it arises out of the material itself. As such, the expansive nature of the gaze is reflexive, albeit inconclusively, as it expresses and describes the network of relations in which the characters, and principally Karrer, subsist.

It is not simply the case, as Kovács suggests, that the movement of the camera relative to that of the characters implies a distancing that leads us to observe them as immobile elements of their environment, for the scenes are constructed in such a way that they are each given a material prologue and epilogue, which has the effect of not only situating the characters in their environment but also of indicating the latent vitality of this background. Tarr has reaffirmed Godard's preference for editing in the camera, which corresponds to his understanding of tracking shots as ones that are inherently concerned with morality, since the equanimity of the camera's gaze in these long sequences brings out the whole world of the characters in the moment of their coexistence: their concrete reality in both its extension and its variation.[13] Rancière discusses this material balancing in terms of the way that Tarr establishes a different mode of physical situation in which 'it is not the individuals who live in places and make use of things. It is the things that first come to them, that surround, penetrate, or reject them' [BT: 33–4/27]. However, for Rancière this is made possible by the way that Tarr works with what he calls (following Flaubert) an 'absolute' sense of style, that is, a style that is not subordinated to a narrative goal but is 'an absolute way of seeing things', one that in being independent of subject matter 'gives to the visible the time to produce its own effect', leading to 'a vision of the world become creation of an autonomous sensible world' [BT: 32–3/26, 69/63].[14] While such an understanding of style is apparently geared towards the revelation of the specific durations of the world before us, as was discussed earlier, in essaying its absoluteness Rancière ignores the question of how the movements of the camera or soundtrack are necessarily related to the material of the film, and thus how the disparity between narrative and aesthetics arises from the milieu.

The scene in *Damnation* that is most representative of this disparity is also one of the most distinctive, in fact it is two scenes that seem to bear no relation to each other or to the scenes before or after them, and these are the two sequences that introduce the dance scene. In a manner that has already become familiar, the first part of this introduction involves a long tracking shot from left to right across the front of the dance hall that follows the passage of the rain across the façade of the building and the crowds that wait impassively in its doorways. The explicit association between the faces of the people and the roughened and dilapidated façade emphasizes the sense of immersive material situation that Rancière discusses, but this aspect is offset by the music, which, although repetitive like all the music in the film, is not downbeat like the accordion music but quite buoyant. However, it turns out to have no relation to the music that we come to hear when we get to see the interior of the hall; it simply accompanies this tracking shot to introduce a sense of expectancy and to mark it off from the preceding scene in which Karrer complains to the barman about growing old. This is the other life that has been in the background through the development of the film, but which we are now being shown in its peculiar vitality. As this shot comes to a close the music gives way to the sound of the rain until there is a cut and we are presented with a very different image. Some time has passed as it is now dark and the rain is falling much more heavily, and before us is the solitary figure of a man dancing enthusiastically in the rain. Much like Karrer he seems unperturbed by the downpour, but the dance he performs bears no relation to the music we have just heard or to that which will appear at the end of this shot; instead, there is simply the sound of the man's steps on the wet paving stones that seem to generate their own rhythm. Slowly the camera pulls back from this scene and into the hall, which is now full of activity, and as it does the music from the band becomes audible, but it is much more upbeat, almost rock and roll, and rhythmically unrelated to the dance that preceded it.

These two scenes contribute nothing to the plot and could have been removed without jeopardizing the narrative; so their significance must lie elsewhere and this would seem to be the contrast between its figures (between the one and the many, the mobile and the stationary, and the preoccupied and the patient), which has underpinned the relation that Karrer has sought to negotiate between himself and his environment. Its introduction at this point in the film therefore suggests a moment of submerged criticality, and when, at the very end of the dance scene, we again see a solitary figure dancing without music we recognize that some kind of transition or decision has occurred. But despite this sense of narrative transition there is also a subcutaneous affect in this sequence in which, whether through its slowness or its stylization, we find our attention expanding beyond the simple line of the plot and becoming involved in another form of experience, one that is not focused on Karrer's story but on its milieu, which bears a material vagrancy that is not entirely entropic. It is here that we can discern the latent political import of the mise en scène, for beneath the morality tale of Karrer's duplicity and decline lies an undercurrent of vitality that, however obscurely, persists.

As Bazin remarks, however 'decisive' the art of Carné in *Le Quai des brumes* or *Le Jour se lève* (1940), 'his editing [*découpage*] remains on the level of the reality he is analysing' [QC: 72/32]. The major change that came about through the work of the Italian neo-realists involved finding a way to respond to the facticity of the world as it is through the use of deep focus and long takes, which for Bazin provide an uninterrupted view of reality within which the viewer's gaze can move at will, thereby allowing for an experience of the world in its ambivalence. In this way, we can see that the world of *Damnation* has taken a middle path between poetic and neo-realism that brings a greater symbolic density to the latter and a greater material density to the former, in order to do justice to the broader sense of realism being pursued. For a photograph is not simply a representation of reality, it also bears, as Bazin insists, its own material presence as well, the reality of the image in the absence of the world, a mechanically produced impression of actuality, which 'realizes the strange paradox of moulding itself to the time of the object and, moreover, taking the imprint of its duration' [QC: 151/97]. Such a moment is not that of a Bergsonian *durée*, not simply because it does not involve an open-ended creativity but also because the time of the mise en scène, in being filmed, is reflected and compounded, doubling its sense of endurance.

Thus the filmic image becomes as ambivalent as reality itself in that it bears an objectivity like its object and also conveys that object into a time outside time, enabling both the subjective and objective times of its reality to be expressed by recording and describing them without uniting them, and instead leaving them in a state of paradoxical co-existence. In doing so, the filmic image, like the literary one, does not just represent the object but also translates it into a moment that it could never experience itself, a moment outside the world, which grants it a (negative) symbolic quality that removes it from simple depiction while yet remaining attached to objective reality at every point. This is the basis of the quality that film has of being like a shadow, 'ghostly, almost illegible', no longer offering portraits of people but 'the disturbing presence of lives arrested in their duration, freed from their destiny' [QC: 14/14]. Film does this because, like the *daimon*, it 'realizes a participant image of nature: a true hallucination', such that the image becomes an object only insofar as the object already bears this image-quality, and the photograph then conveys this image as 'a transfer of reality from the thing to its reproduction' [QC: 16/16]. This does not lead to a complete separation of the image from reality, although Bazin can on occasion seem to suggest this, but rather that the filmic image releases reality into another form while still holding to it through its material contingencies. The screen thus becomes 'a mirror with a deferred [*différé*] reflection, in which the tain retains the image' [QC: 152/97].[15]

It is in this way that the poetic and realist elements of *Damnation* do not merge together but remain distinct even as they inform and refract each other. But it nevertheless departs from the classic form of poetic realism as there is no other world the characters can turn to, no figures of escape or hope that might indicate an alternative way of life. Thus the poetic element must arise from within this world, from out of its own texture and dynamics, and can only do so to the degree that it does not offer any transcendence that would violate the sense of that milieu by introducing something extraneous to it. There is thus a strange paradox about the form of *Damnation*, for it is fully integrated aesthetically but nevertheless offers a narrative that expresses a significant lack of unity. In doing so it offers a view that is true to the world that it engages with, but is not so rigid that it refuses those moments of peculiarity that expose its errancy and disunity. It is out of this disparity that the film can still present an oblique political import, which is significant precisely insofar as it is oblique for in this way it supplies a critique that is more subtle and enduring, since in its discretion it slips under the gaze of the narrative and persists subcutaneously as an indicator of what remains beyond nihilism.

It can be seen that the disparity in *Damnation* between the aesthetic and the representational regimes, as Rancière calls them, conforms to his idea of an instability in the film format that prevents it from presenting simple stories (or fables, in his terms). This tension lies in the way that film mobilizes an audiovisual experience alongside its ostensible narrative that does not fully conform to the intentions of this narrative. Within *Damnation* this lack of unity is at once more obvious and also less explicit, insofar as the relation between narrative and non-narrative elements is apparent but is not presented in any explicit manner. Instead, the relation between them serves to complicate any sense we may attempt to make of the motivation of the film's development, which is why it retains a sense of enigma. The final scene where Karrer encounters the dog is clearly a point of realization or discovery, but it is not entirely clear what this point is or how it has been reached. We could say that, having lost his connections to human society, Karrer has been swallowed up by the landscape, but it is perhaps not until the camera finally comes to rest on a black mass of overturned earth that we recall the same silhouette that was the putative subject of the opening shot and the displacement that this implies, which has been present throughout. In this way, despite the richness and mutually expressive relation of the narrative and the mise en scène, there is still a sense of lack or incomprehension, which is highlighted by the scene on the stairs with the singer's daughter that is all but unnoticeable on the first viewing, or, alternatively, by the mysterious motivations of both the characters (as far as their monologues reveal) and the camera (as its own errancy demonstrates).

Consequently, there is less of an explicit tension between the aesthetic and the representational here than a confusion that undermines the possibility of their being so designated, alongside an extremely rich interchange between the material and the semiotic aspects of the images that yet leaves them enigmatic. It is the latter that I have discussed as the sense of being fully integrated and that leads to the uncertainty that pervades the film in which we find it difficult to determine the status or sense of the images that we see. This notion of the work is closer to Adorno's thinking than to Rancière's, for rather than the two regimes working against each other and thus generating a tension between them, there is an integration of image and narrative in which each derives from and refracts the other leading to the film being fully worked through in a dialectical sense, but nevertheless retaining an enigmatic quality that prevents it from being totally determined. This lacuna is for the most part not sensible; it is, as I have said, subcutaneous, developing slowly and without clear aetiology to displace our sense of the film from both the aesthetic and the representational towards the strangeness of historico-material complication, in which their mutual dialectical inflections are experienced (the historical becoming material in the form of decay, and the material becoming historical in the form of fate, which come together undecidably, as we have seen, in the figure of damnation itself) but without this being fully explicated.[16] Part of this can be grasped but there remains much that is not, as if the thread had become lost along the way so that it is now unclear what it is that is being shown. Like the confusing monologues or long camera movements, which are by turns fascinating or alienating, the film moves in time into a foreign landscape so that how and where this movement has taken us is obscure, which is the nature and reality of the historico-material estrangement at work here.

Because Adorno made no sustained attempt to discuss film, Rancière's work goes some way in showing how a dialectics of film aesthetics might work, but to the same degree it is disappointing that he does no more than apply a pre-existing model to his reading of Tarr. For the sense of style as absolute, which Rancière draws from Flaubert and that is foundational for his understanding of the differing regimes of art, cannot simply be applied to a film like *Damnation* without investigating how its style necessarily arose out of its material as that which derives from and reflects its milieu, as I have shown in regards to the development of the long take, something the notion of 'absolute' style can only obscure. Equally, the notion of aesthetic and representational regimes is not in the end a subtle enough tool to discuss a film where the relation between what is shown and how it is shown comes under pressure from the start. For the difference *between* the images and the soundtrack is already to be found *within* them both in terms of the disparity between their import and their distorted forms. Just as folk rhythms or mechanical sounds are interwoven to displace their natural provenance, so too do images of figures and objects become unfixed, as in the action of the rain that grants materiality an expressiveness while drawing the human into an animal world. Such interrelations then become undecidable when they are doubled by the different movements of the images and the soundtrack, which renders the film inexhaustible to the viewer's own variable and inconclusive experience.

6

Rewriting history

XIV. Parapraxis

A discussion of melancholy becomes necessary here not because of the Romantic relation between insight and suffering but because it is a deeply materialist thinking, a thinking through the body in its slowness, obscurity and heaviness, which is the source of both its difficulties and its significance. Not only does this move the discussion of thought away from a conceptual model and towards a more aesthetic arena but it also indicates the way that writing is bogged down as it becomes engaged in its materiality, both in the text and in the labour of its practice. It is thus that Blanchot finds an irresolvable ambivalence between the ambiguity of expression and the expression of ambiguity in the resistance and evasion of writing. This is the problem that links melancholy to writing, since in both cases it is not possible to make a definitive distinction between what is found and how it is found, leaving an uncertainty about its identity and status; whether it is a thing or its meaning. This ambivalence exposes a breach, for in this space between it is not certain whether it is day or night, dog or wolf, that is met, or if there is something else that is neither, which yields a gap, and it is melancholy that responds to this accident or mistake as it bears the same ambivalence that it perceives. Slippage leads to slippage, as 'one must needs scratch where it itcheth', in Robert Burton's words, 'comfort one sorrow with another, idlenes with idlenes'.[1] This slippage is emphatically mundane as it lacks the transcendental structure of classical tragedy, which would fulfil itself in a greater sphere of meaning, and is instead merely accidental in its disaster. And, crucially, it is a result of misreading, a reading that does not result from ordinary perception, which is marred by its blind spots, but a gaze that is otherwise, which occurs through its blind spots, as it were, a bodily, gestural response that opens its breach and in whose emptiness is found fascination. Thus, this breach is irrevocable and incommensurable, it has no beginning or end but exposes sheer errancy or fatelessness.

To examine the deviations of this melancholic vision I will conclude by turning to Benjamin's 1934 essay on Kafka, which is guided throughout by the diversions of various parables: from Kafka himself, from Jewish and Chinese folklore and, perhaps most significantly, by the story on Potemkin taken from Pushkin, which opens the essay. These parables operate in a manner akin to that of the mosaic of quotations that Benjamin pursued in the *Trauerspiel* and *Passagen* projects, which attempt to allow the work to develop autonomously and contingently through the differential effects that each new citation provides, thus enabling the scholar to uncover previously overlooked aspects of the work by enabling it to reveal itself anew. The motivation for this programme lies in the difficulties of bringing out the truth of a particular work, that is, in the problem of interpretation (which we have seen not only in terms of Blanchot's narratives and film noir, but also within these fields as well). And the fact that Benjamin responds to Kafka's work by following Kafka's own inclination towards parable is significant, for it not only recognizes Kafka's pre-eminent significance as a writer and interpreter of texts but in doing so also brings out the peculiar status of the parable as a means of interpretation.

As the term implies, the parable is that which lies alongside (*para*) the main text, and so its place as an interpretive tool is constrained by the fact that its own existence as a text to be interpreted may lead to a digression in which we are drawn away from the main text and into a parabolic discussion, turning from one diversion to another. This aspect of the parable is what appealed to Kafka, insofar as the parable suspends its own significance as a tool by refusing to be interpreted unambiguously: any clues that it offers are also held in question by the fact that in offering them it also diverts the reader into further questions, perhaps unrelated to the initial question. Thus the relation of the parable to the main text becomes unclear: how can it explain it when it needs explaining itself? What is the relation between the two texts, which we as readers are now suspended within? And, if the parable (*Gleichnis*) is like (*gleich*) another text, then how are we to understand this similarity? These queries are phrased and rephrased by Benjamin as he attempts to draw out the heart of Kafka's concerns as a writer. The strand of this discussion that I will focus on here is that which centres on the relation of writing to history, and the particular temporal turning that Kafka and Benjamin seek to bring out in this relation. The ambiguity of the parable as an interpretive tool is conveyed by Benjamin in the way that he uses two particular tales to bookend his essay: the story by Pushkin that opens the essay and the Jewish folktale that appears at the beginning of the last section, for the fact that these are both stories taken from outside Kafka's work indicates part of Benjamin's method of approaching Kafka by translating his concerns into a parallel context. First, then, is Pushkin, and the story of Potemkin and Shuvalkin; although this is well known, its details must be stressed, for it is in these details that Benjamin finds a way of reading alongside Kafka.

Prince Grigori Potemkin was chief of the Russian army and the most powerful statesman in the court of Catherine the Great, and the only one of her lovers who had managed to retain his position after losing her affections. However, he was of a deeply melancholic disposition, and when this mood took him he was inconsolable and would brook no disturbances. As Pushkin's story relates, on one such occasion Potemkin's depression proved deeper than usual. Days turned to weeks, and still he would not return to the court. The imperial councillors became more and more agitated as the days passed: official documents were mounting up that required his signature, and the empress was becoming angered by the delay. Struggling to know what to do, the councillors were one day discussing the problem when a lowly official by the name of Shuvalkin passed by and asked if he might be given the chance to try to obtain the prince's cooperation. Increasingly desperate, the councillors saw no reason to refuse; so they passed the pile of documents over to Shuvalkin, who calmly strode off through the council chambers, through the main doors to the prince's rooms, and then finally, without pausing, into Potemkin's private study. Potemkin sat on the edge of his bed, dishevelled and chewing his nails, but Shuvalkin approached him, took a pen from his desk, dipped it in ink and placed it in the prince's hand. Potemkin looked up at the young official blankly and then back at the papers, and then one after another he signed them. Triumphant, Shuvalkin returned and presented the pile of signed documents to the councillors, who frantically went through them. Then they stopped and looked round at the young official, and something in their faces showed that the praise that he had been expecting would not be forthcoming. 'What is it?' he asked, and they returned the documents to him wordlessly. Looking through them now for the first time, Shuvalkin saw his own name at the bottom of each page.

'This story is like a herald, storming two hundred years ahead of Kafka's work. The enigma that beclouds it [*sich in ihr wölkt*] is Kafka's' [GS2: 410/795].[2] Thus Benjamin states directly after relating this tale and straightaway we are presented by the dimensions and focus of the subsequent discussion: the relation of the parable to time and the 'enigma that beclouds it'. Indeed it is an enigma, for even now 'two hundred years' have not yet passed since Pushkin penned this story; is this simply a mistake on Benjamin's part, or a point of hyperbole? Or is it a hint of the strange relation that writing bears with history? Before attempting an interpretation of this story, which Benjamin calmly assimilates to Kafka's world (Shuvalkin 'is Kafka's K.') in a manner that only makes it less clear, I will move on to the second of the two parables that I want to discuss: the Jewish folktale that opens the final section of the essay [GS2: 410/795]. In doing so, I will make my own parabolic reading by passing over the body of the essay to take in its outer movements, the curves of its trajectory, as these will draw out more strongly this strange relation of writing and history, which is itself the focus of this second parable, and which in turn underlies the relation between the sociological and theological readings of Kafka that Benjamin sought to juxtapose.

A group of men were sitting together in their local inn one Sabbath evening when their discussion turned to what they would each wish for, should they have the chance. One man said that he would wish for wealth, another said a son-in-law and another a new carpentry bench. When they had each spoken they noticed a beggar they had not seen before who was sitting silently on a bench in the corner, and they asked him what he would wish for. With much hesitation he replied: 'I wish that I was a powerful king who reigned over a large domain, then one night whilst I was asleep the castle would be attacked by my enemies, by dawn they would have defeated the guards and reached my bedroom chambers, thereupon I would be forced to rush from the castle in just my shirt and flee across country, travelling all through the day until I came to this inn.' Surprised, the men asked him what he would have gained by this wish, and the beggar said: 'A shirt' [GS2: 433/812].

Aside from the traditional comic conventions, there is a powerful critique of redemption and transcendence here, and more obscurely, a strange relation of time is sketched out in which the beggar wishes for something that appears to resemble what may have already happened. More precisely, the standard timeframe of wish-fulfilment is usually based on a transformed future, but the beggar has turned this transformation back onto the past, such that the present moment becomes the point at which the wish is fulfilled by virtue of the fact that the past has been rewritten, thereby disavowing any intention towards what might be and focusing instead on what might have been. In doing so, the redemptive aspect of the wish is turned directly back onto the present, which is transformed in only the very slightest of ways, thereby rewriting its transcendent aspect as something much more sober and mundane: rather than escaping from life by way of the fulfilled wish, the beggar simply returns more fully to himself. It is as if nothing has happened and yet everything has changed, which for Blanchot is the definition of the disaster [ED: 7/1].

Returning to Shuvalkin we can now see the profound ambiguity in the relation that the young official finds with the prince, for in placing Shuvalkin's name at the bottom of the official documents, Potemkin has simultaneously raised him up to the highest state of office and cast him down into the lowest disgrace. It is impossible to tell in what way the officials will proceed, for they could carry on the charade and grant Shuvalkin a higher rank in order to verify the documents, or they could find both the documents and their bearer invalid. All this is contained in the blank gaze that Potemkin rests on Shuvalkin as he takes up the pen; at this moment the possibility of both futures is held open as the transgression of Shuvalkin's entrance is returned to him in the inscription of his name. In its refusal to be settled, this ambiguous return captures Potemkin's resistance most fully: in the depths of his melancholic withdrawal he has seized upon a profound temporal and scriptural anomaly and in doing so has resisted the attempts of the officials to draw him into a decision. Shuvalkin thus finds himself, like K., and like the reader, suspended in a trap that is not of his own making, but crucially the trap has not snapped shut. Instead, he is granted a muted transcendence by finding himself aware of his own position within a trap but unable to make any alterations or entreaties to change it, unless he refuses to recognize it as a trap. Kafka expressed this position quite concisely in a late piece:

> Concerning this a man once said: 'Why are you defensive? If you were to follow the parables [*Gleichnissen*] then you would become parables yourselves and thus be free of daily cares.'
> Another said: 'I bet that is also a parable.'
> The first said: 'You have won.'
> The second said: 'But unfortunately only in parable.'
> The first said: 'No, in reality; in parable you have lost.'[3]

The enigma that 'beclouds' these stories, as commentators have never failed to point out, lies with the nature and meaning of the Law in Kafka's and Benjamin's writings.[4] The problem of the relation to the Law appears to be central to Kafka's works, and so it is unsurprising that, after reading Benjamin's essay, Gershom Scholem should write to him to say that it was precisely on this point that he saw him getting into difficulties. Benjamin wrote back to say that he considered 'Kafka's constant insistence on the Law to be the point where his work comes to a standstill, which only means to say that it seems to me that the work cannot be moved in any interpretive direction whatsoever from there'.[5] As a result, the significance of the Law may be such that it actually distracts us from other aspects of Kafka's writings by virtue of this intransigence. Consequently, and following Adorno's suggestion, I will focus on the manner in which Benjamin's essay mobilizes other aspects of Kafka's writings to bypass this intransigent relation, and the area that is most heavily explored here is that of the *gestus*, the non-intentional, accidental physical act that makes itself known in distortions (*Entstellungen*) of the form or movements of the body, and the relation this has to writing, particularly the writing that would seek to respond to the inscriptions of the Law, to read and interpret them.[6]

The presence of these distortions is signalled by the contrasting characters of Shuvalkin and Potemkin: one is young, light-footed, obliging and calm, while the other is old, decrepit, slumbering and recalcitrant. Where one appears unbowed, the other is bowed deeply as if under an invisible weight. But the difference between the two is slight, as the beggar's tale illustrated, for with the stroke of a pen a transition is marked between them. The nature of this transition is what is most difficult to grasp as it appears to operate outside the Law and yet as the very executor of the Law. Moreover, it is only from the position of being bowed that one can truly become unbowed: only from the depths of depression and degradation is it possible to find the transition that releases one from enthrallment. Yet Kafka's writings carry the greatest caution about such a release, as if it were neither possible nor even desirable, for the hardest thing of all is to actually confirm that one is bowed. Furthermore, the search for this invisible mark may be that which first inscribes it. Thus this set of questions opens onto the issue of the melancholic's relation to the world and to time: of how it is possible to twist free from the burden of depression when the means to do so lies only in the insight that melancholy brings. In effect, the problem that Kafka and Benjamin are struggling with here is the same one that Hölderlin discussed under the title of 'the *free* use of the *proper* [*des* Eigenen]', which was the problem of how to come to a free relation to one's history and language without losing oneself in it or abusing it.[7]

It is from this point that Kafka turns aside from the redemptive illusions of myth towards the more humble opening of parable, its 'slight adjustment' (*Geringes zurechtstellen*), as Benjamin calls it, which turns the course of the world to one side [GS2: 432/811].[8] That is, Kafka responds to this problem of how we are to relate to the invisible mark of tradition *through* the parabolic mode of his writings, which does not seek to erase or avoid the mark of the past but repeats it by reinscribing history and language into the present anew, and Benjamin's key example of this is Kafka's rewriting of the story of the Sirens. First, Kafka inverts the traditional rendering of Odysseus's trickery by stating that it was Odysseus's ears that were plugged with wax, rather than his crew's. Then he goes on to say that although this was no defence against the Sirens' song, Odysseus was nevertheless safe because he believed in the power of the wax to save him, to such an extent that his only intention was to pass by the Sirens' lair and not to hear their song. So when he came to their cliff-top dwelling, his eyes were fixed on the distant horizon and his mind on the wax in his ears, so, oblivious, he passed in safety. But Kafka then provides a further inversion that seems to place everything just said in suspension, for the Sirens' greatest weapon was not their song but their silence, and it was with this that they echoed Odysseus's oblivious gaze. Then this too is put in doubt, for we are finally told that Odysseus knew that the Sirens were silent and his pretence of ignoring them was simply a shield to protect him from those who might be threatened by his knowledge, that is, the gods [GS2: 415–16/799].[9]

Whereas in Homer the Sirens sang and Odysseus heard them, in Kafka they are silent and Odysseus ignores them; although convoluted, Kafka's rewriting allows him to place his version in the closest proximity to Homer but with the most extreme differentiation. For Odysseus is again granted the greatest intimacy with the Sirens, just as he was in Homer, but this time it is an intimacy based in oblivion, rather than rapture. Now Odysseus and the Sirens exist in parallel, *para allelo*, by one another, alongside but not touching each other, grounded in a mundane transcendence that does not depart from the world but returns to it in oblivion. Stripped of its mythic transport, the story becomes prosaic and yet it carries a peculiar redemptive quality that lies within its telling, for the transformational opening that it bears is to be found *in* its inversions. Here the narrative no longer describes an event but is that which enables it to occur; it is the opening of a transition that it also relates, just as the beggar in the folktale relates a wish that finds him at its conclusion suddenly returned to his own place. The key to this transition is the oblivion that enables an opening to appear in which such alterations can occur, the same oblivion that enabled Odysseus to believe in the power of the wax and to set his eyes on the horizon, or that enabled Shuvalkin to take the pile of documents into Potemkin's inner chambers.

The parable itself constitutes such an act, insofar as it places itself calmly next to the tradition in such a way that its explanatory power does not indicate if it is there to interpret an existing doctrine, or one that is still to come [GS2: 420/803]. No clue is given in the parable itself as to what it is in relation to; this is the mystery of its simplicity, the ambiguous depth of its blank gaze, which places the very possibility of relation in suspension, awaiting its fulfilment but also deferring its bondage, its decisive judgement. This is the enigma that beclouds Kafka's work, for he can never know whether his writing is operating from within the call of tradition or without, as the invisible mark of tradition occupies the same oblivion as its parabolic reinscription. Oblivion is all there is, this is the source of the distortion, the deviation that affects all, and the only response for Benjamin lies in the continual labour of studying, which in its feverish attentiveness and reinscriptions is the reversal that turns back the winds of tradition and 'transforms existence into writing' [GS2: 437/815]. But, as this reversal into writing, study is no longer an act, a praxis subject to everyday oblivion, but an interpretation, a parable that inhabits it:

> He might understand himself, but what an enormous effort would be required! For it is a storm that blows from out of forgetting. And study is a ride that fights against it. Thus the beggar on the corner bench rides towards his past, in order to catch hold of himself in the figure of the fleeing king. This ride, which is long enough for a life, corresponds to life, which is too short for a ride.
>
> GS2: 436/814

Thus the student can only effect this reversal into parable by exchanging the idle wish for the slight adjustment, the future for the rewritten present, just as the beggar did, and in doing so he finds himself subject to the same change of course that affected Gracchus's ship [GS2: 434/813]. That is, this turning aside from the ordinary course of things is a turning into a deeper oblivion, into a forgetting so profound that it is not only a forgetting of the burden of tradition but also a forgetting to die. For the course of tradition is bounded by a forgetting of death, which guides history by permeating the present with an oblivion that burdens each new generation with an unknown past [GS2: 428/809]. As a result, in myth, transcendence and redemption are marked by a removal from history and a forgetting of the possibility of death, which only replicates the daily oblivion of unknowing that enables tradition to propagate. The step aside that parable performs is instead a turning *into* forgetting that seeks to recall it as such, as the finitude that defines history. As I have shown elsewhere, Blanchot termed this parabolic step 'a dead transcendence', that is, a transcendence that is not, that is dead, and a death that is not, that is transcendent; and although this opens the narrowest of passages between these two extremes and unburdens us of the weight of tradition, it does so only to the extent that it condemns us like Gracchus to an errancy without return [PF: 15/7, 88/83].[10]

Here the distinction between Potemkin and Shuvalkin starts to dissolve, for the bowed posture of the one now becomes the bent figure of the student, while the light step of the other becomes the sign of the condemned following his fate. The gestures of melancholy pass undecidably between the two, preventing us from definitively stating whether the figure is burdened or unburdened by tradition. The gesture is always marked by this oblivion of unknowing, for its singularity persists in secret, in that it remains unmarked, indistinct, by virtue of the enigma of the past that beclouds it. Given this, the only option for the melancholy student is to continually rewrite this passage into the present and thereby displace it, and perhaps this gives a hint as to the excessive signalling that Benjamin ascribes to Pushkin's story, for if it 'is like a herald, storming two hundred years ahead', then this is because the distance that needs to be covered in order to make this transition into the present is always inordinate: 'This ride, which is long enough for a life, corresponds to a life, which is too short for a ride.'[11]

But is the melancholic intent on making this transition into the present, or is the intent rather to deviate from it further – is the subversion of the act more fundamental and actually constitutes a *parapraxis*?[12] Is the deviation here more akin to Bartleby's refusal, which placed action on an errant course by turning it aside with a slight adjustment to the basis of the act [ED: 219/145]? What then is the nature of this slight adjustment but that which returns its oblivion to itself, redoubling it as Odysseus did when confronted with the aporia of being unable to pass the Sirens without hearing or not hearing them. But is this not a turning that then raises critical problems for Benjamin's reading? While Kafka's understanding of time, in which the present is fully permeated by the oblivion of the past, comes to form part of Benjamin's approach to history, Benjamin appears to diverge from this notion with his understanding of critique. For the role of the critic is to find the moment of 'legibility' (*Lesbarkeit*) of the past, which arises in the decisive rupture of remembrance that detaches the present from the movement of time, but the legibility of this moment is precisely what Kafka's work would seem to put into doubt.[13]

Kafka's story about the ride over to the next village appeared in his 1919 collection *Ein Landarzt*; also appearing in this collection were two other parables that dealt with the detachment from time by language, 'Vor dem Gesetz' and 'Eine kaiserliche Botschaft', whose appearance as parables would only be confirmed posthumously by the appearance of the doctrines that they would, in Benjamin's terms, be attempting prematurely to interpret. That is, both parables would seem to be unfolded for the reader by their later appearance in, respectively, *Der Process* (1925) and 'Beim Bau der chinesischen Mauer' (1931), but as both these narratives are themselves unfinished their capacity for enabling the earlier parables to be unfolded is itself deferred [GS2: 420/802]. To understand this more fully it is necessary to examine the relation the parable has with time, and this can be best understood in terms of Blanchot's thought of the *récit*, which, as has been shown, seeks to be a narrative of and from an event. Hence, the '*récit* is not the relating of an event, but that event itself, the approach of that event, the place where it is called to occur, an event that is yet to come and through whose power of attraction the *récit* can hope as well to be fulfilled'. In a manner similar to Kafka's excessive reading of the story of the Sirens, Blanchot gives us too many explications here and ones that appear contradictory; for how can the *récit* be both the event, its approach and its site, and that which nevertheless eventuates from it? But, as we have seen, its time is complex and fragmentary, since it brings out a relation of writing that both precedes and succeeds what occurs, and is thus forever beside it, providing the hollow (and hollowing out) of its event. Blanchot tries again to indicate this:

> The *récit* is movement towards a point, not only unknown, ignored, foreign, but such that it does not seem to have, prior to and outside of this movement, any sort of reality, so imperious however that it is from it alone that the *récit* draws its attraction, in such a way that it cannot even 'begin' before having reached it, but however it is only the *récit* and the unpredictable movement of the *récit* that supplies the space where the point becomes real, powerful, and attractive.[14]

The critical aspect of this transition, which the parable captures, is that which Blanchot describes as a turning from a language of images to an image of language; a language turned back on itself in an attempt to take account of its own emergence but in doing so, as his readings of Char indicated, it becomes no more than its hollowing out [EL: 28/34]. In historical terms this means that the parable operates as the shadow of the past that 'strives to turn towards' its readers in the future, those who will render it legible, and for both Benjamin and Blanchot the fact that this historical relation is 'secret' in no way diminishes the strength of the claim that it asserts; instead it isolates the particular task of the writer.[15] But the essence of the parable is that it never unites with that which it attempts to reach; life is not long enough for that distance to be traversed, and thus its position is that of a past that will never be present. This puts enormous pressure on the possibility of this writing being taken up and read as part of a historical critique and thus places in question the very role of the critic. Although parable and critique are clearly very different in their aims and their modes, they each attempt a particular relation to history, and it is only by examining Benjamin's understanding of critique in his earlier work that it is possible to see how far the parable deviates from its aims and opens up a different relation, one that is perhaps more far-reaching.

XV. Reading melancholy

Benjamin conceives of the critic as one whose work is able to bring about both a historical critique and a critical intervention. However, as we have seen, there is a profound ambivalence in this conception since the nature of reading and writing, tasks essential to the critic, are such that they place the very possibility of criticism in doubt. To show this, it is necessary to examine the dense prologue to Benjamin's *Trauerspiel* study, which contains his most detailed analysis of the role of the critic.

The fundamental problem that concerns Benjamin in the *Erkenntniskritische Vorrede* is that of reading. Although the prologue starts with the relation between philosophical writing and presentation (*Darstellung*), Benjamin makes clear that his understanding of the issue of presentation in critical writing arises out of the necessity and difficulty of finding a way to read history philosophically. The *Trauerspiel* then becomes the means by which this problem is explored, as it raises in an extreme form the issue of language made distant from us both temporally and culturally and thereby indicates how such difficulties in reading become central to any historico-philosophical project. It is from these difficulties that the problems associated with a critical-historical writing arise, and Benjamin uses the first pages of the prologue to describe the nature of the writing that will be required to pursue such a project. The answer he opts for is that of a treatise (*Traktat*) rather than a doctrine (*Lehre*) because a doctrine, he claims, pursues an authoritarian didacticism that the subject matter will not permit, the subject being that of historical truth.

As a result, in order to attempt such a historical reading, the project needs to continually question its own method and presentation, and for

Benjamin the treatise supports this as it avoids coercion or conclusion by relying wholly upon the authority of its citations. However, this means that the treatise cannot attain any authority of its own, for its only method is diversion (*Umweg*): referring us onwards from one text to another, in the same way that this method in reading had guided its writing. Benjamin elaborates this point by stating that the treatise arises from a tireless but endlessly interrupted mode of study that seeks to apprehend historical truth by starting, pausing and then returning, thereby allowing these multiple courses of presentation to develop into a mosaic in which historical truth is able to appear more clearly the less directly it is presented [UDT: 208/2–3]. What Benjamin is suggesting is that it is necessary for us to learn to read by way of the mode of continual interruption that characterizes writing, and from this we will then be able to develop a historical writing. In other words, by adapting our reading to the rhythms of writing, we will be able to find a way of writing that can then respond to our reading. The fractured nature of writing thus becomes the condition not only for reading but also for the mosaic-like treatise that might follow from such a reading, and so its fragmentary rhythm becomes the condition of truth.

Following on from his earlier work, Benjamin discusses this appearance of truth as an 'idea' (*Idee*). But despite the putative proximity to Plato and the early Romantics Benjamin's use of this term is entirely singular and arises from his understanding of the essence of language. It is necessary here to jump ahead to the explanation that Benjamin gives eight pages later, where he states that the idea 'is something linguistic [*ein Sprachliches*]', insofar as it 'is released from the heart of reality as the word', and gives itself gratuitously, that is, outside of any intention, 'in naming'. As he points out, this conception owes more to Adam than to Plato, which indicates the strength of Benjamin's understanding of reading as it begins to resemble a form of annunciation [UDT: 216–17/13–14]. However, although it is the fragmentary rhythm of writing that guides this reading, the truth that is 'made present [*vergegenwärtigt*] in the dance of presented ideas' cannot be appropriated within any writing, for just as this truth is without intention, it is also distinct from any form of knowledge [UDT: 209/4]. Instead, truth only occurs in its own form, rather than in any form that might be given to it, so the demand that is placed upon our reading and writing is that of allowing this singular appearance of truth to emerge; hence the need for a mosaic approach that actively inhibits its own presentational conclusions and thereby gives room for something else to arise.

From here Benjamin turns to the *Symposium*, to elucidate two aspects of Plato's thought that he does take up: first, the notion that truth is beautiful, that is, it appears in the form of the beautiful, which is to some extent dependent on its reader; for this beauty, and this is the second point, is the form in which the 'presentational moment' (*darstellende Moment*) of truth takes place, that is, there is an 'erotics' to truth: truth wants to express itself, and this requires it to be read; thus it calls for its lover so that it can appear in the fullness of its beauty. But truth also flees before the pursuit of its lover, and it is this flight that is the form of truth – as the offspring of its emergence and its pursuit, its *Ursprung* – the form that is also the name in which it both distinguishes and extinguishes itself [UDT: 211/6]. It is through the demands of this naming that the reader becomes, for Benjamin, a philosopher, whose task is midway between that of the scientist, who divides the world into concepts, and the artist, who brings about an image of the world in presentations.

Benjamin's rather singular take on hermeneutic phenomenology, which Heidegger was struggling with in Marburg at the same time, and which Adorno found so damaging to the dialectical potential of Benjamin's work, here takes on its most explicit form, for the aim of the reading that the philosopher is to develop is twofold: to bring phenomena to their truth, and to allow their ideas to appear.[16] While these aims clearly converge, this only increases the hermeneutic difficulties for the reader as it requires an approach that works on two fronts in tandem. Where the inclination to philosophy fails, though, is in its drive to unity that covers over the fragmentary nature of phenomena. But if the philosopher attends to each individual phenomenon by distinguishing it conceptually, he is able to bring out its truth in the presentation of its name or idea, in which it is 'saved' or 'rescued' (*gerettet*) [UDT: 213/9]. This dual process of emergence is made possible by a form of reading and writing similar to that mentioned earlier, as the concepts the philosopher uses cut through the conventional and illusory forms of phenomena and then rearrange them such that they can appear in their truth, as their ideas or names. Concepts are thus the temporary interface, or lens, which focus the convergence of things and names in their truth. But it is through this combined reading and rewriting of phenomena that truth is able to occur in the appearance of its ideas, which means that such reading-writing is the necessary condition for the appearance of truth as it is the medium of its reflexivity.

However, ideas only relate to phenomena indirectly, in the same way that constellations relate to stars, as they are not derived from phenomena nor can phenomena be used to judge their accuracy. Instead, the idea only finds its relation to phenomena in that the latter, once divided and gathered by concepts, find their saved form in the idea. So while it is from the extreme forms of phenomena (those furthest from the grasp of knowledge) that the richest concepts arise, it is in the gathering of these extremes, or eschatology, in the mosaic that the idea appears in its general form, which then fulfils the philosophical aim of exposing the underlying unity of the extremes [UDT: 214–15/10–11]. This presentation of truth in the name is not a revelation but a recollection or anamnesis, for in this reading and writing the truth of ideas themselves becomes 'renewed' by this recollection. Philosophy is thus a quest to bring these names back into their truth as the ideas of things; it is not a creative endeavour that acclaims the sovereignty of the thinker but a service and care for language so that it can appear in its truth, each time singular and finite and thus continually interrupted [UDT: 217/14].

With the general epistemo-critical programme laid out, Benjamin can move on to the specific issue of the *Trauerspiel*. However, he does so by immediately stating that the *Trauerspiel* is an idea [UDT: 218/15]. So before we have even begun studying it, the nature of German baroque drama has been granted the name that reveals its truth: the *Trauerspiel*. Benjamin no doubt feels that this move is necessary in order to justify his decision not to assimilate this particular form of drama to either ancient tragedies or modern dramas, but doing so seemingly pre-empts his reading by claiming that this disregarded mode already has its truth confirmed in its name. However, it is also out of this opening that his writing can find its own mosaic-like beginning: by setting forth the hermeneutic supposition that will allow the object to be read. Equally, this move signals Benjamin's concern with drawing out the broader truth of history as a whole by mobilizing its conceptual extremes. For the study of the *Trauerspiel* is the move that Benjamin makes in order to bring about the presentation of a more fundamental truth about history itself, which will then allow the project as a whole to reflect back onto the broader question from which he began: that of the problem of reading historically.

As he has made clear, coming to an understanding of the nature of history as such requires concepts that can expose the unity of its extremes. In saying this, however, he attempts to distance himself from any philosophical unification by stating that these concepts are not the hypostatization of the reader's perspective, nor are they established by some process of induction or deduction from phenomena; instead they are grounded in the individual forms of phenomena. In making this claim, Benjamin proposes his own sense of the 'origin' of such forms in which they arise out of the process of historical becoming as singular but temporary configurations; 'whirlpools' (*Strudels*) in its currents. While such a notion allows for a limited restorative saving of phenomena in their individuality, it is always incomplete, for it exposes each phenomenon to the truth of history in its totality in which its singularity is grounded solely in its repetition [UDT: 226/24–5]. The task of our reading-writing is then to isolate this origin, to uncover its unique concrete manifestation, so that it can be the trigger through which the work may be brought to its truth, which thereby brings us into relation with the idea of history itself as its *word*, for history only reveals itself in its totality in its 'afterlife', in the ongoing history of its becoming, of which our reading-writing is thus an essential part.[17]

It is this afterlife that is the key to the project as a whole and allows us to answer two of the most pressing problems of the prologue. First, what does 'saving' (*Rettung*) involve? Second, if the idea is unrelated to the phenomenon except as the name in which it is saved, then how do we know when this name is found? As mentioned earlier, the aim of Benjamin's treatise has less to do with the saving of a particular mode of baroque drama and more to do with the issue of coming to understand how to read historically. And this is where the issue of saving becomes most explicit, for the saving of phenomena is only possible by way of its repetition, such that it is never complete and so calls unceasingly for its continued communication (*Mitteilung*).[18] This continually interrupted and repeated communication is how we should understand saving, which is why the *Trauerspiel* is such an important means for uncovering the truth of history, for in its vision of a world of perpetual decline that is replicated in the mourning and decay of its own ruined allegories we find the strongest image, or idea, of a continually interrupted reconfiguration. The idea of historico-philosophical reading and writing, the name in which *its* truth is exposed, *is* the *Trauerspiel*, which means that the truth of this name is only realized in the moment of its presupposition as a result of what it releases, after the fact.

Thus the task of the critic is twofold. First, there is critique: the collection, sifting and analysis of material with a view to bringing out its truth; in this there is both a preservation and resuscitation of the past in its truth. Second, there is its critical aspect, insofar as the retrieval of a hidden truth has an explosive and decisive effect on the moment in which it is retrieved; this is the corollary of bringing out the truth of the material. However, there is a dialectical relation between these two aspects, for it is only possible to bring about a retrieval *through* the decisive rupture of the moment: it is thus naming that (paradoxically) becomes the condition of legibility. This raises an important distinction, for as was found with Potemkin and Shuvalkin, naming in parable has a very different role: while it also reveals the moment of historical transition, it only does so by designating it with the impossibility of deciding; naming here withdraws the moment into an oblivion that refuses decision.

So while the relation between text and interpretation in critique, and the concomitant disruption of time, recalls the mode of the parable, the two remain quite distinct in their historical relation – for there is a suggestion that the careful ministrations of critique enable the singular truths of history to yield to a greater eschatological truth, to a revolutionary or messianic annunciation – in much the same way as mourning (*Trauer*) differs from melancholy in seeking to subsume trauma into its recovery. But for Kafka, there is no room for this teleological perspective as the chiasmus of the moment in critical reading is such that it is not given that the past can speak to us, or that we can hear it. The possibility of such a retrieval is always in doubt, for it only exists in the moment of its passage, thereby suspending its dialectic. As the beggar's wish indicated, it is only by way of a recapitulation of what may not have happened that it is possible for the past to repeat itself, so that he may have the chance to find himself anew in the moment.

But as a recapitulation, the wish is finite and so must itself be repeated, and as such its outcome can never be decisive. This is the finitude that leads the writer into a melancholic withdrawal; unless he comes to accept that there is no possibility for anything other than this repetition, here, perhaps, Blanchot is a more sober guide than Benjamin.

Thus, the possibility of a critical-historical writing lies in the nature of the relation attempted between past and present, in which we find the differing modes of Blanchot's and Benjamin's attempts to engage such a critique and crisis. There is in both parable and critique an inversion of the relation between past and future, as the future, which ordinarily was the sphere of the possible, becomes a closed book insofar as it is beyond any planning or organization, and the past, which ordinarily was the sphere of unchangeable fact, becomes opened to endless alternatives. This repeats the inversion of tense often found in cases of psychic trauma, which arises as the trauma recurs and disrupts the relation between past, present and future, leading to the effects just described.[19] But this means that any critical-historical writing is engaged in a *poiēsis* of trauma as its attention to the singularity of the rupture leads to its recapitulation, exposing this writing to the most serious responsibility of recapitulating trauma. The problem of critical-historical writing is thus one of finding a path that neither lessens the rupture in relation to the present, nor destroys the present through the repetition of its rupture. Blanchot's response to this problem can be found in his understanding of the *récit* as a mode of writing that recapitulates the ruptured passage of history as both rupture and passage, without turning it to a particular end. This point is developed most starkly in *L'Arrêt de mort*, where the narrative starts again after a break by returning to the beginning, so that the second part is both a repetition and a continuation of the first part, rewriting the narrative but also the rupture that perpetually suspends its possibility of going on. In the fragmentary dialogues of the later works this aporetic movement occurs at a more microscopic level, as in the intricate negotiations of the voices in *Celui qui ne m'accompagnait pas* and *L'Attente l'oubli* where each step is both a turning and a return, an affirmation and a negation. In doing so, the separation of the rupture is re-presented, thereby preserving its distance (as in melancholy) instead of absorbing it (as in mourning), and herein we find the demand underlying the anamnesis of this parabolic writing.

But as is found in all cases of melancholic insight, there is a risk here of valorizing the *source* of the trauma, and thereby diminishing its rupture by seeing it as simply part of the essential striving of our becoming human. In doing so, we then turn the source of the trauma into a tyranny to which we must allow ourselves to be subjected, which is part of what is at work in the apparent fatalism found in many films noir. But in our encounter with finitude, nothing is less certain than our survival, and nothing is more ambiguous than the face it presents. For its opaque Law means that it can never simply be tyrannical and thus it is entirely other than any worldly tyranny, and so the subjection it calls forth is more passive than any suffering; it is an exposure to an ambivalence without end rather than the oppressive certainty of tyrannical subjection, and it is thus that it is other (in which is also found Blanchot's response to theology). The encounter here grants an entirely different sense to finitude, one that due to its ambivalence cannot lead to a conflict of striving opponents. Hence, what the muteness of trauma indicates is perhaps more startling and disturbing than it appears at first, as it indicates the possibility of not returning from its parabolic detour, and so leaving its melancholic refusal as a parapraxis that is unavailable to any subjection and thus useless for tyranny.

Although there are similarities between Benjamin's discussions of parable and critique, they are separated by their different relations to history, and the resistance of parable to decision may offer more to the problems of historical reading than critique, which is ostensibly Benjamin's response. For instead of becoming lost in a fascinated contemplation of the fragmentation and disenchantment of history or transforming this dissolution into an allegorical rescue of its lost meaning by restoring the fragmentary pieces, it may be that writing can pass through melancholy to turn back on itself, thus allowing the ambivalence of meaning to itself become the manner in which this ambivalence is reinscribed, as Kafka found in parable. In this way, the transformation of melancholy arises when language becomes suspended in the possibility of relation midway between the muteness of its need to speak and the muteness of its endless lament, alongside or parallel to the cadaver, the only mark of finitude that is true to its ambivalence, whose company writing seeks so as to find its own ambivalence.

In his reading of the *Trauerspiel* Benjamin emphasizes the point that the cadaver is never just a *memento mori* but is always a sign of resurrection [UDT: 392/236–7, 405/254]. But Blanchot, as has become evident, takes a more sceptical path, which also seems closer to the ambivalence that pervades Kafka's thought, as the cadaver is not just a mark of death but a mark of its suspension or rupture, of a death that does not end but remains, and so is undecidably present and absent and neither. As such, the cadaver is a figure of dissembling that insists, except that it is no longer a figure and so does not lead to anything; it is simply an image that resembles itself in its own deterioration. For writing to come close to this ambivalence is for it to follow some of the convolutions that Kafka pursued in his rewriting of the story of the Sirens, as it is a question of writing entering into its own deterioration as it becomes an image of language, which is the convergence on non-writing announced in the disaster. This is not to give up on the possibility of the future but to find in the material resistance of the cadaver the conditions for an entirely different mode of writing and thinking historically.

In these aporetic encounters the movement between a language of images and an image of language is struck as both a decision and its suspension and, as a result, the temporality of writing is removed or diverted from the present. Hence, thought also finds its contemporaneity in these encounters, its own counter-time, for in this non-coincidence thought becomes that which 'addresses us in the present most radically, and in that very gesture addresses us from some other place or time which does not belong to the contemporary, but creates a fissure or caesura in temporality itself'. Such is Hill's proposed description of the 'extreme contemporary', which for this reason 'is neither extreme nor contemporary at all' as both words have now become markers of absence from the present.[20] Thus the transformation of thought in the concrete image does not lead to its end or closure, as its removal from the present is never completely decisive or final. Instead, it remains out of step even as it actualizes itself (since its material context also reformulates itself), but in doing so it becomes a gesture, a thing alongside other things, which is to say that thought encounters its own disaster, the empty form of alienation as such and without respite as an estrangement into sheer material finitude. It is worth returning to Hegel here, for his discussion in the *Phänomenologie* of the negativity inherent to the labour of thinking, its sundering and alienation, occurs alongside the first mention of death and also the first mention of the accidental. As he explains, the activity of analysis is to break up an object so that its originary moments can be revealed in and as thoughts, much as Benjamin had suggested.

> But what is *separated* [*dies* Geschiedne], the non-actual itself, is an essential moment; for it is only because the concrete divides itself and turns itself into the non-actual that it is self-moving. The activity of separating is the force and labour of the *understanding*, the greatest and most astonishing or, rather, the absolute power. The circle, enclosed within itself, is at rest and as substance, which sustains its moments, is an immediate and thus not astonishing relation. But that the accidental as such, separated from its surroundings, which is bound and is actual only in its context with others, attains an existence of its own and an isolated freedom, is the tremendous power of the negative; it is the energy of thinking, of the pure I. Death, if we want to so name that non-actuality, is the most fearful, and to hold fast what is dead requires the greatest force.
> PG: 27/18–19 (emphases in the original)

This is the passage that then leads into a description of the life of the spirit that arises out of this tarrying with the negative and endures it, which here finds its form and force in accidental death. Death is the accidental to the degree that the accidental is the arising of separation as such, the flaw or fault that is also its own ridge. For, if we examine this passage closely, it is apparent that there are two sides to the analysis: while the understanding (*Verstand*) separates the concrete through its force and labour, the concrete is also that which divides itself. So, although the understanding can be called the absolute power because it is that which breaks up the concrete, the accidental that is thereby released into its freedom also does so because of the self-division of the concrete, leaving the status of the element or moment that is released uncertain, which is the origin of ambiguity (as word or thing). It is thus that the accidental is death, the loss or end of thought as it passes into the concrete in its errancy, just as death as the break-up of the concrete is that which leads to the emergence of the accidental in its autonomy, its own existence. This is the power of the negative to which thought must keep hold, and that forms the life of the spirit, a life that in maintaining itself in this devastation (*Verwüstung*) cannot always find itself, no matter how long or how closely it seeks to tarry with it; instead, what is found in the autonomy of the accidental is the deterioration of the subject, its endless self-fragmentation. As a result the understanding becomes a thought *of* contradiction, in both senses of the genitive, in its infinity, and so not merely one-sided [PG: 98–9/99].

Considered in this way, film noir indicates the sociopolitical implications of this ambivalence: the uncertain formations that emerge from a broader manifestation of accidental death, and the demands of thinking it. When we examine films like *Quicksand* (Irving Pichel, 1950) or *Where Danger Lives* (Farrow, 1950), in which the remorseless unfolding of accidents leads to a cascade of irreversible and ever increasing deviations, then it is possible, if we exclude their mandatory moral teleology, to see the effects of a concrete and widespread parapraxis. In these cases each action only leads to further false moves and greater mistakes, which may lead to the death or imprisonment of its protagonists (unless they are just as arbitrarily saved), but from the point of view of the materiality of their existences these mistakes also expose the relentless material innovation that its breaching unleashes. This is no more a question of valorizing the materiality at issue than it is of condemning or suppressing it, since from the point of view of the material these deviations are neither good nor bad, positive or negative, but are simply pointless. Kafka's oft-cited statement about the existence of hope (as recalled by Brod) is rarely taken seriously, for it would require an understanding of 'hope' that is not oriented around the human, which in turn would indicate a sense of 'history' that is to be found in the contingent and accidental.[21] If hope is the belief that things will improve, or at least that 'events' have a positive outcome, then without the human it is these aspects of belief and improvement that are lost, just as the notion of the event is also deteriorated, leaving only a sense of errancy. It is then possible to understand how such a thought can cast light on the sense of a pitiless fate that is central to film noir, for in this case it is merely the fact of irreversible change that is being reflected, fate not as a specific and unalterable destination but rather as an eccentric breaching in which change occurs simply as deviation and fragmentation. Alienation becomes the objective material reality of time, in which there is no return other than its own reflection. The mark of fate runs counter to the mark of tradition, such that alienation becomes the non-sense of history, 'the historical outside of history', in Blanchot's words, which is also the disaster [ED: 68/40]. Fate is thus the mark of an exposure to the opacity of the future, its distortion and deferral, which instead leaves the moment open to another form of event.

There is, then, *no* reason to believe that things will get better. As Hegel remarked, what we learn from history is that generally we never learn from history.[22] This is not an excuse for glib pessimism but rather an indication that in thinking historically we come up against an extreme opacity that holds no meaning and bears no revelation. In thinking historically, if this proceeds without the support of ideological positivisms, we come up against that which cannot be known, an absence or emptiness that pervades history and knowledge, which is its lack of reason. And, in encountering this lack, as we seek to think the contingency of a future without reason, thought finds that 'nothing' is revealed as it is.

NOTES

Chapter 1

1 Compare the first and last versions of the poem from the manuscripts, as contained in Friedrich Hölderlin, *Sämtliche Werke Frankfurter Ausgabe 6: Elegien und Epigramme*, ed. D. E. Sattler and Wolfram Groddeck (Frankfurt am Main: Verlag Roter Stern, 1976), 218 and 261, where the end of stanza seven is as follows:

Aber Herzen an Kraft, wie auf weißer Haide Blümlein,	But hearts of strength bloom, as on the white heath
Da es dürr ist; das Grün aber ernähret das Roß	where it is barren; yet greenery nourishes the horse
Und den Wolf, in den Wildniß, aber des Todes denkt Einer	and the wolf in the wild, but one hardly thinks of
Kaum, und der Jugend Haus fassen die Seher nicht mehr.	death, and the house of youth no longer holds the seer.
Aber doch etwas gilt, allein. Die Regel, die Erde.	But still something counts, alone. The rule, the earth.
Eine Klarheit, die Nacht. Das und das Ruhige kennt	A clarity, the night. That and the calm a sensible,
Ein Verständiger wohl, ein Fürstlicherer, und zeiget	more princely one, knows well and shows
Göttliches, ihrs auch sei lang, wie der Himmel und tief.	divinely, they are too long and deep, like the sky.

Groddeck provides an extensive reading of Hölderlin's revisions in *Hölderlins Elegie 'Brot und Wein' oder 'Die Nacht'* (Frankfurt am Main: Stroemfeld Verlag, 2012). In doing so, he presents a version that is perhaps more conclusive than is acceptable considering that no final version was ever produced. While the seventh stanza is revised more heavily than any of the others, the form that Groddeck presents, after Sattler, attempts to combine the lines into one single reading where Hölderlin's manuscripts only show revision after revision.

2   In an essay from 1946 on Malraux, Blanchot writes the following lines:

> There is no way that the revolution can be defeated. It suffers serious setbacks, and the mistakes of its leaders sometimes lead to catastrophes made more difficult in that those who pay are the masses that it claims to liberate. But, whatever the vicissitudes of the movement, it cannot be brought to a halt [*il n'est pas susceptible d'arrêt*]. As it is linked to a whole, to the entire volume of history considered as a real totality, it does not know genuine rest. It is in this way first of all that the revolution is permanent.

See Blanchot, '*L'Espoir* d'André Malraux', in *La Condition critique, articles, 1945–1998*, ed. Christophe Bident (Paris: Gallimard, 2010), 46; trans. Michael Holland as '*Days of Hope* by André Malraux', *Paragraph* 30.3 (2007): 5–6.

3   See Claude Gauteur, *Jean Renoir, la double méprise 1925–1939* (Paris: Les Editeurs Français Réunis, 1980), 184–5. In an interview with Marcel Oms in 1971, published in *Les Cahiers de la cinémathèque* 5 (1972), Carné recalled that Renoir tried to apologize to Prévert by saying that he had not meant to say that the film was fascist, but that the characters had a fascist core (*tripe*). However, Prévert did not see this as an apology. But in his memoirs, *La Vie à belles dents, souvenirs* (Paris: Jean-Pierre Ollivier, 1975), 117, Carné recalls a slightly different phrase – that Renoir had said that the film's characters called for a fascist beating (*trique*). Further details on the background of the film can be found in Edward Baron Turk, *Child of Paradise: Marcel Carné and the Golden Age of French Cinema* (Cambridge: Harvard University Press, 1989), chapter 6. The remark by the unnamed Vichy official is recalled by Georges Sadoul in his *Dictionary of Films*, ed. and trans. Peter Morris (Berkeley: University of California Press, 1972), 299.

4   François Vinneuil [Lucien Rebatet], '*Le Quai des brumes*', *L'Action française* (20 May 1938). See also Christopher Faulkner, 'Theory and Practice of Film Reviewing in France in the 1930s: Eyes Right (Lucien Rebatet and *Action française* 1936–1939)', *French Cultural Studies* 3.8 (1992): 133–55.

5   Pierre Mac Orlan, *Le Quai des brumes* (Paris: Gallimard, 1927), 55–64. For more on this notion, see Roger W. Baines, '*Inquiétude' in the Work of Pierre Mac Orlan* (Amsterdam: Rodopi, 2000), 197–201. This notion can be usefully compared with the form of colonial disorientation described by Jean Paulhan in 'Aytré, who gets out of the habit', in *Progress in Love on the Slow Side*, trans. Christine Moneera Laennec and Michael Syrotinski (Lincoln: University of Nebraska Press, 1994), 77–96.

6   R. [Lucien Rebatet], 'Note de lecture sur *Thomas l'Obscur*', *Je suis partout* 534 (18 October 1941): 8. It is however notable that one of the most positive and substantial reviews of Blanchot's novel would be published by another figure from the extreme right, Thierry Maulnier, who had been Blanchot's friend and colleague for many years. Maulnier was a very astute critic, and he noticed one of the most significant aspects of *Thomas l'Obscur*, which is not emphasized enough: the tension between a language of extraordinary rigour and elegance and a narrative of the most strange and peculiar transformations.

Although he would interpret this tension along Nietzschean lines, as the tension between the Apollonian and the Dionysian, it is important for present purposes as it indicates how Blanchot is pursuing his examination of the limits and possibilities of language along formal and material lines without necessarily synthesizing them, but rather through their mutual negation. See Maulnier, 'Note de lecture sur *Thomas l'Obscur*', *L'Action française* (28 January 1942): 3. In making this reading Maulnier also associates Blanchot with Lautréamont and Giraudoux as part of the revolutionary poetics that Surrealism sought to approach, which is to say that he perceived the politics of Blanchot's poetics.

7   Jean-Paul Sartre, *Situations 1* (Paris: Gallimard, 1947), 140; trans. Chris Turner as *Critical Essays* (London: Seagull Books, 2010), 213. It is often missed that Sartre does not write 'transcendence' but 'transdescendence', a notion derived from the thought of Jean Wahl (as Sartre makes clear). See Wahl, *Human Existence and Transcendence*, ed. and trans. William C. Hackett and Jeffrey Hanson (Notre Dame: University of Notre Dame Press, 2016), 27–8; and my *Aesthetics of Negativity: Blanchot, Adorno, and Autonomy* (New York: Fordham University Press, 2016), 99–100. Charles Maurras was the 'father' of French fascism, and a supporter of Pétain.

8   Sartre, *Situations 1*, 124; *Critical Essays*, 188–9.

9   Alain Badiou, 'The Three Negations', *Cardozo Law Review* 29.5 (2008): 1877–83. Badiou often slips between referring to a principle of contradiction and a principle of non-contradiction. I have clarified this point.

10 This ambiguity is reflected in a comment from the *Enzyklopädie Logik*, where Hegel states that 'number is thought, but it is thought as a being that is completely external to itself. It does not belong to intuition, because it is thought, but it is thought that has the externality of intuition as its determination'; see *Enzyklopädie der philosophischen Wissenschaften im Grundrisse (1830)*, ed. Wolfgang Bonsiepen and Hans-Christian Lucas (Hamburg: Felix Meiner, 1992), §104, 139; *The Encyclopaedia Logic (with the Zusätze)*, trans. T. F. Geraets et al. (Indianapolis: Hackett, 1991), 165. Confirming this point Hegel remarks in *Vorlesungen über die Geschichte der Philosophie I*, ed. Eva Moldenhauer and Karl Markus Michel (Frankfurt am Main: Suhrkamp, 1971), 110; trans. E. S. Haldane as *Lectures on the History of Philosophy 1* (Lincoln: University of Nebraska Press, 1995), 89, that enumeration is a bad method (*schlechte Manier*). Badiou would reject these criticisms, since for him the being of number is unrelated to quanta but is a rational ontological structure that provides its own order and internal determination derived from set theory and Cantorian infinites; see, in particular, his *Number and Numbers*, trans. Robin Mackay (Cambridge: Polity, 2008). Much has been written about Badiou's use of mathematics, and the argument is far from settled as to its pertinence and implications for ontology, but see Burhanuddin Baki, *Badiou's 'Being and Event' and the Mathematics of Set Theory* (New York: Bloomsbury, 2015), for a sympathetic introduction.

11 Gilles Deleuze and Félix Guattari, *What Is Philosophy?*, trans. Hugh Tomlinson and Graham Burchell (London: Verso, 1994), 156–7.

12 Deleuze, *Logique du sens* (Paris: Minuit, 1969), 177–8; trans. Mark Lester as *The Logic of Sense*, ed. Constantin V. Boundas (New York: Columbia University Press, 1990), 151. See also *Difference and Repetition*, trans. Paul Patton (London: Athlone, 1994), 112–13, where the reading of Blanchot in relation to the death drive derives from Deleuze's earlier reading in 'Coldness and Cruelty', trans. Jean McNeil in *Masochism* (New York: Zone Books, 1989), 30–1. Here it is the notion of repetition, particularly as it is found in Sade's writings, which comes to inform his understanding of the death drive, not as a drive towards death but as the inherent failure of all drives to be satisfied that leads to repetition and the ubiquity of death. See also Deleuze's concurrent reading of the crack (*fêlure*) in Zola's *La Bête humaine* in *Logique du sens*, 378–9/326–7, a novel about the inevitability of failure that led to two notable film (noir) versions by Jean Renoir and Fritz Lang.

13 The same formulation is used in Ovid's *Metamorphoses*, trans. David Raeburn (London: Penguin, 2004):

> the whole of nature displayed but a single face, which men have called chaos: a crude, unstructured mass, nothing but weight without motion, a general conglomeration of matter composed of disparate, incompatible elements … Although the land and the sea and the sky were involved in the great mass, no one could stand on the land or swim in the waves of the sea, and the sky had no light. None of the elements kept its shape, and all were in conflict inside one body: the cold with the hot, the wet with the dry, the soft with the hard, and weight with the weightless. (1: 6–9, 15–20)

14 Scott MacDonald, 'Spaces of Inscription: An Interview with Martin Arnold', *Film Quarterly* 48.1 (1994): 2–11. As Arnold explains, he spent eighteen months working on this sequence from *The Human Jungle*, using a handmade optical printer to break it down into 148,000 images that were then pieced together in a 200-page score. *Pièce touchée*, along with later shorts, *passage à l'acte* (1993), and *Alone. Life Wastes Andy Hardy* (1998), can be found on Arnold's *The Cineseizure* (Index DVD 018, 2007).

15 Blanchot, *L'Attente l'oubli* (Paris: Gallimard, 1962), 32; trans. John Gregg as *Awaiting Oblivion* (Lincoln: University of Nebraska Press, 1997), 19. Anthony Abiragi, 'The Measure of the Outside', *Colloquy* 10 (2005): 102–33. I discuss the formal innovations of this work in *Blanchot and the Outside of Literature* (New York: Bloomsbury, 2019), chapter 7.

16 It is worth noting how this approach develops that of Kant's understanding of beauty, in which the free play of the faculties leads to a thought of form as a purposiveness without purpose, which is also a thought of mere futurity, insofar as there is in this free play an effort to find a conceptual form for the object of beauty and thus an opening of the future as that in which such a form may occur. Contemplation of the beautiful would then bear an orientation to the possibility of the future as such, sheer futurity without a specific form. But, as Adorno notes, it is an aspect of art in its modernity

that the pleasure and harmony that Kant finds in the contemplation of the beautiful cannot be separated from the anxiety and dissonance that occurs in the experience of the sublime [A: 53–4/30–1].

17. Omar Robert Hamilton, *The City Always Wins* (London: Faber & Faber, 2017).

18. Gorgias's treatise, *On nonexistence (Peri tou me ontos)*, is lost but comes down to us via Sextus Empiricus' *Against the Logicians*, ed. and trans. Richard Bett (Cambridge: Cambridge University Press, 2005), 15–19.

Chapter 2

1. This thesis was developed by Herder in his *Kritische Wälder* from 1769, primarily in response to Lessing's *Laokoon*, and it became a key part of his thinking of rhetorical force (*Kraft*); see Johann Gottfried Herder, *Selected Writings on Aesthetics*, ed. and trans. Gregory Moore (Princeton: Princeton University Press, 2006), 140–1. Force as such is to be understood as the relation 'through' (*per*), as opposed to 'next to' (*juxta*) and 'after' (*post*), which refer to relations in space or time. This notion makes it possible to grasp how things move into and out of each other in a kind of dialectic of transformation, and so to make sense of the way that language comes to have an effect. Although poetry differs from painting and music in its formations of space and time, it is because it is made up of arbitrary rather than natural signs that the notion of force can be used to explain how the mind can be affected by signs that are not limited to natural associations, and yet are still borne by way of a sensible materiality. The transformations of sense that take place in poetry are articulated further in the fourth *Kritisches Wäldchen*, for while painting, sculpture and music are related to the senses by which they are primarily received (sight, touch and hearing), poetry exists in and beyond these as the 'sense' of the imagination (*Selected Writings*, 285–7). Poetry thus has a major role in Herder's understanding of the aesthetic nature of human thought as it combines the three modes of space, time and force, and reveals how sense, as that which is both obscure and effective, material and abstract, comes to bear on thought without being wholly cognitive. Unfortunately, Christoph Menke's generalization of Herder's thought in *Force: A Fundamental Concept of Aesthetic Anthropology*, trans. Gerrit Jackson (New York: Fordham University Press, 2013), loses its impact to the degree that it distances itself from this specific formation of linguistic signs. The 'force' of poetry, and of aesthetics more generally, is actually less a force than a contagion, as it depends exactly on the undeclared senses and indeterminate pervasion of material signs and their unexpected effects, a rethinking that has been most usefully taken up by Paul de Man in his analyses of the (aporetic) material and temporal experiences of reading.

2. On Heraclitus's thought of converging-diverging, see Charles H. Kahn, *The Art and Thought of Heraclitus* (Cambridge: Cambridge University Press, 1979), 281–6.

3   Char's response to Sartre arose in a piece written for a special issue of *Empédocle* in 1950 and gave rise to an equally strong endorsement from Bataille two months later; see Char, 'Y a-t-il des incompatibilités?', in *Œuvres complètes*, 658–9; Georges Bataille, *Œuvres complètes* XII (Paris: Gallimard, 1988), 16–28; 'Letter to René Char', trans. Christopher Carsten in *Yale French Studies* 78 (1990): 31–43, which also includes Char's original piece.

4   See Kahn, *The Art and Thought of Heraclitus*, 216–27. This thought is at the heart of Derrida's reading of Hegel and François Jacob in *La vie la mort, séminaire (1975–76)*, ed. Pascale-Anne Brault and Peggy Kamuf (Paris: Seuil, 2019).

5   In making this association with the repression of the drives, in all their unsettling necessity and troubling refusal of form, Blanchot is hinting at an alignment between Freud's *Es* and the *il y a*, instead of the more common association of the latter with Heidegger's *Es gibt*. Of course, the notion of an unconscious drive was developed in various ways by Schelling, Hegel and Schopenhauer, alongside the works of early alienists like Esquirol and Pinel, and so does not refer essentially to psychoanalysis but rather to the *sense* of nature as a *material* force. As de Man notes, this idea leads to a significant reversal: 'Far from seeing language as an instrument in the service of a psychic energy, the possibility now arises that the entire construction of drives, substitutions, repressions, and representations is the aberrant, metaphorical correlative of the absolute randomness of language, prior to any figuration or meaning' (*Allegories of Reading* (New Haven: Yale University Press, 1979), 299).

6   Interestingly, Adorno does not see Plato's thought as constituting a metaphysical doctrine of ideas or theory of forms but as pre-metaphysical in its dialectical interrelation (*methexis*) of the sensuous and the ideal; see the 1965 course, *Metaphysik. Begriff und Probleme*, ed. Rolf Tiedemann (Frankfurt am Main: Suhrkamp, 1998), 29–34; trans. Edmund Jephcott as *Metaphysics: Concept and Problems* (Cambridge: Polity, 2000), 16–19. In doing so he separates Socrates' speech from the anamnesis of ontological truth that comprises Platonism, which thereby enables a comparison with Heidegger's reading of the *Phaedrus* in 1937 where a similar revision takes place, but one that remains within the scope of Platonic idealism:

> As soon as man lets himself be bound by being in his view upon it he is removed [*entrückt*] beyond himself, so that he is stretched as it were between himself and being and is outside himself. This elevation-beyond-oneself and being-drawn-towards being itself is *eros*. And only to the extent that being itself is able to unfold 'erotic' power in its relation to man is man capable of thinking about being itself and of overcoming the oblivion of being.

Martin Heidegger, *Nietzsche. Der Wille zur Macht als Kunst*, ed. Bernd Heimbüchel (Frankfurt am Main: Vittorio Klostermann, 1985), 239–40; trans. David Farrell Krell as *Nietzsche: The Will to Power as Art* (New York: Harper

& Row, 1979), 194. While it is intriguing to find Heidegger discussing *eros*, the most significant aspect of this point is that it arises as part of his reading of Nietzsche's aesthetics, that is, he has seen the profound similarity between Nietzsche and Plato on this point but has remained within the ontological idealism of the latter, rather than seeing how far Nietzsche's thoughts disrupt such a combined reading of *eros*, truth and beauty. It is telling that this depiction of *eros* parallels that of his contemporary discussion of the rift (*Riß*) in the work of art as an originary opening of being, whereas Klossowski will pursue the more Nietzschean disruption of such harmony.

7 I have explored this text further in *Aesthetics of Negativity*, 129–33.
8 In Leslie Hill's words, 'If the intermediary demon betrays, it is not because a possibility of transparent communication is being compromised. Betrayal here is not the betrayal *of* an original state of affairs, but betrayal *as* an original state of affairs' (*Bataille, Klossowski, Blanchot: Writing at the Limit* (Cambridge: Cambridge University Press, 2001), 140).
9 Blanchot, 'Cours des choses', *Lignes* 11 (1990): 189; trans. Zakir Paul as 'Course of Things', in *Political Writings, 1953–1993* (New York: Fordham University Press, 2010), 64. These reflections form part of the programme for the *Revue internationale* and were developed in an article first published in Italian in *Il Menabò* 7 (1964), where Blanchot discusses Yuri Gagarin's trip into space in relation to Levinas's ideas about nomadic and pagan thinking; see 'The Conquest of Space', in *Political Writings*, 70–2. While this article may reflect Blanchot's desire to follow Levinas in distancing himself from Heidegger's thought (although he is no closer to Levinas than he is to Heidegger on this point), the place of the earth in Char's writings cannot be assimilated to a 'pagan' ideology, even if Char would later find an affinity with Heidegger.

These ideas were first raised in an article from 1958, 'L'étrange et l'étranger' (*La Condition critique*, 287), which was a review of Colin Wilson's *The Outsider*, about which Blanchot was justifiably scathing, but which formed the occasion for a discussion of the nature of modern alienation (in Marxist terms and otherwise). At the end of the article Blanchot added a footnote recommending Levinas's recently published essay 'La philosophie et l'idée de l'infini' and suggested that there was a link between the notion of alienation, as he had discussed it, and a thought of *déracinement* that was opposed to Heidegger's 'pagan' *enracinement*. There may be several reasons why Blanchot chose to associate his thought with that of Levinas at this time, the first time he has done so since his brief remarks in 'La littérature et le droit à la mort' ten years earlier, but the sense of *déracinement* moves the notion of alienation into a very different sphere of references, as will be discussed in note 18.
10 Although no mention of Heidegger is made in the original article, an explanatory footnote was added when it was reprinted in *L'Espace littéraire*. Unfortunately, this footnote has been omitted from the English translation.
11 Heidegger, *Holzwege*, ed. Friedrich-Wilhelm von Herrmann (Frankfurt am Main: Vittorio Klostermann, 1977), 32; *Off the Beaten Track*, ed. Julian Young and Kenneth Haynes (Cambridge: Cambridge University Press, 2002), 24.

12 Heidegger, *Wegmarken*, ed. Friedrich-Wilhelm von Herrmann (Frankfurt am Main: Vittorio Klostermann, 1976), 267 ff; *Pathmarks*, ed. William McNeill (Cambridge: Cambridge University Press, 1998), 204 ff.

13 Stéphane Mallarmé, *Œuvres complètes II*, ed. Bertrand Marchal (Paris: Gallimard, 2003), 200–1; *Divagations*, trans. Barbara Johnson (Cambridge: Harvard University Press, 2007), 167. For Rodolphe Gasché this passage indicates that Mallarmé sees being in the same way as Heidegger, since both view rhythm as a form of transcendental imprinting; see 'Joining the Text', in *The Yale Critics: Deconstruction in America*, ed. Jonathan Arac et al. (Minneapolis: University of Minnesota Press, 1983), 162–3, as I will show this is a hasty conclusion.

14 Blanchot, *Thomas l'Obscur, nouvelle version* (Paris: Gallimard, 1992), 27; trans. Robert Lamberton as *Thomas the Obscure*, in *The Station Hill Blanchot Reader: Fiction and Literary Essays*, ed. George Quasha (Barrytown, NY: Station Hill, 1999), 67; *Thomas l'Obscur, première version, 1941* (Paris: Gallimard, 2005), 43–4.

15 In the original article that appeared in *Les Temps modernes*, this citation concludes as follows: 'not only an other world, but *the other* of all worlds, that which is always other than the world – and in relation to the object, is the non-object, and in relation to the course of truth, non-truth, and in relation to reality and the historical revelation of being, non-being and nothingness' (*Les Temps modernes* 79 (1952): 1945; emphasis in the original). It is unclear why Blanchot removed these lines when the article was reprinted in *L'Espace littéraire*, although the later essay shows substantial reductions throughout, largely in terms of clarification, but in this instance there is a sense that Blanchot has also moderated his position in relation to Heidegger in omitting these lines.

16 See my *Blanchot and the Outside of Literature*, part II.

17 Kevin Hart has examined Blanchot's 1953 essay on Char in '"I Hear My Destiny in the Rustling of an Oak": Blanchot's Char', in *Understanding Blanchot, Understanding Modernism*, ed. Christopher Langlois (New York: Bloomsbury, 2018), 183–201, in which Blanchot discusses the relation between poetic and prophetic language.

18 Two reviews in particular stand out for their careful and engaged readings: that by art critic Gaëtan Picon in *Critique* in 1956, 'L'œuvre critique de Maurice Blanchot'; and, six months earlier, the essay by Levinas in *Monde Nouveau*, 'Maurice Blanchot et le regard du poète'. Picon's review focuses on the status of the artwork in relation to the world, and although he faults Blanchot for a perspective that aligns the imaginary with nothingness, failing thus to see the depth of the Hegelian critique that underlies Blanchot's thought, he nevertheless draws out much of what is at stake in the unreal nature of the artwork.

Levinas's review of *L'Espace littéraire* provides a perceptive reading of the innovations of Blanchot's work, although in doing so he translates these innovations – exteriority, errancy, obscurity and so on – into a vocabulary of alterity and transcendence, which is not merely foreign to Blanchot's discussion but also misses the manner in which he rejects the onto-theological foundation of such notions. For example, while Levinas makes it clear that the issues of ethics and transcendence are not part of Blanchot's thought, he still interprets him as saying that 'the authenticity of art must herald an order of justice, the slave morality absent from the Heideggerian city', which converges on the privileged ethical imperative incumbent on desert nomads who experience no certainty apart from their encounter with the other; see 'Maurice Blanchot et le regard du poète', *Monde Nouveau* 98 (1956): 17; trans. Michael B. Smith as 'The Poet's Vision', in *Proper Names* (Stanford: Stanford University Press, 1996), 137. Nevertheless, this remains an important essay as it is Levinas's first article on Blanchot as well as being an early realization of the significance of Blanchot's works, for already Levinas has espied the radical degree to which Blanchot has left the 'pagan enrootedness' of the Heideggerian world and placed its key terms in doubt.

This distinction between pagan and nomad thinking forms a key part of Levinas's thought, and as we have seen it also comes to appear in Blanchot's writings. However, this is not only a misleading and confused distinction, but it also derives from a polemical response to Simone Weil's discussion of *enracinement*. Indeed, the manner in which this distinction is employed by Levinas highlights some of his most forceful ethnocentric judgements. After all, the designation of paganism is not philosophical but theological, as Françoise Dastur has pointed out, and, furthermore, it is a wholly derogatory term applied by monotheism to its opponents; see 'Levinas and Heidegger: Ethics or Ontology?', in *Between Levinas and Heidegger*, ed. John E. Drabinski and Eric S. Nelson (Albany: SUNY Press, 2014), 150–1. The distinction seems to have come about in the ideas of early Jewish thinkers in their relation to the ancient worlds of Athens and Rome, whence the further aspect that links paganism to cities and monotheism to the desert (although in Northern Europe paganism is precisely associated with an antipathy to the city, as Heidegger demonstrated). Such a polemic reflects neither the reality of the classical world nor that of modern Europe to which Levinas applies it, in which Heidegger's thought (and non-Jewish thought more generally) is assimilated to paganism and Israel is associated with the 'homeland' of nomadism. Although he was keen to keep his writings on Judaism separate from his philosophical writings, it is apparent that the two are interwoven in Levinas's thought, with ideas passing backwards and forwards between them, making it impossible to consider his 'philosophical' ideas without registering their theological freight.

While there is much justifiable criticism to be made of the *Blut und Boden* rhetoric of the Third Reich, which Heidegger does not distance himself from – even as he also emphasizes the *Unheimlichkeit* of *Dasein*, its essential not-at-homeness – this cannot be taken as emblematic of European or non-Jewish thinking more generally. Moreover, the privileging of Jewish thought over non-Jewish thought is just as problematic as its inverse, especially when the other regime of desert nomads, the Islamic world, is left out. But the distinction between thought that is rooted in a certain place and that which is marked by exile or migration is worth examining as long as this is not mapped onto ethnic or religious distinctions, especially since Zionism has become a nationalist ideology of the most 'pagan' kind, and those that may have been understood as 'pagan' (ancient or modern) are marked just as strongly by the experience of diaspora. It is unfortunate that Blanchot takes up some of these points from Levinas, as his own readings of Heidegger and Weil are far more balanced and subtle, and his thinking of the errancy of the *neutre* is not the same as the nomadism that Levinas reads into it insofar as it is neither an ethnic nor a religious designation.

Levinas's discussion of this distinction arises in an article from 1952, 'Simone Weil against the Bible', in *Difficult Freedom: Essays on Judaism*, trans. Seán Hand (London: Athlone Press, 1990), 133–41, before reappearing in the review of *L'Espace littéraire* and transferring to his more directly philosophical writings in 1957 in 'Philosophy and the Idea of the Infinite', in *Collected Philosophical Papers*, trans. Alphonso Lingis (Dordrecht: Martinus Nijhoff, 1987), 52–3. See also *Totality and Infinity: An Essay on Exteriority*, trans. Alphonso Lingis (Dordrecht: Martinus Nijhoff, 1979), 47; and 'Heidegger, Gagarin and Us', in *Difficult Freedom*, 231–4. As evidence of the confusion of these terms Levinas later revises this distinction by claiming that 'nothing is more enrooted than the nomad', and stating instead that he now prefers the term 'emigrant'; see *Entre Nous: On Thinking-of-the-Other*, trans. Michael B. Smith and Barbara Harshav (New York: Columbia Press, 1998), 117–18.

19 Hölderlin, 'Anmerkungen zur *Antigonä*', in *Sämtliche Werke 5*, ed. Friedrich Beißner (Stuttgart: Kohlhammer, 1952), 270; *Essays and Letters*, trans. and ed. Jeremy Adler and Charlie Louth (London: Penguin, 2009), 330; see also Beda Allemann, *Hölderlin und Heidegger* (Zurich: Atlantis Verlag, 1954), esp. 13–34.

20 Christophe Bident, *Maurice Blanchot: A Critical Biography*, trans. John McKeane (New York: Fordham University Press, 2019), 528. Blanchot cites from 'Germanien' in the epigraph to *La Part du feu* and elsewhere [PF: 65/59, 129–30/128]. On the latter occasion he uses the more conventional translation of 'entre jour et nuit' for Hölderlin's 'zwischen Tag und Nacht', as he does in *L'Espace littéraire*.

21 The same play on the sense of *frayer* is made in Blanchot's concurrent *récit*, *Celui qui ne m'accompagnait pas* (Paris: Gallimard, 1953), 74–5; trans. Lydia Davis as *The One Who Was Standing Apart from Me*, in *The Station Hill Blanchot Reader*, 294.

22 Lucretius, *De rerum natura*, 2: 219–24. Thomas Nail emphasizes the implications of seeing *corpora* as bodies rather than atoms in his *Lucretius: An Ontology of Motion* (Edinburgh: Edinburgh University Press, 2018).

23 Louis Althusser, *Philosophy of the Encounter: Late Writings, 1978–87*, ed. François Matheron and Oliver Corpet, trans. G. M. Goshgarian (London: Verso, 2006), 167–71, 260–4. See also Michel Serres, *The Birth of Physics*, ed. David Webb, trans. Jack Hawkes (Manchester: Clinamen, 2000); Badiou, *Theory of the Subject*, trans. Bruno Bosteels (London: Continuum, 2009), 57–70; Jacques Derrida, 'My Chances: A Rendezvous with Some Epicurean Stereophonies', trans. Irene Harvey and Avital Ronell in *Taking Chances*, ed. Joseph H. Smith and William Kerrigan (Baltimore: Johns Hopkins University Press, 1984), 1–32. Deleuze's early essay, in *Logique du sens*, 311–12/269–70, reads the clinamen in terms of a plurality of independent causes rather than randomness.

Chapter 3

1. Nino Frank, 'Notre scénario romancé, *Le Quai des brumes*', *Pour vous* 498 (1 June 1938): 14. For more on the early usage of the term 'noir', see Charles O'Brien, 'Film Noir in France: Before the Liberation', *Iris* 21 (1996): 7–20; and Thomas Pillard, 'Une histoire oubliée: la genèse française du terme "film noir" dans les années 1930 et ses implications transnationales', *Transatlantica* 1 (2012).

2. In addition to the titles noted here, the following are helpful guides: Dana Polan, *Power and Paranoia: History, Narrative, and the American Cinema, 1940–1950* (New York: Columbia University Press, 1986); Alain Silver and James Ursini, ed., *Film Noir Reader* (New York: Limelight Editions, 1996); Kelly Oliver and Benigno Trigo, *Noir Anxiety* (Minneapolis: University of Minnesota Press, 2003); Edward Dimendberg, *Film Noir and the Spaces of Modernity* (Cambridge: Harvard University Press, 2004); Mark Osteen, *Nightmare Alley: Film Noir and the American Dream* (Baltimore: Johns Hopkins University Press, 2013); Andrew Spicer and Helen Hanson, ed., *A Companion to Film Noir* (Oxford: Blackwell, 2013); Erik Dussere, *America Is Elsewhere: The Noir Tradition in the Age of Consumer Culture* (Oxford: Oxford University Press, 2014); Robert Miklitsch, *The Red and the Black: American Film Noir in the 1950s* (Urbana: University of Illinois Press, 2017).

3. Blanchot's responses to film are not fully known. Jacqueline Laporte recalls seeing Blanchot at a screening of Ingmar Bergman's *The Silence* (1963); see *Cahiers de l'Herne*, 'Maurice Blanchot' (2014): 102; she also mentions his regard for Murnau, Welles, Ophüls and Ozu, as well as for *Les Enfants du Paradis* (Carné, 1945) and *Casque d'Or* (Jacques Becker, 1951). Blanchot also sat on the jury for the prix Réjane in 1938 and 1939, which awarded prizes for young stage and screen actors, the years when poetic realism was at its height. Brief discussions of Blanchot in relation to film noir can be found in Oliver Harris, 'Film Noir Fascination: Outside History, but Historically So', *Cinema Journal* 43.1 (2003): 3–24; and, more broadly, Elisabeth Bronfen, *Night Passages: Philosophy, Literature, and Film*, trans. David Brenner (New York: Columbia University Press, 2013). Mention should also be made to the work of P. Adams Sitney, *Modernist Montage* (New York: Columbia University Press, 1990); and Noël Burch, *Theory of Film Practice*, trans. Helen R. Lane (Princeton: Princeton University Press, 1981), 150–1, who were among the first to attempt to link Blanchot's writings to film studies.

4. Siegfried Kracauer had remarked on the false status of the happy ending in *From Caligari to Hitler: A Psychological History of the German Film* (Princeton: Princeton University Press, 1947), 100–1, where, in relation to *Der Letzte Mann* (F. W. Murnau, 1924), he stated that its happy ending was not merely a satire on what was already a Hollywood convention but, by presenting its resolution in such unbelievable terms, it also indicated that the only alternative to the world of contingency and decline that the film had thus far shown lay in blatant illusion and fantasy, which thus only confirms the initial proposition of the film.

5 Sadoul, 'Films noirs et bilans roses', *Les Lettres françaises* 172 (3 September 1947): 7.

6 Jorge Luis Borges, 'An Overwhelming Film', in *Selected Non-Fictions*, ed. Eliot Weinberger, trans. Esther Allen et al. (London: Penguin, 1999), 259. This line is from G. K. Chesterton's Father Brown story, 'The Head of Caesar' (1913): '"What we all dread most", said the priest in a low voice, "is a maze with *no* centre. That is why atheism is only a nightmare"' (emphasis in the original). Blanchot's comments come from his reading of Borges in *Le Livre à venir* (Paris: Gallimard, 1959), 130; trans. Charlotte Mandell as *The Book to Come* (Stanford: Stanford University Press, 2003), 93.

7 Sartre, 'New Writing in France', *Vogue* 106.1 (1 July 1945): 84–5; and 'Quand Hollywood veut faire penser …', *L'Écran français* 5 (1 August 1945): 3–4, 15. Sartre saw *Citizen Kane* while in New York, over a year before it was released in France, and was not impressed. In his view, cinema should operate in the present tense as a medium of transparent action that the audience can engage in, and so Welles's extensive use of flashback and the sophisticated camerawork and editing that went along with this do not lead to a work that has the vitality and relevance of a novel but simply to a narrative in the past tense. This cinematic error arises out of a more basic political failing, as he says; everything is dead because it is merely an intellectual exercise that is cut off from the masses. (It is significant that Sartre would later claim not to recognize this essay, to such a degree that he would even suggest that it might not have been written by him. As such, it was not reprinted in any of the volumes of *Situations* or his *Écrits*, and only reappeared in his writings in the augmented volume of *Situations 2* in 2012.)

8 Lotte H. Eisner, *The Haunted Screen: Expressionism in the German Cinema and the Influence of Max Reinhardt*, trans. Roger Greaves (Berkeley: University of California Press, 1969), 47–56. As Thomas Elsaesser points out in *Weimar Cinema and After: Germany's Historical Imaginary* (London: Routledge, 2000), 422, Eisner's book is more helpful for what it suggests about contemporary films than as a reading of Expressionist cinema.

9 This essay had originally appeared in English as 'Spengler Today', *Studies in Philosophy and Social Science* 9 (1941): 305–25 (the name that the *Zeitschrift für Sozialforschung* used in exile), while Adorno was living in New York. I will cite from the later *Prismen* version, which includes Adorno's substantial revisions, but, of the passages I cite, only this first one and the later remark about modern art differ from the earlier version.

10 Oswald Spengler, *The Decline of the West, Volume II: Perspectives of World-History*, trans. Charles Francis Atkinson (New York: Alfred A. Knopf, 1928), 100, 102.

11 Royal S. Brown, *Overtones and Undertones: Reading Film Music* (Berkeley: University of California Press, 1994), 121–2.

12 See especially the reviews by Manny Farber in *The New Republic* 111 (24 July 1944): 103; and James Agee in *The Nation* 159 (14 October 1944): 445.

13 Robert B. Pippin's *Fatalism in American Film Noir* (Charlottesville: University of Virginia Press, 2012), concerns itself solely with the epistemological problems of agency: what film noir says about what an individual thinks they know and thinks they can do in any given situation. The films he discusses are then treated as texts that can be decoded to demonstrate these issues. While he makes a strong case for the philosophical importance and singularity of film noir, in many ways agency is the least interesting aspect of these films, since it is not the issue of why characters act as they do but rather the nature of the milieu that they find themselves in, and the implications this has, that make these films distinctive. Subordinating the rest of the complex structure of films noir to concerns about agency loses sight of the historical and material problems they raise in relation to the very possibility of action, especially with regards to the role of contingency, as I have shown in *Double Indemnity*. Pippin's later reading of *Vertigo* in *The Philosophical Hitchcock* (Chicago: University of Chicago Press, 2017) is more extensive but adopts the same approach, which Hitchcock's film only complicates, for although it may offer greater scope for studying the basis for actions it also renders this problem inherently obscure. In general, the issue of agency in film noir has been explored more usefully by Robert von Hallberg in *'The Maltese Falcon' to 'Body of Lies': Spies, Noirs, and Trust* (Albuquerque: University of New Mexico Press, 2015).

14 The dating of *Double Indemnity* is not often remarked upon but its backdating apparently enabled Wilder to show a well-stocked supermarket, rather than one suffering under wartime rationing, thus emphasizing the banality and materiality of the criminals' minds. Equally, 1938 was the last year before the war began, which would have complicated the story unduly, for in the intervening years the very nature of what would constitute an event or an accident would change. The same rationale could lie behind the backdating of *L'Arrêt de mort* and *D'Entre les morts* and oddly both these stories, like *Double Indemnity*, are grounded in erroneous dates from 1938 and 1940. Wilder's film also slips up in mentioning *The Philadelphia Story* (George Cukor, 1940) and a song by Johnny Mercer that only appeared in 1942.

Cain's original story was based on the real case of Albert Snyder, who was killed in Queens in 1927 by his wife and her lover for his insurance money, which, because of its combination of adultery and greed, and the sloppy nature of the crime, became a very sensational story. Cain, and later, Chandler and Wilder, made the story more elegant, which only leads to a greater emphasis on the strangeness of the motivation of the killers. For more on the Snyder case, see Penelope Pelizzon and Nancy West, 'Multiple Indemnity: Film Noir, James M. Cain, and Adaptations of a Tabloid Case', *Narrative* 13.3 (2005): 211–37.

15 J. P. Telotte provides a helpful reading of the deceptive dynamics of Neff's voiceover in *Voices in the Dark: The Narrative Patterns of Film Noir* (Urbana: University of Illinois Press, 1989), 40–56.

16 The sexual tensions between the main characters of the film have led to many psychoanalytical readings, of which the most developed is probably the essay

by Hugh S. Manon, 'Some Like It Cold: Fetishism in Billy Wilder's *Double Indemnity*', *Cinema Journal* 44.4 (2005): 18–43.

17   Raymond Saleilles, *Les Accidents de travail et la responsabilité civile (essai d'un théorie objective de la responsabilité délictuelle)* (Paris: Arthur Rousseau, 1897), 36. Michel Foucault, 'About the Concept of the "Dangerous Individual" in Nineteenth-Century Legal Psychiatry', trans. Alain Baudot and Jane Couchman in *Power*, ed. James D. Faubion (London: Penguin, 2000), 197. Preliminary attempts to develop this reading of the history of insurance have been conducted by François Ewald and Daniel Defert in *The Foucault Effect: Studies in Governmentality*, ed. Graham Burchell et al. (Hemel Hempstead, UK: Harvester Wheatsheaf, 1991), 197–233; and Thomas Lemke, *Foucault's Analysis of Modern Governmentality: A Critique of Political Reason*, trans. Erik Butler (London: Verso, 2019), 216–28. See also Joan Copjec, 'The Phenomenal Nonphenomenal: Private Space in Film Noir', in *Shades of Noir: A Reader*, ed. Joan Copjec (London: Verso, 1993), esp. 167–72.

18   Foucault, 'About the Concept of the "Dangerous Individual"', 200.

19   The phrase is from Ducasse's *Poésies*; see Lautréamont, *Œuvres complètes* (Paris: José Corti, 1961), 362; *'Maldoror' and the Complete Works*, trans. Alexis Lykiard (Cambridge, MA: Exact Change, 1994), 224.

20   *Double Indemnity* was released in Paris at the end of July 1946 as *Assurance sur la mort*. Two weeks later it was reviewed in *L'Écran français* by Jean-Pierre Barrot.

21   Frank, 'Un nouveau genre "policier", l'aventure criminelle', *L'Écran français* 61 (28 August 1946): 8–10; trans. Alain Silver as 'A New Kind of Police Drama: The Criminal Adventure', in *Film Noir Reader 2*, ed. Alain Silver and James Ursini (New York: Limelight Editions, 1999), 15–19. The idea of a 'fantastique social' was developed by Mac Orlan in his essay 'Le fantastique', *L'Art cinématographique* 1 (1926): 1–19, to indicate that the nature of the fantastic had changed in the age of modern industrialization, and that its sources should be sought in the urban world of vice and criminality rather than in any supernatural agencies, a notion that would become central to the poetic realist films of the late 1930s, especially *Le Quai des brumes* (Baines provides a detailed overview of the background of this term in *'Inquiétude' in the Work of Pierre Mac Orlan*, chapters 1 and 2). It is thus significant that Frank should use this term in seeking to describe the new crime films appearing in America in the 1940s, but that he would also place it in quotation marks to indicate the changes its new context had brought.

22   See especially Sheri Chinen Biesen, *Blackout: World War II and the Origins of Film Noir* (Baltimore: Johns Hopkins University Press, 2005), 96–111. Further background on the development of the film can be found in Richard Schickel, *Double Indemnity* (London: BFI, 1992).

23   As has been widely discussed, the ending of the film originally featured Neff's execution in a gas chamber, followed by Keyes's lonely walk away from the execution room. The fact that Wilder removed this ending has often been adduced to a negative audience reaction at the film's previews but, as Jonathan

Auerbach writes, it also provides a more damning closure to the story to have Neff dying in the office; see *Dark Borders: Film Noir and American Citizenship* (Durham, NC: Duke University Press, 2011), 57–89. James Naremore, *More than Night: Film Noir in Its Contexts* (Berkeley: University of California Press, 2008), 81–95, takes the opposing view that the original ending would have provided a grim realization of the widespread Taylorization of life and death.

Auerbach also links the film to the rising issue of white-collar crime, and the ennui of the *Angestellten* that Kracauer had first discussed, which is explored more broadly by Gerd Gemünden in *A Foreign Affair: Billy Wilder's American Films* (New York: Berghahn, 2008). The issue of white-collar crime was just beginning to emerge within criminology in the 1940s, and it says much that the problem of criminality occurring in individuals who are ostensibly successful and securely established in society is still perplexing. However, the idea that crime may be engendered by the same structures that permit of social success, through the emphasis on profiteering and a lack of accountability coupled with a sense that such crimes appear 'victimless', suggests that its likelihood is not merely possible but inevitable, a fact that Wilder's film makes quite clear.

24 Kracauer, 'Hollywood's Terror Films: Do They Reflect an American State of Mind?', in *American Writings: Essays on Film and Popular Culture*, ed. Johannes von Moltke and Kristy Rawson (Berkeley: University of California Press, 2012), 41. This article originally appeared in *Commentary* 2.2 (August 1946): 132–6, at the request of Clement Greenberg. *Commentary* was the journal of the American Jewish Committee and was associated with the Institute for Social Research at Columbia University.

25 Kracauer, 'Hollywood's Terror Films', 44–5. Kracauer's blindness to the implicit socio-historical commentary in these films (*The Dark Corner* and *The Spiral Staircase*, particularly) may be symptomatic of his position as a critic seeking to find explicit responses to contemporary social ills, but it is also evidence of the complexity of film noir that viewers both now and then tend to see only one aspect of what is at work, whether it is in terms of style or pathology, for this one-sided view obscures the integration of these aspects as well as their disparities.

26 Alongside these reflexive moments it is important to recognize the role played within film noir narratives by the parallel discourses of painting, psychoanalysis and music, which tacitly direct our attention back to the visual, dialogic and aural forms of the work. While a large amount has been written on the place of music and psychoanalysis in film noir, the relation with painting is less widely discussed, not just for its effect on the visual appearance of the films but also in terms of the depiction of the role of artists within society; see especially Kent Minturn, 'Peinture Noire: Abstract Expressionism and Film Noir', in *Film Noir Reader 2*, 270–309.

27 This fascinating story has been described by David Jenemann in *Adorno in America* (Minneapolis: University of Minnesota Press, 2007), 128–47. The film was to have depicted an accident in which a woman falls from a

subway train and the subsequent discussions among the other passengers as to whether she was pushed. Following the research conducted at Berkeley the film sought to develop its enquiry indirectly so as to allow multiple viewpoints to develop, which would lead the viewer to consider their own perspectives on the event. Although it was backed by the American Jewish Committee as an examination of anti-Semitism, which allowed Horkheimer and Adorno to gather significant interest in the project, its didacticism ultimately prevented it from becoming a viable product. As Kracauer showed in 'Those Movies with a Message', *Harper's* 196 (June 1948): 567–72 (*American Writings*, 72–81), the manipulative approach of problem pictures like *Crossfire*, *The Long Night* (Anatole Litvak, 1947) and *Boomerang!* (Elia Kazan, 1947) often came to resemble that of the problems they were trying to discuss. Kracauer had in fact helped with the script of *Below the Surface*, along with other writers and scholars, including the anthropologist Margaret Mead.

28 Richard Maltby, 'Film Noir: The Politics of the Maladjusted Text', *Journal of American Studies* 18.1 (1984): 49–71, remains one of the best readings of the difficult problem of assessing the representative status of film noir.

29 Adorno, 'Über epische Naivetät', in *Noten zur Literatur*, ed. Rolf Tiedemann (Frankfurt am Main: Suhrkamp, 1974), 38; trans. Shierry Weber Nicholsen as 'On Epic Naiveté', in *Notes to Literature: Volume I* (New York: Columbia University Press, 1991), 27. This essay was written in 1943 as part of *Dialektik der Aufklärung*.

30 Adorno, 'Über epische Naivetät', 39–40; 'On Epic Naiveté', 29.

31 Irving Howe, 'Hollywood Terror Films Mirror of Social Decay', *Labor Action* 10.37 (16 September 1946): 3.

32 The film gris cycle is a group of thirteen films noir with left-wing leanings that were identified by Thom Andersen in his 1985 article 'Red Hollywood', which has been reprinted with commentaries in Frank Krutnik et al., ed., *'Un-American' Hollywood: Politics and Film in the Blacklist Era* (New Brunswick: Rutgers University Press, 2007), esp. 257–8. It is enough to recall the number of Hollywood figures targeted by the blacklist, and the effects this had on the course of film noir after 1951, to realize the significant level of social critique these films had begun to develop (and Andersen has only selected the most notable ones). For, in place of the tendency to understand criminality in relation to socio-historical structures, later crime films pursued different approaches that focused on the cynical subsumption of the individual into the para-national entity of the criminal syndicate, or the innate foreignness of the criminal individual as an irrational psychopath. In both cases the aetiology of crime is reified. On these points, see in particular Brian Neve, *Film and Politics in America: A Social Tradition* (London: Routledge, 1992); and Jonathan Munby, *Public Enemies, Public Heroes: Screening the Gangster from 'Little Caesar' to 'Touch of Evil'* (Chicago: University of Chicago Press, 1999).

33 Karin de Boer offers a helpful but narrow reading that focuses on the conceptual role of contradiction in 'Hegel's Account of Contradiction in the *Science of Logic* Reconsidered', *Journal of the History of Philosophy*

48.3 (2010): 345–74; while Todd McGowan provides a more expansive reading in *Emancipation after Hegel: Achieving a Contradictory Revolution* (New York: Columbia University Press, 2019), chapter 1. Badiou's account of contradiction in 'The Three Negations' does not treat Hegel's reading in *Wissenschaft der Logik*; indeed, in none of Badiou's readings of Hegel's *Logik* does he concern himself with this chapter in the Doctrine of Essence, although this may be because it had already received considerable attention from Lenin and Mao, among others.

Chapter 4

1 The word used here, *arrête*, is a coinage combining the words for ridge (*arête*) and arrest (*arrêt*). Blanchot does not often use such puns but its occurrence here is clearly fortuitous.
2 Derrida, 'Survivre', in *Parages* (Paris: Galilée, 1986), 159; trans. James Hulbert as 'Living On', in *Parages*, ed. John P. Leavey (Stanford: Stanford University Press, 2011), 139.
3 In addition to the cover copy of *L'Arrêt de mort*, Blanchot also refers to Poe's 'Ligeia' in a contemporary article, 'Du merveilleux' (*La Condition critique*, 123). Jeff Fort has very successfully explored the role of the ghostly woman in Blanchot's *récit* in *The Imperative to Write* (New York: Fordham University Press, 2014), chapter 6.
4 Boileau-Narcejac, *D'Entre les morts* (Paris: Denoël, 1954); trans. Geoffrey Sainsbury as *The Living and the Dead* (London: Hutchinson, 1956). The phrase 'd'entre les morts' is used throughout the 1872 Darby translation of the Bible in reference to the saying, 'resurrection from the dead'. When Hitchcock's film was released in France at the end of 1958 it was given the title *Sueurs froides*, consequently the title of the source book was changed, as was the case with its translation. The dubbed French version of the film also changed the names of two characters: Judy became Lucie, and Midge became Betty.

Hitchcock's decision to set the film in San Francisco makes sense considering he was working in Hollywood and needed somewhere that could combine the wealth of the shipping industry, within which Elster works (like Gévigne in the book), with the distinctive architecture and topography of a bohemian city with its clear elements of style, history and class. The other differences with the book are the inclusion of the character of Midge and the decision to bring the moment of the revelation of Elster's plan to an earlier position in the narrative. Otherwise, the stories are very similar, although Flavières is a more sensitive character than Scottie, more vulnerable to the seductions of the mystery. *D'Entre les morts* also focuses more strongly on the hiatus of the war, which separates the two parts of the narrative and during which Flavières works as a lawyer in Dakar. When he returns to Paris he sees Madeleine in the background of a newsreel report of De Gaulle's arrival in Marseilles, which leads him to look for her there. Much is made of the Orphic dimensions of Flavières's quest: he gives her a lighter inscribed with the motto 'À Eurydice ressuscitée' after rescuing her from the Seine, associates her with his memories of exploring caves in his childhood and persistently views her in terms of images.

5 Hill discusses the peculiar dates in *L'Arrêt de mort* in *Blanchot: Extreme Contemporary* (London: Routledge, 1997), 146–50. See also Bident, *Maurice Blanchot*, 82–7.

6 This way of phrasing is associated with Kafka, as is shown by Hill in *Bataille, Klossowski, Blanchot*, 208–13.

7 See the earlier edition of *L'Arrêt de mort* (Paris: Gallimard, 1948), 148. This version is still available despite the new edition appearing in 1971, so the two differing versions of the ending can be read side by side. Indeed, the only difference between the two versions, aside from the missing epilogue, is the fact that the second version (which was not marked as revised or amended in any way) is no longer called a *récit*, which may or may not be related to its absent ending. Much discussion of this conundrum has been made, but the most important readings are by Pierre Madaule, *Une Tâche sérieuse?* (Paris: Gallimard, 1973); Roger Laporte, 'White Night', trans. Marshall Olds, *SubStance* 14 (1976): 58–66; J. Hillis Miller, *Versions of Pygmalion* (Cambridge: Harvard University Press, 1990), 179–210; and Christopher Fynsk, *Language and Relation: … That There Is Language* (Stanford: Stanford University Press, 1996), 245–71. See also Marie-Claire Ropars-Wuilleumier, 'Film Reader of Text', trans. Kimball Lockhart, *Diacritics* 15.1 (1985): 18–30, for a provocative analysis of how the blind spot in *L'Arrêt de mort* corresponds to that in Alain Resnais's *Hiroshima mon amour* (1959).

8 So extensive has the literature on *Vertigo* become that there are now essays on the history of *Vertigo*-criticism; see Kriss Ravetto-Biagioli, '*Vertigo* and the Vertiginous History of Film Theory', *Camera Obscura* 25.3 (2011): 101–39; and Tim Groves, '*Vertigo* and the Maelstrom of Criticism', *Screening the Past* 32 (2011). Amid the wealth of Marxist, semiotic, psychoanalytical, feminist and structural studies, the most helpful general readings can be found in Robin Wood, *Hitchcock's Films Revisited* (London: Faber & Faber, 1989), 108–30; William Rothman, '*Vertigo*: The Unknown Woman in Hitchcock', in *The 'I' of the Camera: Essays in Film Criticism, History, and Aesthetics* (Cambridge: Cambridge University Press, 1988), 121–40; Katie Trumpener, 'Fragments of the Mirror: Self-Reference, Mise-en-Abyme, *Vertigo*', in *Hitchcock's Rereleased Films: From 'Rope' to 'Vertigo'*, ed. Walter Raubicheck and Walter Srebnick (Detroit: Wayne State University Press, 1991), 175–88; Murray Pomerance, *An Eye for Hitchcock* (New Brunswick: Rutgers University Press, 2004), 214–60; and Katalin Makkai, ed., *Vertigo* (London: Routledge, 2013). Given the importance of the locations in the film some very interesting work has been done on its geography; see Douglas A. Cunningham, ed., *The San Francisco of Hitchcock's 'Vertigo'* (Lanham, MD: Scarecrow Press, 2011).

9 Blanchot, *Celui qui ne m'accompagnait pas*, 41; *The One Who Was Standing Apart From Me*, 279.

10 The work Poe is probably referring to is *Saducismus Triumphatus*, a compendium of writings about the continued existence of witchcraft and other

supernatural activities, published after Glanvill's death in 1680. However, the quotation appears to be Poe's own invention.

11   The place of women in Blanchot's writings deserves a more critical, but also a more sensitive response. It is not the case that women are subjected to certain positions in his writings that treat them only as types, any more than the male characters are; rather, subjectivity as such is rethought on the basis of its distortion in and through literature. Derrida provides a preliminary outline of these issues in 'La loi du genre', in *Parages*; trans. Avital Ronell as 'The Law of Genre', in *Parages*, where he states that Blanchot avoids treating women as mere emblems of the female gender, but as *women*, individual and variable figures, which 'makes an opening for the event, the performance, the aleatory, the encounter' (*Parages*, 278–9/241). Although helpful in the way that it highlights the alterity inherent in encounters for Blanchot, this rethinking is not without its own problems.

12   See Wood, *Hitchcock's Films Revisited*, 111. This point is taken up by James F. Maxfield in 'A Dreamer and His Dream: Another Way of Looking at Hitchcock's *Vertigo*', *Film Criticism* 14.3 (1990): 3–13; and Chris Marker, 'A Free Replay (Notes on *Vertigo*)', in *Projections 4½*, ed. John Boorman and Walter Donohue (London: Faber & Faber, 1995), 123–30, who suggests that the second half of the film is Scottie's dream while he remains in his catatonic state.

13   Hitchcock's explanation of the 'MacGuffin' occurs in his interview with François Truffaut in 1962; see *Hitchcock* (New York: Simon and Schuster, 1984), 138–9. The link with Hegel has been made clear by Mladen Dolar in 'Being and MacGuffin', *Crisis and Critique* 4.1 (2017): 82–101, where he examines the opening of *Wissenschaft der Logik* as one in which nothing is the impulse.

14   Considering the richness and importance of the vertigo motif, it is intriguing to note that the studio was very resistant to Hitchcock using this title. They tried for several months to come up with alternatives and suggested over forty choices that circled around the themes of the woman, the face, the mask, deceit, shadows, time and so on; see Dan Auiler, *'Vertigo': The Making of a Hitchcock Classic* (New York: St. Martin's Press, 1998), 68, 113. The French title is evidence of the mis-step that was avoided by Hitchcock's insistence, but this resistance is also symptomatic of the way that early viewers of the film did not grasp what was significant about it, and failed to recognize the importance of its differences from Hitchcock's other films. A point underlined by the fact that none of his other films ends on such a note of despair, although *The Wrong Man* (1956) comes close, for in both these films the crime is solved but at such a cost that any sense of victory or success is lost. Such a pessimistic mood may have been closer to Hitchcock's own understanding of the ubiquitous grip of crime, but it can only produce a very sombre experience for the viewer, which his commercial instincts otherwise sought to avoid.

15   Herbert Marcuse, *Hegels Ontologie und die Grundlegung einer Theorie der Geschichtlichkeit* (Frankfurt: Vittorio Klostermann, 1932), 109–10; trans. Seyla Benhabib as *Hegel's Ontology and the Theory of Historicity*

(Cambridge: MIT Press, 1987), 97, citing Hegel's *Wissenschaft der Logik* [WL1: 389/550] (emphasis in the original).

16 Useful studies of Hegel's notion of contingency can be found in Stephen Houlgate, 'Necessity and Contingency in Hegel's *Science of Logic*', *The Owl of Minerva* 27.1 (1995): 37–49; and Adrian Johnston, 'Contingency, Pure Contingency – Without Any Further Determination: Modal Categories in Hegelian Logic', *Russian Journal of Philosophy and Humanities* 1.2 (2017): 23–48.

17 Jean Hyppolite, *Logique et existence, essai sur la logique de Hegel* (Paris: Presses Universitaires de France, 1953), 131–2; trans. Leonard Lawlor and Amit Sen as *Logic and Existence* (Albany: SUNY Press, 1997), 102 (emphasis in the original).

18 Foucault, *L'Ordre du discours* (Paris: Gallimard, 1971), 77–8; trans. Ian McLeod as 'The Order of Discourse', in *Untying the Text: A Post-Structuralist Reader*, ed. Robert Young (London: Routledge, 1981), 75. This discussion develops what he had said a year earlier in a eulogy for Hyppolite; see 'Jean Hyppolite, 1907–1968', *Revue de métaphysique et de morale* 74.2 (1969): 131–6. It should be apparent that Foucault is not using 'non-philosophy' in the later technical sense developed by François Laruelle.

19 Blanchot, *Faux pas* (Paris: Gallimard, 1943), 19; trans. Charlotte Mandell as *Faux Pas* (Stanford: Stanford University Press, 2001), 11. See my *Aesthetics of Negativity*, 104–8, for a commentary on these lines.

20 Calum Watt, *Blanchot and the Moving Image: Fascination and Spectatorship* (Oxford: Legenda, 2017), esp. 44–52. Although Watt does not go far enough in showing how Blanchot's thoughts on the image diverge from those of Deleuze and Rancière, his work is an excellent analysis and insightfully pieces together the traits of a possible Blanchotian reading of cinema. This association is not foreign to Blanchot's thought, as there is a significant episode in the first version of *Thomas l'Obscur* where Thomas goes to the cinema and experiences a strange inversion of sense similar to that found in the scene in the photography shop in *Le Très-Haut*; see *Thomas l'Obscur, première version*, 175 ff. This episode is discussed by Crispin T. Lee in *Haptic Experience in the Writings of Georges Bataille, Maurice Blanchot, and Michel Serres* (Oxford: Peter Lang, 2014), 152–9, but unfortunately, despite a detailed reading, he does not link it to the profound physical disturbances of Blanchot's later novel. On the latter, see my *Blanchot and the Outside of Literature*, 56 ff.

Chapter 5

1 Poetic realism has been widely studied, especially in terms of its relation to American noir, but the best analysis remains that by Dudley Andrew, *Mists of Regret: Culture and Sensibility in Classic French Film* (Princeton: Princeton University Press, 1995). See also Ginette Vincendeau, 'Noir Is Also a French Word: The French Antecedents of Film Noir', in *The Movie Book of Film Noir*, ed. Ian Cameron (London: Studio Vista, 1992), 49–58.

2 As Kovács notes, this song was written by Víg as a parody of mournful love songs when he was with the rock group Trabant in the early 1980s, but it has subsequently become very popular [CBT: 152].

3 I have used the subtitles on the DVD of *Damnation* produced by Artificial Eye (ART 249: 2003); unfortunately no details are given as to who made these subtitles. Kovács provides some quotations from the film that he has translated himself, but for the sake of consistency and availability I have remained with those on the DVD.

4 Rancière extends the reference to Bergson by referring to Deleuze's work on the time-image (although neither is mentioned directly) when, in regard to the camerawork of *Damnation*, he states that 'from this point on a Béla Tarr film will be an assemblage of these crystals of time in which the "cosmic" pressure is concentrated. More than all others, his images deserve to be called time-images, images in which duration is made manifest' [BT: 41/34]. But Deleuze's time-image is crystalline because shots of different temporal relations are edited together in it without effacing their autonomy and incommensurability, which makes the actuality of time visible as an interval of becoming, and for which he finds the most concrete examples in the films of Resnais and Ozu. *Damnation* does not operate under this logic at all, since it is not becoming that is made manifest in its long takes but the *Seinesgleichen* of the everyday, as Robert Musil would call it, its continuing existence as the same. If Rancière is attempting to reclaim the notions of duration and time-image from their original contexts (as his critique of Deleuze in *Film Fables*, trans. Emiliano Battista (Oxford: Berg, 2006), 107–23, suggests), then the point is still problematic, since what the long takes in *Damnation* indicate is the endless decay of time, or at most its slow turning on the spot, wherein there is not lived experience but limbo.

   Rancière corrects this point in a recent article, 'Béla Tarr: The Poetics and the Politics of Fiction', in *Slow Cinema*, ed. Tiago de Luca and Nuno Barradas Jorge (Edinburgh: Edinburgh University Press, 2016), 245–60, when he argues that the 'blocks of time' in Tarr's films 'are not crystal images as Deleuze defines them', instead 'they construct time as the lived experience of the possibility or impossibility of movement', but despite this change he then returns to his discussion of time as expectation. This article is reprinted in a major collection edited by Corinne Maury and Sylvie Rollet, *Béla Tarr, de la colère au tourment* (Crisnée: Yellow Now, 2016).

5 Although the context is not film, Adorno usefully states that 'in the long, contemplative look that first unfolds people and things the urge towards the object is always broken, reflected. Consideration [*Betrachtung*] without force, from which all happiness of truth comes, is dependent on the fact that he who considers does not assimilate the object: nearness of distance' [MM: 98/89–90].

6 The process by which music animates the cinematic image is emphasized by Adorno and Eisler in their treatment of film music:

> The bodily image as a phenomenon in itself lacks motivation for movement; only indirectly [*abgeleitet*], mediatedly, do we realize that the

> images are moving, that the reified impression of reality seems to have kept a touch of just that spontaneity that was withdrawn from it by its fixation: that the petrified marker [*Kenntliche*] is testifying to a kind of life of its own. At this point music intervenes, as it were supplying gravity, muscular energy, and a feeling of corporeity [*Körpergefühl*]. It is thus in its aesthetic effect a stimulus of motion, not its reduplication.
>
> KF: 77/52

Despite his criticisms of the culture industry, film is important for Adorno because it is an audiovisual medium, which means that it is uniquely gifted with the possibility of engaging with the divergent trends of the auditory (towards the subjective) and the visual (towards the objective), a contradiction that film music should make productive, rather than trying to obliterate it [KF: 71/48]. Martin Seel pursues this possibility further in his 'Sitting Unobserved: Adorno's Outline for an Aesthetics of Cinema', trans. Steven Lindberg in *Adorno: The Possibility of the Impossible*, ed. Nicolaus Schafhausen (Berlin: Lukas & Sternberg, 2003), 25–30.

7   In general, Rancière is insensitive to the fact that the films directed by Tarr are not *auteur* pieces, quite the opposite; Tarr is committed to the collaborative practices developed in his early works and *Damnation* is clearly introduced as a film by Krasznahorkai, Medvigy, Pauer, Víg, Hranitzky and Tarr.

8   One of the earliest responses to Tarr's works came from Jonathan Rosenbaum, who in 1990 wrote in relation to *Damnation* that 'the story and the mise en scène are constructed in counterpoint to one another, like the separate melodic lines in a fugue', so that the space and time of the film is constructed as much by the movements of the camera and soundtrack as it is by those of the characters and plot; see *Placing Movies: The Practice of Film Criticism* (Berkeley: University of California Press, 1995), 57–8. Hence, what we are watching is not the movements of the characters per se but a specific mise en scène in which the characters play only one part.

9   As Miriam Hansen points out in *Cinema and Experience: Kracauer, Benjamin, Adorno* (Berkeley: University of California Press, 2012), 207–50, Adorno raises three major problems for an aesthetics of film (arising out of the falsely natural analogies between photography and objectivity, editing and temporality, and sound and image): first, the sense in which film's susceptibility to the material world facilitates a non-critical immersion; second, the manner in which visual montage becomes naturalized as a convention of narrative disruption; and third, the way that the construction of image-sequences operates like the instructive codes of writing. What is significant about *Damnation* is the way that the relation between image and soundtrack disrupts all three of these modes through which film risks becoming a commodity.

It is notable, albeit unfortunate, that recent attempts to discuss the emergence of 'slow cinema', as is exemplified by Tarr's films, have failed to respond to these three problems, finding instead that the slowness of these films gives rise to a sense of wonder or contemplation that ignores the commoditization inherent in such modes. See, for example, Ira Jaffe, *Slow Movies: Countering* the *Cinema of Action* (New York: Wallflower Press, 2014); and Lutz Koepnick, *The Long Take: Art Cinema and the Wondrous* (Minneapolis: University of Minnesota Press, 2017). The problem with categories like wonder is their lack of critical capacity, as can be seen in Koepnick's discussion of Tarr's *Werckmeister Harmonies*. For while he recognizes the film's sociopolitical commentary, as well as its meaningless realism, he retreats from these points (and their implicit tension) to claim that the film draws the viewer into a different mode of experience, a new form of perception and of time, which leads to mere contemplation of its mystery, a simple vicarious experience of difference, without content.

10 This is the point that Adorno will take up in his later sketch, 'Filmtransparente', in *Ohne Leitbild*, ed. Rolf Tiedemann (Frankfurt: Suhrkamp, 1977), 355; trans. Thomas Y. Levin as 'Transparencies on Film', in *The Culture Industry*, ed. J. M. Bernstein (London: Routledge, 1991), 180. See also Nicole Brenez, 'T. W. Adorno, Cinema In Spite of Itself – but Cinema All the Same', trans. Olivier Delers and Ross Chambers, *Cultural Studies Review* 13.1 (2007): 70–88, for a useful overview of the ways in which Adorno thinks film may avoid this potential trap.

11 On this point Tarr is very clear: what we see in *Damnation* is what is actually there in these dilapidated former mining towns. On the other hand, Pauer provides a fascinating insight into how this realism was constructed out of many different locations, such that what we see is not anywhere in particular, but everywhere [CBT: 62–3].

12 The deliberately artistic quality of the film also indicates its cultural and historical context, as Kovács details. For example, there is the conspicuous presence of figures from the Hungarian underground artworld, like Pauer (who will provide the set and costume design, and also play the barman, a role he will reprise with variations in the remainder of Tarr's films up until *The Man from London* (2007)), Krasznahorkai and Víg. But there is also the figure of the young man who dances on his own at the end of the long dance scene, who is explicitly citing a similar dance he had performed in a short film by László Najmányi, *The Emperor's Message* (1975), and whom Tarr hired for that purpose [CBT: 70]. It is telling then that *Damnation* would be roundly condemned by Hungarian critics when it was released but would become a success on the international film festival circuit, and would subsequently become very influential for later Hungarian filmmakers.

13 For Jean-Luc Godard's comments on tracking shots, see the discussion of *Hiroshima mon amour* in Jean Domarchi et al., 'Hiroshima, notre amour', in *Cahiers du cinéma, the 1950s: Neo-Realism, Hollywood, New Wave*, ed. Jim Hillier (London: Routledge, 1985), 62. Tarr refers to Godard in Kovács [CBT: 53]. It is as such that the techniques of Tarr and Medvigy do not converge on the apparent independence of camera movement attempted by Lars von Trier through the 'Automavision' technique developed for *The Boss of It All* (2006).

14 Rancière is recalling the letter that Flaubert wrote to Louise Colet in January 1852 in which he notes that prose bears a style that is absolute insofar as it can say anything or nothing. This discovery is central to Rancière's notion

of the aesthetic regime of art and its displacement of the representational regime, which he discusses especially in *Mute Speech*, trans. James Swenson (New York: Columbia University Press, 2011) and *The Politics of Literature*, trans. Julie Rose (Cambridge: Polity, 2011). As Rancière shows, the apparently unadorned nature of prose, which grants it the ability to say anything, bears an absolute status that is contradictory, insofar as its lack of rhetorical hierarchy is politically democratic but linguistically material, which is then taken up in the divergent tendencies of writers like Zola and Mallarmé. In translating this idea from literature to cinema, in relation to Tarr, Rancière drops the nuances of this analysis in favour of an absolute vision whose sole quality is that of revealing the *durée* of a world by abstaining from any plot, blurring the internal tensions of Flaubert's discovery and obscuring its material basis.

Although his reading of Tarr is hampered by this lack of depth, in *Film Fables* Rancière goes into more detail on how his understanding of the differing regimes of art operates in relation to film. The aesthetic regime of film does not surpass the representational regime of theatre simply by displacing dramatic plotlines with a sensitivity to materiality, as that would suggest that cinema is subsumed into the aesthetic, which is clearly not the case. Instead, the passivity of the camera's gaze, which opens it up to the materiality of the audiovisual, also renders it vulnerable to market forces that draw it back into a representational framework. So the task for the artistic filmmaker is to counter this passivity by emphasizing the activity of the machinic gaze through montage or, as we have seen, obtrusive camera movements, or even through a revived but transformed dramatic narrative (in the Brechtian tropes adopted by Fassbinder or Trier, or the reductions deployed by Bresson or Haneke). There is thus no simple teleology to this dialectic as the aesthetic may have to go by way of the representational in order to counter it, which entails its own countering by the representational, in which neither achieve dominance.

Despite this potential, Rancière's model still lacks the subtlety of Adorno's understanding of aesthetic material because it lacks a worked-out dialectic of natural history that would situate artworks in their contexts, and because his attention to the antagonism of the two regimes omits those aspects of inassimilable negativity that would destabilize their dialectical interaction. Ultimately, there is too little attention paid to how the matter of the aesthetic and the representational assist and resist conceptualization, which only a thorough and careful analysis of particular works can reveal. As a result, his analysis of the two regimes remains at the level of narrative affect, rather than seeking, or being able, to understand the film's construction as a work.

15 It is significant that both Blanchot and Bazin refer to the peculiarity of images that are made by taking a physical impression of objects, like the Turin Shroud or the veil of Veronica, as is mentioned in *L'Arrêt de mort*:

> On the wall of his office there was an excellent photograph of the Turin Sudario, a photograph in which he saw two images superimposed on one another: one of Christ and one of Veronica; and as a matter of fact I distinctly saw, behind the figure of Christ, the features of a woman's

face – extremely beautiful, even magnificent in its strangely proud expression.

AM: 19–20/136–7

Conversely, Bazin wrote in 1945 that 'the Turin Shroud realizes the synthesis of the relic and the photograph', and while cinema is the 'veil of Veronica on the face of human suffering', photography achieves this effect because it takes an impression of an object in the same way as a death mask [QC: 14/14, 34/163]. There is little of substance that can be made of the relation between Blanchot and Bazin, despite their contemporaneity, but what is of interest is the way that their thoughts on the image, and its relation to space, time and materiality, allow for a mutually informing approach to cinematic and literary works. Something of this understanding can be grasped when it is recalled that the veil of Veronica refers to a cloth that was given to Jesus as he carried the cross up to Golgotha, so that he could wipe the sweat and blood from his face, which means that it records an impression of Jesus' face, as Bazin notes, not Veronica's, as Blanchot writes. However, the cloth that Veronica provided was her own veil, which would suggest that in Blanchot's reading it had also recorded the outlines of her own face, perhaps retroactively reproduced as it absorbed the marks of Jesus' face, although, of course, this has nothing to do with the Turin Shroud. The photograph seen in *L'Arrêt de mort* is thus a very strange artefact as it is not an image of the veil of Veronica or the Turin Shroud, but something else that seems to merge the two together. That Blanchot refers to the Turin Sudario rather than the Turin Shroud would seem to confirm this conflation, since a *sudarium* is a face cloth or veil, whereas a shroud would be called a *sindon*. (Kevin Hart, *The Dark Gaze: Maurice Blanchot and the Sacred* (Chicago: University of Chicago Press, 2004), 169–70, discusses this point but does not recognize the deliberate conflation.) But, as Bazin pointed out, the Turin Shroud is not just an image of a past reality, a photograph, it is also its material instance or remains, a relic. Such is the confusion borne by literary and cinematic images that it casts doubt on whether the image is of something else or of itself. The figure of Veronica becomes a central part of Madaule's response to *L'Arrêt de mort* in *Véronique et les chastes* (Dijon: Ulysse, 1988); see also his correspondence with Blanchot, *Correspondance 1953–2002* (Paris: Gallimard, 2012).

16 Adorno, *Ästhetische Theorie*, ed. Gretel Adorno and Rolf Tiedemann (Frankfurt: Suhrkamp, 1971), 191–2; trans. Robert Hullot-Kentor as *Aesthetic Theory* (Minneapolis: University of Minnesota Press, 1997), 126–7.

Chapter 6

1 Robert Burton, *The Anatomy of Melancholy*, ed. Thomas C. Faulkner et al. (Oxford: Clarendon Press, 1989), 7.

2 Benjamin's source for this story was the 1924 edition of Pushkin's *Anekdoten und Tischgespräche*, edited by Johannes von Günther, where the clerk

who enters Potemkin's chambers is called Petuschkow (after the Russian Petushkov); see Benjamin, *Gesammelte Schriften II*, ed. Rolf Tiedemann and Hermann Schweppenhäuser (Frankfurt am Main: Suhrkamp, 1977), 1271; Aleksandr Pushkin, 'Table-Talk', trans. Mary Hobson in *The Complete Works of Aleksandr Pushkin*, vol. 15 (Downham Market, UK: Milner & Co., 2003), 101. That Benjamin changed this name to Schuwalkin (perhaps from *Schalke*, meaning 'rogue'), thereby repeating the act of re-signing the text, is perhaps in response to the appearance of this anecdote in Bloch's *Spuren* in 1930, where the name of the clerk is countersigned with the closer and perhaps accidental variation of Petukow. As Benjamin complained in a letter to Scholem in 1929, Bloch's forthcoming volume contained much that had been 'borrowed' from his own as yet unpublished writings; see Ernst Bloch, 'Potemkin's Signature', in *Traces*, trans. Anthony A. Nassar (Stanford: Stanford University Press, 2006), 88–9; Benjamin, *Selected Writings: Volume 2 1927–1934*, ed. Michael W. Jennings et al. (Cambridge: Harvard University Press, 1999), 834.

Carol Jacobs thinks the opposite, for although she mentions the fact that Benjamin had referred to Pushkin's anecdote in his first hashish protocol in December 1927, she suggests that it was Benjamin who had borrowed the story from Bloch; see *In the Language of Walter Benjamin* (Baltimore: Johns Hopkins University Press, 1999), 122–3. This should only remind us of the difficulty of determining the author, and thus the status, of a signature, since it does not bear any verifying mark of provenance (without countersigning it further) but merely presents itself as its own authority, the prosaic mark of fate that has to be borne come what may. Pushkin's story has no greater authority, as it was based on a popular story that circulated in St. Petersburg during the 1820s and 1830s along with many others that featured Potemkin, and even Petushkov, who, bearing a name that means 'cockerel' (much like Pulcinella in the Commedia dell'arte), appears to be a comic type common to these stories.

3 Kafka, *Nachgelassene Schriften und Fragmente II*, ed. Jost Schillemeit (Frankfurt am Main: Fischer, 1992), 532; 'On Parables', in *The Great Wall of China and Other Short Works*, trans. Malcolm Pasley (London: Penguin, 1991), 184. David Schur discusses this piece in *The Way of Oblivion: Heraclitus and Kafka* (Cambridge: Harvard University Press, 1998), 196–211; see also Henry Sussman, 'The Herald: A Reading of Walter Benjamin's Kafka Study', *Diacritics* 7.1 (1977): 42–54, who examines the indifference that arises from the reversals of parable.

4 See, for example, the extensive analysis by Gasché in 'Kafka's Law: In the Field of Forces between Judaism and Hellenism', *MLN* 117.5 (2002): 971–1002.

5 Gershom Scholem, ed., *The Correspondence of Walter Benjamin and Gershom Scholem 1932–1940*, trans. Gary Smith and Andre Lefevere (Cambridge: Harvard University Press, 1989), 123, 127, 135–6.

6 Part of the reason why Benjamin wants to avoid the concept of the Law is that he feels that it removes the parable-character of parables and leaves them as uninterpretable symbols. The cloudiness of the parables is instead better understood through their gestures, as Adorno describes in his 1953 essay on Kafka, where he insists that the reader should pursue 'the incommensurable,

opaque details, the blind spots. That Leni's fingers are connected by a web or that the executioners look like tenors is more important than the excursus on the Law'. As he goes on to show, such gestures 'are the traces of experience that become covered over by signification', for the 'gesture is the "So it is", while language, whose configuration should be truth, as broken, is untruth'. Thus, these gestures need to be interpreted, for only then will the ambivalent image of fate light up within them [P: 258–60/248–9]. These points are extended from those Adorno had raised in a letter responding to Benjamin's essay, in which he remarked that there is more than merely 'cloud' to Kafka's parables, instead 'they are to be thoroughly dialecticised', which 'must remain the innermost intention of any interpretation of Kafka'; see Adorno and Benjamin, *The Complete Correspondence 1928–1940*, ed. Henri Lonitz, trans. Nicholas Walker (Cambridge: Polity, 1999), 69; see also Werner Hamacher, *Premises: Essays on Philosophy and Literature from Kant to Celan*, trans. Peter Fenves (Stanford: Stanford University Press, 1996), 294–336; and Samuel Weber, *Benjamin's -abilities* (Cambridge: Harvard University Press, 2008), 202–8.

7 Hölderlin, letter to Casimir Ulrich Böhlendorff, 4 December 1801, *Sämtliche Werke*, vol. 6, ed. Friedrich Beißner (Stuttgart: Kohlhammer, 1954), 426; *Essays and Letters*, 208.

8 Scholem claimed that the notion of a slight deviation originated with himself but he also notes that it appeared in Bloch's *Spuren*, like the story from Pushkin; see *The Correspondence of Walter Benjamin and Gershom Scholem*, 123. Adorno also recognized his own thoughts in this idea, for in his letter to Benjamin on the Kafka essay he speaks in similar terms of the possibility that 'almost nothing has made everything well again', a line from the libretto for his unfinished opera *Der Schatz des Indianer-Joe*, which Benjamin had heavily criticized earlier in that year. The significance of this point is that this convergence of political and mystical thought on the nature of radical change suggests that its imperceptible quality is a mark of its uncertainty and unpredictability, so it can only be prepared for, perhaps endlessly. Such a quality forms the 'cloudy spot' of the parables, the gesture that might realize their non-identity, but only insofar as they are not identified as parables.

9 Kafka, *Nachgelassene Schriften und Fragmente II*, 40–2; 'The Silence of the Sirens', in *The Great Wall of China and Other Short Works*, 101–2. In contrast to Kafka's account, the readings provided by Adorno and Blanchot of Odysseus's encounter with the Sirens seem almost conventional. As Vivian Liska has shown in 'Two Sirens Singing: Literature as Contestation in Blanchot and Adorno', in *The Power of Contestation: Perspectives on Maurice Blanchot*, ed. Kevin Hart and Geoffrey H. Hartman (Baltimore: Johns Hopkins University Press, 2004), 80–100, both Blanchot and Adorno criticize Odysseus for his refusal to allow himself to experience the power of the Sirens' song (understood in terms of the power of literature or myth), which exemplifies its subordination to instrumental thought, but both then find that this failure is recouped in the *Odyssey* itself, in which the power of the song persists even as its author disappears, and persists crucially in the secular but still potent form of prose or, for Blanchot, the *récit*. On this account, Kafka's version has

collapsed these two levels into one so that it is not possible to discern where the failure of one approach merges with the success of the other.

10 Allen, *Aesthetics of Negativity*, 109–10.

11 Benjamin is referring to Kafka's tale 'Das nächste Dorf'; see *Drucke zu Lebzeiten*, ed. Wolf Kittler et al. (Frankfurt am Main: Fischer, 1994), 280; 'The Next Village', in *The Transformation and Other Stories*, trans. Malcolm Pasley (London: Penguin, 1992), 174, which reads in its entirety: 'My grandfather used to say: "Life is astonishingly short. When I look back now it is all so condensed in my memory that I can hardly understand, for example, how a young man can decide to ride over to the next village, without his being afraid – quite apart from unfortunate accidents – that the whole span of a normal happy life is far from being adequate to such a ride."'

12 For the sake of clarity, I should add that my use of 'parapraxis' does not refer to Freud. As is well known, parapraxis was the word James Strachey and Alan Tyson used to translate Freud's term *Fehlleistung* (failed act) in their 1960 translation of *Zur Psychopathologie des Alltagslebens*. In its popular usage, parapraxis has come to mean a (Freudian) slip of the tongue, whereas in Freud's sense of the term *Fehlleistung* refers to any action in which the failure of one intention and the success of another combine within the same performance, whether in reading or writing, listening or speaking, or in other actions. While my use of parapraxis bears some similarity with this understanding, it is based on the more literal sense of a deviation from the modes of ordinary praxis, without regard for any speculative unconscious intentions. Sebastiano Timpanaro, *The Freudian Slip: Psychoanalysis and Textual Criticism*, trans. Kate Soper (London: Verso, 1976), provides a much-needed critique from a Marxist and philological point of view, but despite the self-evidently tendentious nature of Freud's thought on this point the notion of *Fehlleistungen* remains relatively undiscussed.

13 Benjamin, *Das Passagen-Werk*, ed. Rolf Tiedemann (Frankfurt am Main: Suhrkamp, 1982), 577–8; *The Arcades Project*, trans. Howard Eiland and Kevin McLaughlin (Cambridge: Harvard University Press, 1999), 462–3.

14 Blanchot, *Le Livre à venir*, 13; *The Book to Come*, 6–7. As Walter Strauss has noted in 'Siren-Language: Kafka and Blanchot', *SubStance* 14 (1976): 18–33, there is a striking resemblance between Blanchot's understanding of the *récit* and the tradition of the German *Novelle*. See, in particular, Martin Swales, *The German 'Novelle'* (Princeton: Princeton University Press, 1977), 19–58, who provides a careful examination of how the *Novelle* evolved as a narrative that attempted to deal with the singularity of the event.

15 Benjamin, *Gesammelte Schriften I*, ed. Rolf Tiedemann and Hermann Schweppenhäuser (Frankfurt am Main: Suhrkamp, 1974), 694; *Selected Writings: Volume 4, 1938–1940*, ed. Michael W. Jennings (Cambridge: Harvard University Press, 2003), 390. Benjamin's theses on the concept of history were originally published in French, in the same issue of *Les Temps modernes* that featured Blanchot's long article on Sade, so it is likely that Blanchot knew them, especially considering his contemporary interest in revolutionary thought.

16 In a letter to Kracauer in May 1930, Adorno complained about Benjamin's prologue to the *Trauerspiel* study, and in particular its 'blatant, historically oblivious, and in the end veritably mythological Platonism, which not by accident must take frequent recourse to phenomenology', and, according to Adorno, Benjamin later conceded these points in conversation with him, cited in Gary Smith, 'Thinking through Benjamin', in *Benjamin: Philosophy, History, Aesthetics*, ed. Gary Smith (Chicago: University of Chicago Press, 1989), xxvii and xli. However, this did not prevent Adorno from recognizing the major significance of Benjamin's study, as he taught a course on it in the summer of 1931 and again the following winter, providing the link between his first public lectures on the actuality of philosophy and the idea of natural-history; see 'Adornos Seminar vom Sommersemester 1932 über Benjamins Ursprung des deutschen Trauerspiels. Protokolle', *Frankfurter Adorno Blätter* 4 (1995): 52–77. But most important of all, from the perspective of Adorno's later development, was his study of Kierkegaard, which, as both Benjamin and Scholem recognized, effectively translated the methods and themes of Benjamin's book into an analysis of the nineteenth-century bourgeois intellectual; see Adorno and Benjamin, *Complete Correspondence*, 20–1. It is very revealing then that it was Horkheimer who accepted this work as Adorno's *Habilitationsschrift*, since he had been involved in rejecting Benjamin's *Trauerspiel* study as his *Habilitationsschrift* six years earlier. (This note revises the one in the first version of this essay.)

17 Benjamin refers here to one of his earlier papers, 'Die Aufgabe des Übersetzers'. In this piece translation is the exemplary mode in which 'afterlife' is to be understood, but it should be noted that Benjamin uses three terms to characterize this process – *Fortleben*, *Überleben* and *Nachleben* – which emphasize the different aspects of, respectively, living on, survival and afterlife; see Benjamin, *Gesammelte Schriften IV*, ed. Rolf Tiedemann and Hermann Schweppenhäuser (Frankfurt am Main: Suhrkamp, 1982), 9–21; *Selected Writings: Volume 1 1913–1926*, ed. Marcus Bullock and Michael W. Jennings (Cambridge: Harvard University Press, 1996), 253–63.

18 Here again Benjamin is drawing upon earlier work, this time it is his 1916 sketch 'Über Sprache überhaupt und über die Sprache des Menschen', in which the essence of language is understood to be its communicability and what it communicates is itself; see *Gesammelte Schriften II*, 140–57; *Selected Writings: Volume 1*, 62–74. This enables Benjamin to make the transition from Adam's pure language of names to the decadent status of modern languages, for in this communication language loses itself and becomes a play of mourning.

19 As is explained in Cathy Caruth, 'An Interview with Jean Laplanche', in *Topologies of Trauma: Essays on the Limit of Knowledge and Memory*, ed. Linda Belau and Petar Ramadanovic (New York: Other Press, 2002), 104–6, the complex *Nachträglichkeit* of trauma operates both forwards from and backwards to its absent origin, thereby persistently calling for and yet undermining any narrative response. (Many thanks to Anna Johnson for pointing out this very cogent discussion.) Caruth's *Unclaimed Experience: Trauma, Narrative, and History* (Baltimore: Johns Hopkins

University Press, 1996), 25–56, focuses on this aporia in a reading of *Hiroshima mon amour* as an attempt to respond to trauma by way of its recitation.

20 Hill, *Blanchot*, 224.

21 Max Brod recalls a conversation from the end of February 1920 in which Kafka said that 'we are nihilistic thoughts arising in God's head' on one of his bad days. Brod attempts to relate this idea to Gnosticism, but Kafka rejects it. Instead, in more Hegelian terms, considering what is said about *Wissenschaft der Logik* being the exposition of God before the creation, such nihilistic thoughts would refer to the *Schlecht* infinite, the hopeless unravelling of absolute knowing. This conversation was first published in an article by Brod, 'Der Dichter Franz Kafka', *Die neue Rundschau* 32.1 (1921): 1210–16, and then appeared in a slightly different version in his biography of Kafka in 1937. Benjamin cites from the first version in his article on Kafka [GS2: 414/798].

22 Hegel, *Vorlesungen über die Philosophie der Weltgeschichte*, ed. Karl Brehmer et al. (Hamburg: Felix Meiner, 1996), 10; *Lectures on the Philosophy of World History, Volume I: Manuscripts of the Introduction and the Lectures of 1822–1823*, trans. Robert F. Brown and Peter C. Hodgson (Oxford: Oxford University Press, 2011), 138. On this point see the very interesting reading by Frank Ruda in *Abolishing Freedom: A Plea for a Contemporary Use of Fatalism* (Lincoln: University of Nebraska Press, 2016), chapter 4.

INDEX

Abiragi, A. 16, 150
accidents 4, 44, 45, 48, 53, 56, 57–9, 60, 64–6, 70, 72, 73, 74, 79, 80, 86, 88, 89, 91–3, 98, 100, 102, 103, 105, 116, 127, 131, 143–4
Adorno, T. W. 26–7, 38, 49, 55–6, 70–2, 118, 119, 125, 126, 131, 138, 150–1, 152, 158, 161–2, 167–8, 169, 170, 172–3, 175
alienation 4, 44, 45, 48, 49, 50, 51, 54, 56, 57, 60, 70, 72, 73, 74, 101, 102, 114, 125, 143, 144–5, 153
Allemann, B. 41, 156
Althusser, L. 11, 44–5, 156
Aristotle 8–9, 32, 45
Arnold, M. 14–15, 150
artwork 30, 31, 34, 36–9, 72, 154, 170

Badiou, A. 8–12, 25, 34, 100, 149, 163
Baines, R. W. 148, 160
Bataille, G. 39–40, 42, 152
Bazin, A. 123–4, 170–1
Benjamin, W. 128–40, 142, 171–2, 175
Bergson, H. 115–16, 123, 167
Blanchot, M. 1, 4, 5, 7–8, 9–12, 15–17, 21–6, 30–44, 49, 53, 54, 77–89, 94–6, 100, 102, 103, 104–6, 127, 128, 130, 134–6, 141, 142, 145, 148–9, 150, 152–8, 163–6, 170–1, 173, 174
Bloch, E. 172, 173
Boileau, P. 81, 163
Borde, R. 49–54, 67
Borges, J. L. 53, 158
Brod, M. 144, 176
Burton, R. 127, 171

Camus, A. 41, 65
Carné, M. 4–8, 47–8, 107, 123, 148

Char, R. 4, 17, 22–6, 29–31, 33, 35–6, 38, 42–3, 135, 152, 153, 154
Chaumeton, É. 49–54, 67
Chesterton, G. K. 158
chiaroscuro 1, 54–5, 57
clinamen 44, 84, 99, 156
contingency 1, 4, 6, 17, 19, 29, 30, 35, 44, 45, 51–4, 59, 60, 64, 66, 67, 72–5, 82, 86, 88, 89, 91, 93, 94, 100–3, 120, 124, 128, 144, 145, 157, 159, 166
contradiction 9–10, 14, 24, 25, 29, 49, 52, 54, 55, 72, 73–5, 86, 97, 102–3, 118, 135, 144, 149, 162–3, 168, 170
criminality 30, 51, 52, 53, 65, 66–7, 73, 100–1, 160, 161, 162

Damnation (Tarr, 1987) 4, 70, 107–26, 167–9
Deleuze, G. 12–13, 78, 100, 149–50, 156, 167
De Man, P. 151, 152
Derrida, J. 44, 78–9, 152, 156, 163, 165
desire 4, 23, 25–30, 42, 51, 61, 63, 64, 74, 82, 83, 85, 104, 113, 120
Diana/Actaeon 28, 64, 98
disaster 5, 10, 12, 14, 28, 29, 30, 34, 49, 83, 93, 99, 100, 103–5, 130, 142, 143, 145
Double Indemnity (Wilder, 1944) 4, 52, 57–68, 73–5, 159, 160
drives 13, 26, 150, 152
Ducasse, I. 67, 160

écart 33, 39, 42, 43–4, 85
Eisler, H. 70, 118, 167–8

INDEX

Eisner, L. H. 54–5, 57, 158
elemental 31–3, 43
eros 27–8, 152–3
event 1, 2–3, 4, 9–10, 12–13, 14, 19, 24, 28, 29, 32–8, 44–5, 48, 60, 72–3, 74, 78–9, 80, 83–5, 94–6, 99, 100, 104, 105, 106, 119, 133, 135, 144, 145, 165, 174
expressionism 54–5, 57, 158

fantastique social 5, 68, 160
fate 6, 19, 40, 45, 47, 48, 87, 88, 89, 91, 93, 100, 101, 125, 127, 134, 144–5, 172, 173
film noir 1, 5, 7, 15, 18–19, 45, 48–54, 55, 56, 57, 67–70, 71–3, 100, 144–5
Flaubert, G. 122, 126, 169–70
Foucault, M. 66–7, 103–4, 160, 166
Frank, N. 47–8, 67–8, 69, 71, 157, 160
Freud, S. 29, 45, 152, 174

Gasché, R. 154, 172
Glanvill, J. 94, 164–5
Godard, J.-L. 49, 121, 169
Görgei, A. 108, 110–11
Gorgias, 18, 36, 151
Gracchus, 15, 134

Hamilton, O. R. 18, 151
Hansen, M. 168
Hart, K. 154, 171
Hegel, G. W. F. 11, 18, 27, 33, 35, 36, 38, 39, 73–4, 75, 95, 100–3, 105, 143–4, 145, 149, 152, 154, 162–3, 165–6, 176
Heidegger, M. 2, 23, 24, 30–9, 40, 41, 42, 43, 45, 83, 87, 100, 102, 103, 138, 152–3, 154–6
Heraclitus 22, 23, 25, 26, 29, 151, 152
Herder, J. G. 21, 29, 151
Hill, L. 143, 153, 164
Hitchcock, A. 81, 86, 89–99, 100, 114, 159, 163, 164, 165
Hölderlin, F. 1–2, 10, 18, 22, 23, 24, 35, 36, 38, 40–3, 45, 57, 132, 147, 156, 173
Horkheimer, M. 70, 162, 175

Howe, I. 72–3, 162
Hyppolite, J. 102–4, 166

insurance 57–8, 60–1, 66–7, 160

Janus 13–14, 15, 17

Kafka, F. 4, 7, 15, 30, 42, 70, 113, 128–35, 140, 142, 144, 164, 172–4, 176
Kant, I. 11, 27, 150–1
Klossowski, P. 28–9, 153
Koepnick, L. 169
Kojève, A. 102
Kovács, A. B. 111, 119, 120–1, 167, 169
Kracauer, S. 55, 68–9, 72, 157, 161, 162, 175

Lang, F. 52, 70, 150
Laporte, J. 157
Lenin, V. I. 11, 30, 163
Levinas, E. 30, 31, 104, 153, 154–6
Lucretius 44, 45, 156

MacGuffin 97, 165
Mac Orlan, P. 5, 6, 148, 160
Madaule, P. 164, 171
Mallarmé, S. 10, 22, 23, 32, 42, 43, 95, 154, 170
Marcuse, H. 100, 165–6
Marxism 3, 72, 153, 164, 174
Maulnier, T. 148–9
Medvigy, G. 108, 169
melancholy, 15, 88, 90, 127, 129, 131, 132, 134, 140, 141, 142, 171
Menke, C. 151
Merleau-Ponty, M. 31, 44

Narcejac, T. 81, 163
Neutre 23, 25, 26, 156
New Year's Day 13, 29
Nietzsche, F. 87, 149, 152–3
non-philosophy 103–4, 166
number 11–12, 149

Odysseus 132–3, 134, 173
Orpheus 38
Ovid 13–14, 150

paganism 30, 153, 155
parable 128–31, 132, 133–6, 140, 141, 142, 172, 173
parapraxis 34, 134, 142, 144, 174
Pauer, G. 108, 109, 169
Paulhan, J. 43, 148
Pippin, R. B. 159
Plato 26–8, 137, 152–3, 175
Poe, E. A. 80, 81, 89, 91, 93–5
poetic realism 5, 50, 54, 107, 124, 157, 160, 166
Potemkin, G. 1289, 130–1, 133, 134, 140, 172
Prévert, J. 5, 6, 148
Pushkin, A. 128–9, 134, 171–2, 173

Quai des brumes, Le (Carné, 1938) 4–7, 47–8, 123, 148, 157, 160

Rancière, J. 114–16, 117, 119, 122, 124, 125, 126, 166, 167, 168, 169–70
Rebatet, L. 5–7, 47, 148
Renoir, J. 4, 5, 148, 150
Resnais, A. 164, 167
revolution 2–4, 13, 15, 17–18, 26, 27, 28, 30, 41, 44, 148, 149, 174

Rosenbaum, J. 168

Sadoul, G. 5, 53, 148, 158
Saleilles, R. 66, 160
Sartre, J.-P. 5, 7–8, 24, 32, 35, 53, 54, 70, 149, 152, 158
Serres, M. 44, 156
Scholem, G. 131, 172, 173, 175
Sophocles 40
Spengler, O. 55–7, 158

Tarr, B. 4, 70, 107–26, 167–70
trauma 29, 89, 92, 93, 96, 140–2, 175–6
Trauerspiel 128, 136, 139, 140, 142, 175
Trotsky, L. 3

Vertigo (Hitchcock, 1958) 4, 81, 89–99, 159, 164, 165
Víg, M. 108, 117, 118, 167, 169

Wahl, J. 149
Watt, C. 166
Welles, O. 6, 157, 158
Wilder, B. 51, 52, 68, 159, 160–1
Wood, R. 96, 164, 165